Date Due

FE 4 '53			
FE 18 '53	DEC 18 '56		
	JAN 4 '56		
MR 19 '53			
AP 8 5	FEB '57		
FE 16 '54	FEB 16 '69		
	FEB 21 '03		
MR 19 54			
MR 11 55			
AP 20 55			
FE 28 56			
AP 11 56			
APR 25 56			
MAY 16 '56			
DEC 3 56			

— Painting by Virginia Broderi

Saint Thérèse of the Child Jesus

The Rose Unpetaled

SAINT THÉRÈSE
OF
THE CHILD JESUS

From *Une Parole de Dieu: Sainte Thérèse de l'Enfant-Jesus.* Crowned by the French Academy. BLANCHE MORTEVEILLE.

Translated by MOTHER PAULA, O.S.B. St. Cecilia's Abbey, Ryde, Isle of Wight

THE BRUCE PUBLISHING COMPANY
MILWAUKEE

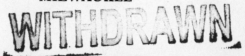

Nihil obstat: **H. B. RIES**, Censor librorum
Imprimatur: ✠ MOYSES E. KILEY, Archiepiscopus Milwaukiensis

*"And what is this Little Way that you
would teach to souls?"*
*"It is the Way of Spiritual Childhood,
the way of trust and absolute
self-surrender."*

17663

PREFACE BY THE GENERAL EDITOR

BLANCHE MORTEVEILLE has contributed a new and authentic Life of Thérèse of the Child Jesus. The book was honored by the French Academy. It is based on the Saint's own writings, and on notes and reminiscences derived from those most close to her.

Freely interwoven with the narrative are valuable interpretations and present-day applications, while due recourse is had to leading studies in this field. The result is an equally attractive and practical work, pitched in a popular key, and of personal pertinence to every reader. Above all, it truly conveys to us the spirit of St. Thérèse.

Her "secret of sanctity," as it is called, the Way of Spiritual Childhood, expresses her peculiar mission, the message she had been sent to teach.

Verbum Dei, "A Word from God," Pope Pius XI magnificently called her, and no title could fit her better. She is God's word to the present and to future generations, the Voice of the Eternal made audible and intelligible to us in her very self. She not merely speaks to us God's message but she incorporates it in her life and being, the message most necessary for the entire world to learn and take to heart if it would be saved.

That message is her *Little Way,* which she herself defines for us as *the Way of Spiritual Childhood, the way of trust and complete self-abandonment.*

"There is a call to the faithful of every nation," said the great Pope of World War I, Benedict XV, "no matter what may be their age, sex, or condition in life, to enter wholeheartedly upon the Little Way which led Soeur Thérèse to the summit of heroic virtue."

iii

Large words these, spoken by a sovereign pontiff, but not larger than Thérèse's own predictions of what God meant to accomplish through her in the course of the centuries to come. Yet all her prophecies have been fulfilled up to the present, even to the very letter. There is consequently no reason to doubt about the future. In her we behold reiterated to all the world the Divine Paradox of greatness in littleness.

Do we wonder, then, at Pope Pius XI's exhortation "that the faithful followers of Christ *study her life attentively* in order to imitate her and become themselves 'as little children' "?

For that special purpose the present book, with its frequent interpretations and explanations, is particularly adapted. The fascination inseparable from the story itself is not lessened but enhanced by these. The book supplies us with what further we wish to know. It makes pleasantly possible the fulfillment of the papal desire regarding the attentive study of the life of St. Thérèse by everyone. Of all her clients, one of the greatest and most constant was the illustrious Pope Pius XI himself, who turned to her in all his problems, built to her a shrine in the Vatican Gardens, and owed to her a miraculous cure.

In our Lord's own teaching on Spiritual Childhood we find a threefold lesson: first, that *we must become* "as little children"; second, that *unless we do so* we shall not enter the Kingdom of Heaven; and third, that whosoever "shall humble himself as this little child, he is *the greater* in the Kingdom of Heaven."

There would consequently seem to have been nothing of higher importance in the eyes of Christ than Spiritual Childhood. It contains the very essence of the one thing He would have us learn from Him: to be "meek and humble of heart." It is the same Divine Paradox which the Little Flower teaches: that to be Christlike, we must be childlike. What tenderness in our Lord's own cry: *Abba,* "Father!"

All who truly understand the Little Flower know there is in her the most wonderful resemblance to Mary. Like her she was too little to fail in humility.

"I am too little to be guilty of vanity," she said, "and too little to prove my humility by high-sounding words. I prefer, therefore, to own in all simplicity that 'He that is mighty hath done great things to me,' and the greatest of all is that He has shown me my littleness and how of myself I am incapable of any good."

That resemblance to Mary we further behold in the charm of her purity, in the beauty of her soul, in the sweetness with which she endured sacrifices the most difficult, and sufferings the most intense, in her winsomeness combined with an inflexible strength, and in her unbounded zeal to serve the cause of God, over all the earth, and to the end of time.

Glancing at the manuscript of her life into which her very soul has passed, she was moved to remark: "Ah, well I know it, all the world will love me!" Is there not in this a distant echo, as it were, of Mary's words that "Henceforth all generations shall call me blessed"? So too, in her confident assertion that in heaven God could deny her nothing since "from the age of three" she never had refused Him anything on earth, is there not a touch of the queenship of Mary?

In a word, her Little Way, like the way of Mary, was that of trusting confidence and complete self-oblation, all transfused by the blinding beauty of a supernatural love ineffable in its intensity, until, as had been foretold by her, she died in a very ecstasy of love: "All my smallest desires have been realized. . . . Then the greatest of all must be realized as well — to die of love." It is so we believe that Mary died, of an excess of love.

Nothing sentimental will be found in St. Thérèse's Little Way. Thus Pope Pius sums up the virtues comprised in it: "Sincere humility of heart, utter fidelity to duty wheresoever God has placed us, readiness for self-sacrifice, affectionate surrender to God's loving guidance, charity above all — that charity which is genuine love of God and a tender affection for Jesus who so tenderly has loved us, charity which 'is patient, is kind . . . beareth all things, hopeth all things, endureth all things.' Such is the Little Way." Add to this the words of Pope Benedict XV: "The Way of Spiritual Childhood is the path which leads to eternal life."

I have preferred throughout this introduction to allow, as far as possible, the Church herself to speak, in the persons of her supreme pontiffs. "Easy and sure," they pronounce her Little Way to be, yet capable of leading souls to the very heights of spiritual perfection. No one, therefore, can go wrong in following it. "O Jesus! would that I could tell all little souls of Thine ineffable condescension," exclaims the Little Flower. "I feel that if by any possibility Thou couldst find one weaker than my own, Thou wouldst take delight in loading her with still greater favors, provided that she abandoned herself with entire confidence to Thine Infinite Mercy."

And here a brief word may still contribute to greater clearness on this subject. While the Way of Spiritual Childhood may appear to take on many forms, when described more at length by the Little Flower herself or by the supreme pontiffs, yet its essential qualities are always expressed in just two words: *confidence* and *self-surrender*. These she conceives of as leading up to what is the crown of all, *love*.

In this very relation we may refer to another and sublime devotion conceived by Thérèse under the guidance of the Holy Spirit, which has spread throughout the universal Church. It is her Oblation as a Victim of Holocaust to God's Merciful Love. But this, like all else of consequence will be found amply treated by the author.

There is just one point more that calls for passing attention here. Since Thérèse's Little Way of Spiritual Childhood is ultimately taken from the Sacred Scriptures — why do we speak of it as new?

The newness of St. Thérèse's message to the world, like that of the Poverello, St. Francis of Assisi, consisted in an intense perception of the scriptural truth in question and in an entirely original application made of it. Most important of all, her teaching was actualized, vitalized, and rendered unforgettable to future generations by the undying example of the Saint herself.

It is Thérèse's exceptional personality that draws mankind.

It is her simplicity; her childlike intimacies with God; her love and daring; her marvellous qualities of intellect, heart and soul; her continued sweetness amid the most heroic asceticism, suffering and anguish of all her being; and not least, the wonderful ingenuity of her spiritual inventions that won over to her all mankind, and above all, the Heart of Christ Himself. She threw Him the flowers of her "little Sacrifices" and won Him by caresses. That, she remarks, "is why I shall be so well received."

"I intend," she said, "to find a means of attaining Heaven by a little way, very short and very straight, a little way which is *wholly new.*" Considering herself unable to climb the high stairway of perfection, she cast herself, as a little one, with *trust* and *self-abandonment*, into the arms of Jesus, to be carried up in them past all the many landings, to the very summit of holiness. That was her "Lift of Love." Indeed the *newness* of her Little Way, with all its happy devices, was manifested by the manner in which it took at once all the world by storm.

Nor would age have made any difference in her method of life. For were she to live until eighty, the Saint protested, she would never change her way. Like the Little Mary, in the scripture passage applied to her, Thérèse, too, was ever "playing before the Lord," intent only upon giving Him pleasure.

Verbum Dei, "A word from God!" — that to all who know her, is and ever will be St. Thérèse, a gleam of sunshine amid gloom, a freshness of roses and morning dew in an old and jaded world.

In almost lyric terms the saintly Pope Pius X wrote of her: "Verily she has blossomed as a lily, and has shed abroad the lily's pleasing perfume. She has put forth a rich fruitage of divine grace, and praised to the full her Lord and blessed Him in His works."

Such was his conclusion after reading the *Autobiography* of the Little Flower, whose fragrance is wafted no less through the volume here offered, with its reverential treatment of the Saint and its faithful dependence on her words. As for the literary value of the present work, we need but allude once more to the exceptional distinction conferred upon it: its crowning by the French Academy, shortly before the outbreak of World War II.

When making her choice of a translator for our English version, the author turned for advice to Thérèse's own Carmel of Lisieux, where three of the Saint's own sisters were then still living. The choice fell upon the Benedictine nuns of St. Cecilia's Abbey, Ryde, Isle of Wight, England. It was with the Benedictines that the Little Flower had been in closest association during her schoolgirl days, and it was a Benedictine nun who now successfully performed the task of offering an English translation in the spirit of the original, the spirit of St. Thérèse.

A valuable Appendix has been added by the English translator, while for various adaptations and additions the Editor stands responsible. The effort has been to make of this a standard contribution to our literature on St. Thérèse of the Child Jesus and the Holy Face in English-speaking countries.

The title selected for this translation is that chosen by Thérèse herself for the poem in which she sought to sum up her own life's dream, imaging herself as *La Rose Effeuillée,* "The Rose Unpetaled." It was the symbol of her eagerness to immolate herself for Christ entirely, in purest love.*

JOSEPH HUSSLEIN, S.J., PH.D.,
General Editor, Religion and Culture Series

St. Louis University
Christmas Day, 1941

* Cf. Poem, pp. 250, 251.

CONTENTS

ENGLISH TRANSLATION OF THE LETTER FROM CARDINAL PACELLI TO MADEMOISELLE BLANCHE MORTEVEILLE

SECRETARIAT OF STATE
OF HIS HOLINESS

FROM THE VATICAN
January 16, 1937

MADEMOISELLE,

The Holy Father has had great pleasure in accepting the book which you so kindly sent Him concerning the Carmelite Virgin of Lisieux, "Saint Thérèse of the Child Jesus."

His Holiness thanks you for this gift and for the thoughtful kindness which prompted it.

As a pledge of His paternal benevolence and of the Divine Blessing on you and yours, He sends you the Apostolic Blessing.

Thanking you very sincerely for the copy which you have been kind enough to offer me, I take this opportunity of assuring you of my religious devotedness.

E. CARD. PACELLI

(His Eminence Cardinal Eugenio Pacelli was elected Pope on March 2, 1939, and took the name of Pius XII.)

THE ROSE UNPETALED

PART ONE

CHAPTER I

A HAPPY CHILDHOOD

1. *The Little White Flower*

ON JANUARY 4, 1873, the sacrament of baptism was administered in the Church of *Notre Dame* at Alençon. The babe, just two days old, was surrounded by a happy family, while the young godfather and the thirteen-year-old godmother replied with great earnestness to the priest's questions:

"What dost thou ask of the Church of God?"

"Faith."

"What doth Faith obtain for thee?"

"Eternal life."

"If then thou wilt attain to eternal life, keep the commandments: 'Thou shalt love the Lord Thy God with thy whole heart, and with thy whole soul, and with thy whole mind, and thy neighbour as thyself.' "

When the ritual prayers were ended, the group proceeded to the baptistery, situated in the first chapel on the left of the ancient gothic church, and the priest, pouring holy water three times on the child's forehead, pronounced these words:

"Marie, Françoise, Thérèse, I baptise you in the name of the Father, and of the Son, and of the Holy Ghost."

I do not know if the *Te Deum* was sung, as is the custom in certain dioceses, but the whole of heaven must have resounded with hymns of praise and thanksgiving. The child, who was one day to become St. Thérèse of the Child Jesus, had just been made a member of God's family.

A child of God! How eminently she was to live up to that title! The supernatural life and the gifts of the Holy Ghost imparted to her soul were to attain their full development; accompanied ever by the perfect correspondence of her strong,

3

unfailing will. Her sanctity was to be the magnificent and harmonious development of the graces received at baptism. But the marvellous destiny of Thérèse Martin was as yet unknown to all.

Carefully wrapped in a warm, fur-lined cloak on that cold, wintry afternoon, the little girl was taken home to her mother, for whom the postponement of baptism — due to the godfather's absence — had been a cause of great anxiety and regret. Now joy reigned supreme.

Four little girls gathered delightedly round the cot where their baby sister lay sleeping, while the mother watched her little one with tender love. Madame Martin had already lost four children in their early childhood and feared that Thérèse would also wing her flight to heaven.

As the days passed, it soon became evident that the little flower was already drooping on its tender stalk. Happiness gave place to anxiety, and, one evening, the doctor declared that nothing could save the child but a good foster-mother. Immediately the poor mother would have set out in quest of one she knew, had it been possible, but it was night, a night heavy with anxiety. But at the first break of day, Madame Martin left home with all haste. Some miles from Alençon there lived a good woman, Rose Taillé, the wife of a farmer, who had already nursed one of her children. The woman consented willingly, and at once left to save Thérèse's life, but on her arrival found that the baby was dying.

Heartbroken, the mother threw herself on her knees in prayer, and, with tears, implored St. Joseph's aid. The little one seemed to revive, and lifted her head, where she lay on the nurse's knees, but only to fall back a moment later, with her eyes closed, as if in death.

"O my God! blessed be Thy Holy Will!" sobbed Madame Martin. Then, through her tears, she looked again at her child. Suddenly the baby seemed to return to life, opened her eyes and smiled at her mother. Thérèse's life had been spared.

As Rose Taillé was obliged to return home and attend to

her husband and children, she bore off the little nursling in her arms. Thus it came about that in the rustic surroundings of a farm of Lower Normandy, in the company of the humble and lowly, like the Child Jesus at Bethlehem. Thérèse gradually became a bonny babe, golden haired, pink cheeked, lively and gay, and her progress was noted by the happy mother at every visit.

Thérèse's parents were well-to-do citizens, exemplary in the faithful accomplishment of their daily work and the duties of their family life. For the past three years they had lived at *Rue Saint-Blaise* in a pretty house of reddish brick and white stone, which Madame Martin had inherited from her family. Yet both husband and wife, in earlier days, had dreamed of other things.

Louis Martin, son of a Captain in the Imperial Army, had shown a certain aptitude for the trade of watchmaker. But in course of time higher aspirations made themselves heard in his soul. So it came to pass that one September morning, in 1843, he climbed the mountain of the Great St. Bernard, with the purpose of becoming a monk in this pure solitude. He wished to consecrate himself entirely to God and to the service of charity. The superior questioned the young aspirant on his knowledge of Latin, essential for admission into the monastery, and found him unprepared. Disappointed, the young man descended the mountain slope. But his enthusiasm had only been checked, for he set to work courageously on his studies until ill-health obliged him to abandon them. At length, then, he returned to his work as watchmaker, and some time later opened a jeweller's shop.

In the same way, Zélie Guérin, daughter of a brave soldier who had also taken part in the Napoleonic wars, presented herself one day at the Convent of the Sisters of Charity at Alençon. Her desire was to serve God by devoting her life to the poor, and in consequence she set out to seek admission among the daughters of St. Vincent de Paul. The mother superior listened to her request, and then, without further ado, assured her that this was not her vocation. Surprise and disappointment were soon followed by humble acceptance of that decision, and Zélie Guérin patiently abided the further indications of divine providence. She had not long to wait.

One day, when crossing St. Leonard's bridge that spans the Sarthe, Mademoiselle Guérin chanced to meet a young man whose dignified attitude and reserved manner attracted her attention. At the same moment she heard an inner voice saying: "It is he whom I have chosen for you."

On July 13, 1858, holy church blessed the union of Louis Martin and Zélie Guérin; the bride was twenty-seven, the bridegroom thirty-five.

As a young girl, Madame Martin had taken up the attractive profession of lace making and was unusually proficient in the art of designing and making the artistic Alençon point-lace. Notwithstanding her new duties, she did not abandon this enterprise, which had gradually grown to be an important work. In 1870, Monsieur Martin in fact handed over his entire business as a jeweller to his nephew, in order to share that of his wife.

Known and esteemed by the whole of Alençon, the Martins were seemingly no different from any other well-to-do family of the town, but in their pleasant home one felt the presence of their Sovereign Lord. Unseen, He here reigned supreme and held the first place in both their hearts. Not vowed to God in the religious state, as originally planned by each of them, they were nonetheless enrolled in His service alone. His choice for them of the married state had been clear, and they in turn built up in an eminently supernatural manner their entire family life. Faithfully they followed out the Divine Will. Its dispensations, though inscrutable to them, are luminous now in this our day. They were to be father and mother to a great saint — one who was called to bear a message and fulfil a mission of unique significance in the Church of God.

2. *Her Childhood Traits*

On April 2, 1874, Thérèse was returned to her own home, fresh as a little spring flower whose petals were soon to unfold in charming beauty. "My first recollections," she wrote long after, "were of loving smiles and tender caresses."

Madame Martin herself traces delightful pictures of the baby's loving ways, in letters addressed to her two eldest daughters, Marie and Pauline, then at school at the Convent of the Visitation at Mans, where their aunt was a nun. For sitting in her usual place by the window, working at her point-lace, Madame Martin had been keeping an attentive eye on her darling.

"Here is Baby," she writes, "who has just run up to kiss me and stroke my face with her tiny hand. But her caresses are not altogether disinterested! I can see she wants something to play with. The dear little mite refuses to leave me and follows me about everywhere."

Such is the sweet slavery of motherhood. Thérèse would not leave her mother's side. Despite her love for the garden, she could not be induced to remain there without her cherished "Mamma."

"It is a real picture to see her toddling around," reads another letter. "You should see her at the foot of the stairs, much too high for her little legs; at every step she calls out for encouragement: 'Mamma, Mamma.' There are as many calls of 'Mamma' as there are steps to ascend, and, if by chance I forget to answer, she remains where she is and will go neither back nor forward."

When Monsieur Martin returned home from business, Thérèse would run to meet him. Her favorite amusement then was to sit down on one of his boots, playing ride-a-cock-horse. "In this fashion he used to carry me as long as I wished, through house and garden." And how she enjoyed it! When Madame Martin laughingly reproached her husband for spoiling the baby, he would answer: "Well, why not? She is the Queen." Then, taking the child in his arms and lifting her very high, he would lovingly carry her on his shoulder.

She was indeed a charming little girl, lively, affectionate, ardent, sweet tempered, and full of mischief.

"I think she is more of a little rogue than any of you were," wrote Madame Martin, with a touch of maternal pride, "and she is so frank and straightforward at the same time."

The child was, indeed, like a ray of sunshine in the house. Never wearied, she loved to run about as fast as her little legs would carry her, or play with her sister Céline. Though older by three years and a half, Céline was her inseparable companion.

On receiving a bantam cock and hen from her nurse, Thérèse at once gave the cock to her sister. Every day after dinner, Céline used to catch the bantams, and the two little girls then played contentedly at a corner of the fire-place. One morning, the tiny child took it into her head to get out of her little cot and climb into Céline's. After hunting high and low, the nurse at length discovered her small charge, who exclaimed, as she gave Céline a big hug: "Leave us alone, Louise. We are like the little white bantams, we cannot be separated."

The child's little heart, exceptionally sensitive and loving, was brimming over with tender affection for her dear ones. "You can hardly imagine how much I loved my father and mother," she tells us.[1] But be it noted at once — for the fact is sufficiently rare to be worth noting — that the parents' love for their little girl was in no way blind. They realised the dangers that threatened such an attractive child, and they were determined not to make of her a "spoilt child." She herself remarks: "I must say that Papa did not spoil me."

To give an instance here. Monsieur Martin had erected a swing for his little daughters in the tiny garden. There Thérèse was one day swinging herself, and as he chanced to pass by he said:

"Come and give me a kiss, little Queen."

"Come and get it yourself, Papa!" was the pert retort.

She had spoken without reflection, but the tone sounded slightly rebellious, and so Monsieur Martin gave her no further

[1] The quotations from the *Autobiography* of the Saint are so numerous throughout this book that the references will not be given. The passages quoted will easily be recognised.

attention and promptly continued his walk. Marie, her eldest
sister and godmother, scolded the little girl for her behaviour.
At once, the little mite jumped off the swing, and running after
her father, loudly asked pardon for her naughtiness, the whole
house resounding with her sobs of contrition.

One morning, again, when Madame Martin wanted to kiss
her little daughter before going out, Thérèse hid under the
clothes, saying in the tone of a spoilt child: "I don't want anyone to look at me." The wise mother withdrew, showing her
displeasure. Two minutes later, the little one was running
downstairs after her, stumbling over her long night-dress.
"Mamma," she said, throwing herself on her knees, "I was
so naughty, do forgive me!"

Such tiny incidents suffice to prove the gentle firmness of the
parents and the sweet character of the child, whose little conscience inclined quite naturally toward good, because it had
been rightly guided from its first awakening.

We must not imagine, however, that Thérèse resembled those
amazing little saints, who from the cradle were the cause of
wonder and astonishment to all who came near them. She was
delightful and extremely gifted, but, at that early age, there
was nothing unusually striking to reveal her future sanctity.
When playing with Céline she would sometimes give her a push,
but at once would run to her mother to confess her little fault.

"She has an idea that she will be more easily forgiven if she
accuses herself," writes her mother. This was indeed the case,
though no one made light of her faults.

Writing one day to Pauline, after a few words in praise of
Céline, Madame Martin continued: "As to the little mite, one
cannot tell how she will turn out. She is so young and heedless.
She has not nearly so sweet a disposition as her sister, and her
stubbornness is almost invincible. When she has said 'no,' nothing
will make her yield; one could leave her all day in the cellar
without getting her to say 'yes'; she would sooner sleep there."

However, it was never necessary for Madame Martin to have
recourse to such means of correction. In the words which follow,

she hastens to admit that such remarks are exaggerated: "But all this is not really serious; we find our baby very sweet, even with her childish faults."

Most assuredly, the lively little girl possessed "character"; she knew what she wanted, and she wanted that with all her might. That, in fact, was a quality which, rightly directed, made her a saint, by God's grace.

Also, as a result of her extreme sensitiveness, she was liable to sudden and complete reaction, which often became the occasion of great merit. But she was far from being a difficult character, and divine grace was soon to work on her strength of will. Madame Martin knew this better than anyone, and the Saint herself remarks: "Then, as always, one kind word was enough to make me understand and regret when I had done wrong."

In her humility, Thérèse insists on what she calls her "faults." She tells us that she had "a very great self-love," and relates a striking little incident to prove the fact.

Just to test the child's disposition, Madame Martin had offered her little girl a halfpenny — a little fortune for a child in those days — on condition that she would kiss the ground. Thereupon the tiny form was drawn up to its full height, and prompt was the reply:

"Oh no, Mamma, I would rather go without the halfpenny!"

Still another incident is recounted by Thérèse. It happened on an occasion when the family had been invited to the country to see some friends.

"Mamma told Marie to put on my prettiest frock, but not to let me have bare arms; I did not say a word, but I thought to myself: 'All the same, I should have looked much prettier with bare arms.'"

In her *Autobiography*, written years later, the Carmelite concludes gravely: "With such a disposition, if I had been brought up by careless parents, I should certainly have become very wicked and perhaps lost my soul."

Let us not be surprised at the severity of this self-condemnation. The saints have a clearer vision than we have, for they are nearer to God, the Eternal Truth. Like all human nature wounded by original sin, the child had her weak points, but these tendencies, corrected from their first appearance, served her, as she herself tells us, "as so many means of advancing in the way of perfection." In short, hers was a fine character, rich, and extraordinarily well balanced, in which the good qualities far exceeded the defects.

"There is nothing worse than the corruption of the excellent," ancient writers tell us. Here on the contrary, is a case of perfecting what was "excellent." Her heart, her intelligence, and her will were all of the highest order, and under the direction of excellent parents, so admirably fitted to guide her, they were constantly turned toward good and to whatever was most perfect.

3. In the World of the Supernatural

And here we come, at this early period, to the first manifestations of the supernatural life in her soul. As soon as the childish lips could lisp, Madame Martin had joined Thérèse's tiny hands and taught her a short, simple prayer. This the little girl quickly learned and loved to repeat. The happy mother was pleased to write: "She says her prayers like a little angel, and knows so well how to speak to God." On Sundays, she used to go to church during Vespers, and dearly loved this visit, which she called her "Mass."

On one occasion, when her little heart was overflowing with affection and sought the most beautiful gift to express her loving wishes for her mother's supreme happiness, she threw her arms around her dearly loved mother and exclaimed:

"O Mamma darling, how I wish you would die!"

Somewhat taken aback by such a strange wish, Madame Martin scolded the little one, who looked at her with astonishment. "But I want you to go to heaven, and you say we must die to go there."

In her outbursts of affection for her father, she wanted him to die too! Due to the maternal instructions, carefully adapted to her childish mind, heaven had become for her a vision of infinite beauty and joy, and had an irresistible attraction for her. But her mother had also taught her that in order to go to heaven she must be very good, and then explained what happens to the wicked. To make certain her instruction was fully understood Madame Martin then put the question:

"If Thérèse was not good, what would happen?"

The child listened attentively, with a look of anxiety in her eyes. Then, seized with a happy thought, she exclaimed: "So if I were not good, I should go to hell? Oh no, I know what I would do. I would fly to you in heaven, and you would hold me very tight in your arms! How could God take me away?" Consoled by this reflection, Thérèse was no longer afraid, and Madame Martin — suiting the action to the word — took her little treasure into her arms, caressing her.

The Holy Spirit had already begun His work in her soul. "When I was only just learning to talk, and Mamma asked: 'What are you thinking about?' my answer always was: 'Pauline.' Sometimes I heard people say that Pauline would be a nun, and, without quite knowing what it meant, I thought: 'I shall be a nun, too.' This is one of my first recollections, and I never changed my mind."

Thérèse was, therefore, at the age of two, already brought into contact, however vaguely as yet, with the idea of the most perfect life. It was the example of her own dear sister, soon to be her "little mother" and later her superior at Carmel, which drew her on in her quest of the Divine Lover.

One of the most vivid recollections of her childhood was the First Communion Day of her third sister, Léonie, by whom, too, she was greatly cherished. Like the elder girls, Léonie loved to take care of her little sister, and used to sing sweet songs to lull her to sleep.

Marie, the eldest, having finished her studies, had just left the Convent school of the Visitation and now occupied herself with the little ones. From her Céline was learning to read and write. This meant that Thérèse as well wanted to be present at all the lessons and, if permitted, would sit there motionless. But she was so small that the young mistress would not always allow her to continue this practice, much to her displeasure.

"One day," relates Marie, "I saw her trying to open the door of my room, but she was still too small to reach the handle. . . ." What would she do? Was she going to cry? or would she call someone to her aid? No, finding herself helpless, she contented herself with lying down at the door to show her grief. To us this act of mute protestation may appear a touching sight, but Madame Martin remained firm: "You must not let her do that." The next day, then, the same thing happened.

"Thérèse darling," said Marie, "you are displeasing the Infant Jesus."

With her large expressive eyes, the child looked steadfastly at her sister. "Displeasing the Infant Jesus! Oh, no!" And from that day, the scene was never renewed. For the love of the Holy Child Jesus, Thérèse was ready to overcome all her faults.

"From the age of three, I have never refused good God anything," is the memorable statement Thérèse could humbly and innocently make of herself. A saint, indeed, is one whose will is wholly united to the will of God, and who never says "No" to Him. Thérèse's life was one loving and docile "Yes," acquiescing to every manifestation of the divine Will.

As everything in her life was to appear easy and accessible to us all, her first steps in asceticism were very simple, practised in her childish way. When Marie returned from the Convent school, she brought with her a special little string of beads given by the nuns to their pupils that they might keep count of their little sacrifices. The beads were movable, and one could be moved forward for each sacrifice accomplished. The big sister had given similar strings of beads to Céline and Thérèse, and the little ones were intensely interested.

"Even Thérèse is anxious to make sacrifices!" wrote Madame Martin, who was amazed to see the child repeatedly putting her hand in her pocket to pull a bead forward because she had made another little sacrifice.

Already, this small girl was mortifying herself more attentively than many a religious grown old in the cloister. It was to be thus all her life. The rosary of little sacrifices never ceased to slip through her generous hands. And what wisdom in the choice of the sacrifices! They are seen in the ordinary circumstances of daily life, and especially in her dealings with her neighbour. Marie noted the efforts made by Thérèse to give way to her sisters, particularly to her playmate Céline. The determined little character was learning self-control; her strength of will was acquiring virtue, without the least constraint from others.

"How happy I was at that age!" she tells us, "I was beginning to enjoy life; goodness itself seemed full of charm. Probably my character was the same as it is now, for even then I had great self-command. I made it a practice never to complain when my things were taken, and, if I were unjustly accused, I preferred to keep silence rather than excuse myself. There was no merit in this, for I did it naturally."

Note the quality of the sacrifices. They were of the kind most appreciated in the most fervent Novitiates. "These 'natural' acts," remarks Monsignor Laveille, the eminent historian of the Saint, "were nevertheless accomplished for God's sake, with the definite intention of pleasing Him. The little one lived under the constant guidance of the Holy Spirit." Love already reigned supreme in the heart of this child, causing her to find the yoke of the Lord sweet and His burden light.

4. *Nature Speaks to the Child*

In the happy home in *Rue Saint-Blaise,* life flowed on sweetly and peacefully. Monsieur Martin owned a property, at the gates of the town; it was called *Le Pavillon*[2] because the tiny building stood in the midst of a large garden, full of flowers and fruit trees. This house was a great attraction for the children, and Thérèse always recalled with joy the happy days when her father took her to their "Summer-house." But her special delight

[2] The Summer-house.

were the Sunday outings, because her mother, too, was able to join the family in those long walks, as she was obliged to abandon her point-lace on the day of rest.

Thérèse never forgot the deep impression made on her childish mind on such occasions by the sight of the broad fields bright with flowers, the vast horizons, the immensity of the blue sky, and the tall trees with their leafy branches. All nature charmed her and lifted her soul to heaven. To the pure heart of this little child, nature was somewhat as it had been in the garden of Paradise to our first parents. All the created beauty that entranced her admiring eyes spoke to her of the Creator, who is Himself infinite beauty.

We can picture to ourselves the fair-haired little girl playing in the green meadow on the sunny mornings of late spring. She loved to gather flowers with Céline, singing happily to herself as she arranged her little bouquets, which seemed to her wondrously beautiful. Then she would run to her beloved papa and mamma to have them duly admired. She was happy in the company of those she loved; indeed she needed all her dear ones round her to be perfectly happy!

On her return home, she would put her flowers in front of her mother's beautiful statue of our Lady. During the month of May, a whole room was set apart and arranged as an oratory. Madame Martin had a great devotion to our Lady and would charge her eldest daughter to decorate the improvised chapel as beautifully as possible, adorning the walls with garlands, hawthorn, and flowers of every kind. Early on the fresh spring mornings, as soon as she was dressed, Thérèse would run to the beautiful altar which filled her with wonder and delight; there she would say her prayers, while her little heart overflowed with joy.

"If you only knew how gay and mischievous she is," wrote Marie in a letter to Pauline. "I am lost in admiration. Everyone at home pets and caresses her."

In the midst of these transports of joy, however, Thérèse continued her little sacrifices. One Sunday, as she returned from her walk, laden with cornflowers, daisies, and buttercups, she met her grandmother, Madame Martin. After the customary greetings, the old lady asked as a present her little grand-daughter's bouquet for her own altar at home. Silently, the child gave up her flowers, one by one, even to the last, but the sacrifice was so great that she could hardly keep back the tears. Though they shone in her eyes they did not fall, and were seen only by God — and Céline.

We have two portraits of Thérèse at this period of her life. The first is a photograph. The child is standing with her hand resting on the back of a chair. Her round, healthy, baby face is lit up by the large, candid, expressive eyes; the features are regular, the tiny mouth is not smiling.[3] We are told that Thérèse was afraid of the photographer. No one, however, would suspect that. The general impression is one of dignity and strength, and we are filled with reverence in contemplating the childish face.

The second portrait represents Thérèse on her mother's knee and is the work of her sister, Céline. Madame Martin is just as we imagine her to be; the features denote singular energy, up-rightness, and intelligence; there is a very beautiful expression in her eyes, enhanced by the smooth dark hair parted in the middle; the mouth is firm, the whole attitude dignified and affectionate. One hand gently caresses the child, whose head is resting on her mother's shoulder. As for Thérèse, her golden curls, tied with a ribbon, cluster round her white forehead; her eyes have the same depth of expression that we notice in the photograph, but this time the mouth is smiling, a sweet, resolute smile, which will be one of the Saint's most charming means of practising virtue. The little girl is prettily dressed in a white, short-sleeved frock, tied with a wide sash. Madame Martin wears a dress of tartan plaid and her lace collar is pinned with a cameo. It is a picture of maternal and filial happiness surrounded by material prosperity, under which

[3] Speaking of Thérèse's small mouth, an admiring nurse said it was "as big as one of her eyes" (*grande comme un z'yeux*).

might be written those words of Thérèse: "Truly, everything on earth smiled at me; I found flowers strewn at every step." This is an authentic portrait of the happy little girl, whose awakening faculties were flooded with joy; nothing had ever wounded or deceived her; her fresh little heart had met nothing but love. It was only fitting that her father and mother, so wonderfully prepared by God for their great work, should be for their child a living reflection of His Tenderness and Infinite Goodness.

Thérèse's mission was to sing of Love, and to prove that Love is accessible to all. In her sublime way, she taught souls to respond by Love to God's merciful Love for man.

Never did she forget those early lessons of affection taught in the delightful home of her early childhood. She had but to transfer to the supernatural order the loving total abandonment which she practised toward her parents, and the unhesitating confidence which she had in them. She would never be afraid of God.

CHAPTER II

THÉRÈSE'S FIRST SORROW

"HOW quickly the sunny years of childhood passed away."
In these words, with a suppressed sigh, Thérèse ends the account
of her earliest memories.

But in her wonderful spirit of faith, she bids us not to be
disconcerted at her coming trials, and at once offers us the
reason: "Since I was to be the Spouse of Our Lord at such an
early age, it was necessary that I should suffer from my childhood." Under the sufferings imposed lay hidden a divine love
of predilection.

1. *The Valiant Woman*

One February morning, in 1877, Madame Martin received
a letter from the Visitation Convent at Le Mans, containing
news of her sister's death: "Our beloved Sister Marie-Dosithéa,"
it read, "ended her saintly life early to-day by a most edifying
death. Her calmness of mind and her serenity of spirit were
admirable to the end. One evening she said to our Mother:
'Oh dear Mother, I can do nothing but love and trust and
abandon myself to God. Help me to thank Him for this grace.'"

Madame Martin had loved and revered Sister Marie-Dosithéa,
and her early dream as a young girl had been to follow her
sister's example in giving herself wholly to God. Later she had
confided to her the education of her daughters.

Yet the admiration felt for such a holy death did not lessen
her great sorrow at the loss of her sister. Added to this grief
were serious anxieties, for she knew too well that she herself
was doomed to an early death.

Before her marriage, she had on a certain occasion given

herself a sharp knock on the corner of a table. The slight swelling that formed on her breast was not alarming at first, but a tumor developed in the breast. The inexorable disease, thus started, was doing its work relentlessly. With great courage she had kept the dread secret to herself as long as that was possible. Now, however, toward the end of 1876, her suffering had become intolerable, and she decided to consult a doctor. After examination, he wrote out a prescription, but did not succeed in deceiving the patient.

"Of what use will that be?" she asked him.

"None at all," replied the doctor, unable to evade her direct question. "I do that to please the patients."

Zélie Martin had long been mistress of her emotions; she returned home and calmly took up her ordinary duties. Her brother, a chemist at Lisieux, was not, however, so resigned to this first verdict. He hoped that a successful operation would be possible, and persuaded his sister to come to Lisieux, where he consulted an experienced surgeon.

The vedict was decisive: "It is too late."

On her return home, Madame Martin wrote to her brother and sister-in-law, expressing her gratitude: "You give yourselves far too much trouble on my account, I do not deserve so much attention, my life is not so precious. . . ."

Truly, this simple daughter of France was queenly in her courtesy and virtue. Madame Martin looked death in the face without fear. With her husband's help she put her affairs in order, sold her lace-making connection, and wrote to Lisieux: "I am now going to live a retired life . . . and from every point of view I think it is time. . . ."

She knew well that this life of retired ease, so different from that which she had hitherto led, would not last long. She had worked too hard. Her husband, her children, and her employees could all bear witness to that. They had seen her for many long years fulfilling her numerous duties with such careful attention that nothing was ever neglected. God was served first, and every morning the mother of the family attended the early

Mass at half-past five or six o'clock, before beginning her daily duties.

As mistress of the house, attentive to the well-being of all, she brought up her children with loving care and attended to their every need, even spending long nights at their bedside when they were ill, without ever interrupting her ordinary work. Energy of character and serenity of spirit characterised all her actions. Her manifold duties were accomplished with perfect ease. In all simplicity, she counted on the divine assistance. "It was only the grace of God that kept me up," she wrote, after a serious illness of her eldest daughter.

Her lace making had been almost a recreation for her. "I am really happy only when sitting at my window, working at my point-lace," she used to say. For in her case it was far more than merely manual work. Madame Martin's exquisite taste found full scope in the choice and the assembling of the pieces of lace which her workers brought her, and from her fingers fell fragile and delicate wonders which easily found admiring purchasers.

Family gatherings and a few friendships were the only diversions in this laborious life. In her letters, nearly all addressed to near relatives, we have the keynote of this strong and tender soul. In 1871, having lost four children,[1] she wrote to her sister-in-law:

"When I closed the eyes of my dear little children, and when I buried them, I suffered greatly, but I was always resigned in my sorrow. Everyone said to me: 'It would have been much better never to have had those children.' I could not bear such remarks. My sufferings and anxieties are not to be compared with the eternal happiness of my little ones."

This noble resignation was as the signature to the prayer made by Zélie Guérin before her marriage:

"O my God, since I am not worthy to be Thy spouse like my sister, I shall enter the married state to fulfil Thy Holy

---

[1] Two little sons and two little daughters had died at an early age.

Will; I beseech Thee to make me the mother of many children, who will all be consecrated to Thee."

The souls of four little children already in heaven, and five daughters destined to be religious on earth, of whom one was to be a canonised saint — that was the answer from heaven!

In the year 1877, Madame Martin could not foresee the glory that the future would bring; she could only think with anxiety of the unfinished education of her three younger daughters. Fortunately, Marie had completed her studies, and Pauline was soon to leave school. Both girls were serious minded and gifted with charming qualities, which were accompanied by an ardent piety that foretold their future call to the religious life. But Léonie was only thirteen, Céline had hardly begun her lessons, and Thérèse was not yet five years old!

2. *A Pilgrimage to Lourdes*

The mother's heart was torn with grief at the thought that Sister Marie-Dosithéa was no longer in this world, for she had often said to herself: "I shall confide my daughters to my sister's care." She began to invoke her sister and to pray to the Blessed Virgin. If only God would give her time to accomplish her task to the end! But the saints know well that our poor petitions are often unenlightened and not in accordance with God's Will. So, though her disease grew worse, the invalid mother did not lose courage.

"I shall go to Lourdes," she said, "Our Lady will cure me there."

Though her life seemed quite ordinary outwardly, Madame Martin's thoughts were constantly with God and the inhabitants of heaven, and her confidence in the Mother of God had been rewarded by exceptional favours. Thus, one day, in her girlhood, on the Feast of the Immaculate Conception, Zélie Guérin had heard these unexpected words:

"Have Alençon lace made."

It was as a result of this message from heaven, that she

began her enterprise which was crowned with such complete success.

The second supernatural indication, already mentioned here, concerned her marriage with Louis Martin.

On still another occasion, our Lady had deigned to console her at a time of grief and anxiety. After the death, namely, of her little girl Hélène,[2] so tenderly loved and regretted, the poor mother was praying one day before her beautiful statue of the Blessed Virgin. She felt uneasy because her child had once told a slight untruth, and was wondering sadly if the child were in Purgatory, when a voice came from the statue: "She is here at my side." The memory of such favours stimulated the faith and confidence of the poor sufferer in her present anxieties.

In the spring of the year 1877, several pilgrimages were organised for Lourdes. Madame Martin joined that from Angers and on June 18 set out for our Lady's shrine with her three eldest daughters. What fervent supplications were addressed to the Virgin Mary at Lourdes and at Alençon!

The journey was tiring, the heat oppressive, the food poor. Madame Martin bore all these inconveniences uncomplainingly, but she was quite exhausted before reaching the journey's end.

Every Lourdes' pilgrim has felt that mysterious Presence which here welcomes, strengthens, and caresses with its irresistible sweetness. We do not know what the Blessed Virgin said to the heart of her faithful servant during the hours spent in prayer at the grotto of miracles, but, from what followed, we may affirm that Zélie Martin received wonderful graces of strength and resignation at Lourdes. Although she bathed four times in the waters to which our Lady so often gives miraculous powers, she felt no relief whatever. Then she understood: our Lady did not intend to cure her.

In her simple way, she wrote to Lisieux: "I should have been doubly happy to be cured for your sakes. Alas! Our Lady said to me, as to Bernadette: 'I shall make you happy, not in this world, but in the next.'"

---

[2] Hélène died at the age of five.

Poor mother! on her pilgrimage of pain and supplication, could she but have heard, in anticipation, the far-off echoes of another pilgrimage, that would take place in this very spot, just fifty-seven years later, when the statue of her youngest daughter would be erected here with joyous acclamation! Could she but have known that a relic of her Thérèse — a bone from one of those little feet that ran so eagerly to her — would be enshrined and borne on the shoulders of devout seminarists, whilst the enthusiastic crowd would sing new canticles in her honour:

> Athrill with pleasure,
> Fair Normandy
> Brings thee its treasure,
> O Maid Marie!

But only in heaven was she to know of these wonders. To-day she would leave Lourdes — uncured!

The pilgrims cast a farewell glance over the beautiful landscape hallowed by the Virgin's Apparition. For the last time they beheld the mountains green with verdure, the blue waters of the river Gave pursuing their rapid course, and the great Basilica, with its new white stone, cutting a majestic silhouette against the sky, above the holy grotto where Mary had spoken and smiled. But slowly the train began to move, and the grotto gradually disappeared from view. Their visit to Lourdes was ended; they were bound northward once more.

Marie, Pauline, and Léonie, worn out with sorrow and supplication, were silent. We know, O Mother of Mercy, that the most precious favours obtained at Lourdes are not those which our earthly eyes can look upon, but those wrought in the heart. To the amazement of her daughters, Madame Martin began to join wholeheartedly in the hymns of the pilgrimage.

Meanwhile, Monsieur Martin had passed a week of anxious waiting at Alençon, expecting to receive the longed-for telegram at any moment, but there was no news of a miracle. Informed of the return journey, he took Céline and Thérèse by the hand and hastened to the station. The little girls, always so happy to go out with their father, must have chatted less than usual as they passed through the sunny streets on this bright day in June. Without understanding the gravity of the situation, they knew that their mother was ill and were much surprised that our Lady had not cured her after all their prayers.

When the train steamed into the station, Madame Martin appeared at the door of the carriage. With supernatural cheerfulness, she alighted from the train as gaily as if she had been cured. Her husband could not believe his eyes, but decided to follow her example in courage and cheerfulness. "That renewed his courage, and restored joy to the household again," wrote the courageous invalid, in a letter to Lisieux. Nevertheless, she knew she was seriously ill, and, in the depths of her heart, she felt the extreme bitterness of the sacrifice.

Pauline returned to the Visitation Convent where she was to finish her studies. To this beloved daughter, the mother opened her heart as to a friend in whom she could confide: "Do not expect much happiness in this world, or you will have too many disappointments. As for me, I know what to expect from earthly joys; if I did not hope for those of heaven, I should be very unhappy."[3]

3. *Shadow of God's Hand*

Madame Martin had known many trials, the most poignant of which had been the loss of her four children in their early childhood, but she still possessed those things which represent happiness here below — an excellent husband, five delightful children, and the future assured by easy circumstances. Now, suddenly, she was called to prepare for the long separation!

But Thérèse's mother had always lived under the clear light of the supernatural. She was a fervent Tertiary of St. Francis and faithful in fulfilling her religious duties, observing fast days even in the year of her death. The lives of the saints filled her with a holy enthusiasm. "I do nothing but dream of solitude and the cloister," she wrote to Pauline, after reading the life

---

[3] Letter dated June 25, 1877.

of St. Jane Frances de Chantal; "I should like to live a long
time so as to be able to retire into solitude when all my children
are educated." Her ambition was to become a saint.

God took her at her word, but in His own good way. All
the aspirations of this devout soul were to be fulfilled in these
few weeks of intense physical suffering so heroically borne, and
of sacrifices so generously accepted.

The poor invalid would have liked to return once more to
Lisieux, to pay one last visit to her brother and sister-in-law,
and to take with her Thérèse, who had never visited that town.
But travelling was no longer possible for her. In her correspondence we find these words, perhaps the last that the mother
wrote about her child: "My Thérèse is really a darling; I can
assure you she will know how to look after herself."

Reverently we follow her at the last stations of this Way of
the Cross. In July, the pain became unbearable, allowing the
poor sufferer neither sleep nor rest, but her soul remained strong
and resigned: "I must not lose a minute of the time that still
remains; these are days of grace which will never return. I wish
to profit by them."

On the First Friday of August, notwithstanding her intense
sufferings, Madame Martin succeeded in going to the Church
of *Notre Dame* to assist at Mass for the last time. Shortly after
that date, Monsieur Martin decided that his two youngest
children could no longer remain near their mother. She had
taken care of them as long as that had been possible, but now,
alas, the sacrifice of a separation had to be imposed, for the
drama had become too tragic for their childish feelings.

Though received in a friendly household which welcomed
them each day, Céline and Thérèse felt like "poor little exiles."
Their thoughts were with their dying mother, and when they
received fruit, Céline's only desire was to keep it for her darling
Mamma. "But our beloved mother was already too ill to eat
any earthly fruit," wrote the Saint later in her *Autobiography,*
"she would never more be satisfied but in heaven, by the vision
of God's glory."

One last ray of sunshine brightened those dark days. Before the children's holidays began, Marie arranged a charming distribution of prizes for her little sisters, to whom she acted as teacher in all subjects. She decorated her room with wreaths and garlands of roses and periwinkle, spread a carpet on the floor, and placed two armchairs for her father and mother, who presided at the ceremony. "Yes," wrote the youthful teacher to her aunt at Lisieux, "Mamma also wished to assist at our prize giving. The two little ones were in white, and you should have seen with what triumphant faces they came to receive their books and wreaths. Papa and Mamma distributed the rewards, and I called up my pupils."

The curtain falls on this last happy scene of family life.

Those who have watched at the bedside of dear ones may know what can be endured by the poor human frame consumed in the last throes of that dread disease which afflicted Madame Martin. With her crucifix before her eyes, she now awaited the consummation of her martyrdom.

On August 26, it became evident that the time had come to administer the sacrament of extreme unction. Monsieur Martin went to the church for the priest. Then, with the utmost reverence, he accompanied his Lord and Master, who deigned to visit his home. With humble submission to the divine Will, his daughters knelt and adored, as Jesus entered the house where He was served so faithfully. Thérèse was present. Years later, she wrote: "The touching ceremony of extreme unction made a deep impression on me. I can still see the place where I knelt, and hear my poor father's sobs." When the ceremony was over, Monsieur Martin accompanied the priest back to the church, notwithstanding the grief that oppressed his heart.

On August 28, half an hour after midnight, at the age of forty-six, Zélie Martin gave back her pure soul to God. In spite of their tears, her daughters, who had so lovingly watched at her bedside, noticed the expression of heavenly serenity which her face assumed in death. Monsieur Martin took his youngest child in his arms, and, overcoming his emotion, carried her to the bed where her mother lay. "Come," he said gently, "come and kiss your dear mother for the last time."

"And without a word, I put my lips to my darling mother's icy forehead." Thérèse's childish mouth felt the coldness of death and she never forgot the impression it made on her. Deep and serious thoughts filled her soul; her precocious intelligence and sensibility took note of everything, though outwardly she remained calm. "I do not think that I cried much," she tells us.

Left alone for a moment in the passage, she found herself in front of a long empty box placed upright against the wall. The child stood still and gazed thoughtfully at the coffin; she had never seen one before, but she understood; it seemed to her "very big and very sad." However, she did not run away. With all her courage, she gazed long and fixedly at that coffin. It was a saint's first meditation on her last end.

The sad rites which accompany death were accomplished; the Requiem Mass in the Church of *Notre Dame* and the final prayers at the cemetery were over. The sight of the five pale-faced orphans in deep mourning was really heart-rending; the two little ones looked so frail in their black dresses.

"We were all five together, looking sadly at one another," wrote Thérèse later, when recalling this sad day. Touched with compassion, the nurse who had looked after the two youngest children since their infancy, exclaimed: "Poor little things, you have no mother now!" Céline threw herself into Marie's arms, exclaiming: "You will be my mother." Thérèse was about to imitate her, when a sudden thought stopped her; she feared that Pauline might be hurt if she did not have a little girl too. So, pleadingly, she laid her fair head on her sister's breast and said: "Pauline will be *my* mother."

To what an extent this new bond united the two sisters, Thérèse's whole life will show.

CHAPTER III

NEW HORIZONS

1. *At les Buissonnets*[1]

THE house in the *Rue Saint-Blaise* was silent. It no longer echoed with joyous shouts and children's games, for Madame Martin's children bore their sorrow silently. The elder girls looked after the little ones, and put their mother's room in order. As they handled the familiar objects, the heart-rending reality of the long separation made itself felt ever more intensely. Monsieur Martin thought of his children's future. At the age of fifty-four he was now a widower with five daughters, of whom the two youngest were only children. Who was to replace their incomparable mother?

During her agony, Madame Martin had fixed a long, suppliant look upon her sister-in-law, who had hastened to her bedside from Lisieux. The dying woman could no longer speak, but the devoted Madame Guérin guessed her wish; with generous sympathy, the kindhearted aunt promised to be a mother to her five nieces. This seemed to Monsieur Martin a providential sign, and so, after a week's hesitation, during which he received many suggestions, the father of the family decided that he would live henceforth at Lisieux.

The sacrifice was a big one, for he loved the pleasant town where he had lived for so many years; he loved his friends, the old familiar haunts, the beautiful garden of the *Pavillon,* and the house in the *Rue Saint-Blaise,* so full of tender memories. He would have to leave all these happy ties with the past, and transplant his life into entirely new surroundings. But his own

---

[1] This was the name of the house at Lisieux. The word is somewhat like the English word "shrubbery."

happiness mattered little; the welfare of his children came first. At Lisieux, they would have the affectionate help of their aunt, and the enlightened protection of their uncle, a man of true moral and intellectual worth.

Monsieur Guérin undertook to find a suitable home, and, on September 10, he suggested *les Buissonnets,* a house which satisfied his brother-in-law. Shortly after the Feast of All Saints, the five orphans said good-by to Alençon, though Monsieur Martin remained behind to finish settling his affairs.

Travellers who happened to be at Lisieux station on that November evening may have noticed the little group of five girls, the youngest of whom looked unusually pretty with her golden hair falling softly on her black dress. But who could have guessed that this little girl would make illustrious, within a few decades of years, the name of the modest Norman town.

Thérèse tells us with charming frankness that she felt no grief at leaving Alençon. She was at the age when children love a change of surroundings, and when every new horizon seems to them a wonderful discovery. It was therefore with pleasure that the little Queen took possession of her new town. Her sad little heart expanded at the kind reception of the Guérins, and she always remembered the warm welcome they gave to the lonely orphans. Many years later, she wrote: "I can still see my little cousins Jeanne and Marie waiting for us on the doorstep with my aunt." Jeanne was a little older than Céline, and Marie was two years older than Thérèse, so the children soon became good playmates. That evening, the orphans dined and slept under this hospitable roof, and the next morning their uncle took them to their new home, *les Buissonnets.*

Monsieur Guérin had made a happy choice. The house, which was of pink brick and white stone, like that at Alençon, stood in the midst of pleasant shrubbery and was situated in an airy part of the town. There were a few big trees, some grass-plots, and flowers — everything in fact that could please a little girl so fond of nature. Describing this new home and the first impression it made on her, Thérèse wrote: "The house charmed me; there was a turret commanding an extensive view, a flower garden in front of the house, and another large garden at the back; everything was delightfully new to my childish mind."

The first impression made by Lisieux on the elder sisters, however, was not nearly so agreeable. Notwithstanding its old picturesque houses and avenues, the town seemed to them rather gloomy. The black smoke rising from the factory chimneys, the greyer sky, the damp atmosphere — all these disadvantages made them regret their departure from the town which held for them so many tender memories. Nevertheless, they set to work courageously to organise their new life. In spite of their youth, Marie and Pauline, aged eighteen and seventeen respectively, soon showed themselves equal to their new duties. Capably and conscientiously, with a wisdom beyond their age, they accomplished their housekeeping duties, showed great devotedness to their father, and were vigilant in the care of their little sisters.

God had taken possession of their hearts; He had given them His choicest graces. Later, He would call them to be His spouses, but, before that happy day, He gave them a task to accomplish which is their most glorious achievement here below — the education of a saint.

Madame Martin had cultivated Thérèse's soul "with an unusually sure, strong, and tender hand." The motherless little girl needed to be formed with the same loving affection, which would not spoil her by overtenderness. The task was all the more delicate because her sensitive little heart, so very affectionate, had received a severe blow at her mother's death; indeed the shock had been so great that her temperament seemed to have been affected by it.

"Immediately after my mother's death, my naturally happy disposition changed completely. Instead of being lively and demonstrative as I had been, I became timid, shy, and extremely sensitive; a look was enough to make me dissolve into tears. I could not bear to be with strangers and was only happy in my own family circle."

What efforts Thérèse made to keep back those tears, always ready to start to her eyes! God would one day give her the strength to master her emotions to such an extent that they would not even be noticed, but that was to be many years later. She would then be fourteen.

During this time of trial, however, her will remained firm; she practised virtue "without feeling its sweetness." "As I grew older," she tells us, "I loved God more and more; I tried to please Jesus in all my actions, taking great care never to offend Him." Our Lord was pleased with His little handmaid, whose only ambition was to do His Will and to respond to His divine love.

Monsieur Martin, Marie, and Pauline cooperated as zealous agents in the divine task, preserving that atmosphere of tender affection which was necessary for the delicate child's development. In the intimacy of the family circle, the little flower began to unfold its delicate petals.

During these early years, it was Pauline who took special care of her little sister. Later Thérèse expressed her admiration for the method of education employed by her "little mother": "I sometimes wonder how you managed to bring me up with so much tenderness without spoiling me, for you did not pass over the slightest fault. It is true you never scolded me without cause, but I knew well that you would never change your mind once a thing was decided upon." On the other hand, Pauline was able to testify to her pupil's obedience: "I do not remember that she ever once disobeyed me."

2. Doings of a Small Child

Five years old! That is the age when a child is awakened in the morning by the sweetness of a mother's kiss, and plays all day long, making ever fresh discoveries; it is the age also when a child begins to take an interest in books covered with mysterious black signs. Thérèse was learning to read. The first word she could read alone was heaven; and she ran to her father to announce her new achievement. She knew well where to find him, for the retired watchmaker liked to withdraw to the little tower at the top of the house, where he would read, write, and meditate. Since his wife's death, his contemplative vocation had revived. The child had free access to his retreat, and was frequently the sweet little companion of this lover of solitude and recollection. Very often they were alone, for Marie and Pauline were busy in the house, while Léonie and Céline were day-boarders at the Benedictine Abbey of Notre Dame du Pré at the other end of the town.

The father and his little daughter often went out together. Slowly, to suit Thérèse's step, they traversed the streets lined with old Norman houses so picturesque with their pointed gables and crossbeams of sculptured wood. Every day they would go into one of the churches to visit the Blessed Sacrament — into the cathedral, or St. James's church, or that of *Saint Désir*. One day they entered the Carmelite Chapel.

"Look, little Queen," whispered Monsieur Martin, "behind those big gratings, there are holy nuns who are always praying to almighty God." Thérèse's big, innocent eyes gazed earnestly at the grating of the Carmelite Convent where nine years later she was to be cloistered.

Sometimes the outing was prolonged, for Monsieur Martin was very fond of fishing and used to take his little daughter with him to the banks of the Touques. Those were happy days for the child, for whom nature held such charm. Her father had given her a fishing-rod; imitating his action, she used to fish in the rapid waters, but fishing was a pastime of which she soon grew tired.

At times, she sat on the grass, listening to the far-off sounds and the murmur of the wind in the tall poplars. "Sometimes, distant strains of music came to my ears from a military band in the town, and imparted a sweet melancholy to my thoughts," she wrote later, when recalling her childhood's memories for Mother Agnes of Jesus. Thérèse was, indeed, a little girl of the nineteenth century, whose poetic feelings were tinged with romanticism in the manner of Lamartine, but her healthy and vigorous temperament would not allow her to indulge in long and idle reveries. Everything around her was beautiful, and she loved nature intensely, but her soul yearned for something greater; her thoughts became deep and serious. "Earth seemed a place of exile and I dreamed of heaven. . . ." That was the only dream that could satisfy the ardent soul of this young child.

One day, a storm took the anglers by surprise. The thunder rumbled alarmingly and they were surrounded by vivid flashes of lightning. Suddenly there was a harsh strident sound — lightning had struck in a field close by! When God gave His law to Moses on Mount Sinai, thunder was heard, the lightning flashed, and the people in the camp trembled; but thunder and lightning did not frighten this little child, for the law of fear was not for her. It seemed to her that God was very near, and the thought delighted her. Monsieur Martin, however, had other thoughts, for the rain was coming down in torrents; catching up his little Queen in his arms, he carried her home at top speed. The road home was a long, ascending path which Monsieur Martin had good-humouredly styled "the path to Paradise."

After their morning walks, Thérèse learned her lessons and then played till dinner time. When Monsieur Martin worked in the garden, clipping the trees or watering his flowers, she would romp near him or play at quiet games. In a little corner of one of the flower beds, near the laundry, she would amuse herself by making tiny altars which seemed to her very wonderful, or else she would play at making herb-tea from the bark of trees, and then present it in a pretty little cup to her good father who would smilingly pretend to drink.

To-day, Thérèse's childish toys are exposed in a large glass case at *Les Buissonnets,* for the house has become a most precious reliquary. They are the beautiful toys of a child, who kept with great care the presents that were lavished on her — the stove on which she prepared her "teas," her shrimp basket, her skipping-rope, her bird-cage, and her doll lying in a little cot, which was made on the model of those used by children in 1880. Visitors may also see her catechism — known by heart — from which she learned to know God.

Women to-day, recalling their own early reminiscences, would doubtless draw up a rather similar list of their childhood's treasures. So it is consoling to think that this little saint was just like other children. We expect wonderful deeds and love to hear of miracles, and consequently may fail to penetrate deeper than surface appearances.

Thérèse's sanctity was never of the "sensational" kind. Had God asked her to stand on a milestone at the corner of the road and preach the gospel to the passers-by, as He asked St. Rose of Viterbo when still a child; or had He told her to build herself a little hermitage at the bottom of the garden where she could devote her time to prayer and contemplation with just a few lemon-pips for food, as He told St. Rose of Lima, Thérèse would have obeyed without hesitation. But the mission entrusted to her was of a different kind. The lesson God has deigned to teach us through St. Thérèse of Lisieux is that we can all sanctify ourselves in the ordinary circumstances of everyday life, no matter where we are placed.

The Holy Child at Nazareth lived like other children of His age. Are we quite sure that we would have recognised Him? "Sanctity consists essentially in union with God and in love with which we accomplish our ordinary actions," wrote Father Petitot in his admirable book on the Saint.[2] These words might be written in letters of gold on each of St. Thérèse's toys.

At the end of her simple day — after the happy evening hour when, perched on her father's knee, she had listened to him singing the old French songs in his beautiful voice, as if to lull her to sleep — the little one, safely tucked up in bed, would ask her "little mother": "Have I been good to-day? Is our Lord pleased with me? . . ." Each time the answer was awaited with anxiety, for the only thing that mattered was to please God.

[2] *Une renaissance spirituelle: Sainte Thérèse de Lisieux.*

If Pauline had said "No," she would have spent the whole night in tears; but with a last tender kiss, Pauline would answer "Yes," thus setting the child's mind at rest. Thérèse would then fall into the pure, sweet sleep of little ones.

3. *In Tune With the Church*

Thus the human and the divine harmonised sweetly in this happy home. There was nothing out of the ordinary nor excessive in the pious duties of this well-ordered life. Exteriorly, it resembled the sweet simplicity of Nazareth.

In spite of the grief which had cast its shadow over the little household, the joys of family life still remained pure and serene, and the feasts of the liturgy were as so many bright flowers scattered along the grey warp of the ordinary days. How much more beautiful life is when lived in union with the feasts of holy Church than when it is spent amid the bustle and agitation of this world! This truth was a consoling reality to each member of Thérèse's finely attuned family.

In the evening, when her big sisters read aloud some pages of Dom Guéranger's *Liturgical Year,* the little girl listened and understood. Soon she knew all the feasts which our holy Mother the Church offers to our loving devotion throughout the year. She loved to venerate the spotless purity of virgins, the martyrs' royal purple, the feasts of the Immaculate Virgin Mary, and, above all, feasts of our Lord.

In preparation for Christmas, Thérèse prepared the crib for the infant Jesus, her little Brother. At the Epiphany, she offered her treasures, like the three wise kings. Then, as the Child-God advanced in age at Nazareth, she learned with Him the great law of work, and the love which is content to lie hidden under the humblest actions. During Lent, when the Church dons purple vestments as a sign of sorrow and mourning, she multiplied her little sacrifices to console Jesus in His sufferings. When the joyous *Alleluia* resounded in the glad springtime, then — beyond the Easter eggs, with their gay ribbons, and the chocolate bells — the devout child perceived the triumphant joy of the mystery which uplifts the whole of Christendom: *Jesus is risen and can die no more.*

At the Ascension, when Jesus arose into heaven, she accompanied Him in His triumph, and at Pentecost the Holy Spirit enkindled her soul. Sweetly He came to console her orphaned heart. And so, continuously, God's tenderness was seen through the veil of His Mysteries.

The Feast of Corpus Christi, indeed, was a day of radiant happiness for Thérèse, when, beneath the blue dome of heaven, the majestic procession advanced, amid the perfume of flowers and incense. Dressed in white, with a wreath of flowers resting on her golden curls, the little girl walked near the canopy. Unceasingly, she drew forth the fragrant rose petals from her light basket and threw them high into the air, like her companions, in honour of Jesus in the Sacred Host. But her gesture was more assured than theirs, and her zeal was more ardent, for she wished her petals to touch the golden monstrance. What joy when she succeeded!

Had Thérèse lived in Galilee, she certainly would have been among those happy little children who ran up to the Divine Master, to see Him and touch Him. Unhesitatingly she would have dared to rest at His Sacred Heart. Her innocent boldness was to win for her a kingdom, for she was one day to become the Queen of Little Ones!

With enraptured happiness Thérèse remembered these feast-days. In her opinion they came too rarely, but fortunately there was one which came round every week, a feast-day of obligation — the Feast of God, the day of rest.

In the beautiful cathedral, with its two unequal spires, Thérèse assisted at High Mass with her father. The Martins had their places reserved in a side chapel, but came nearer the pulpit for sermons. All the parishioners of St. Peter's Cathedral knew the handsome, white-bearded Monsieur Martin and his pretty little daughter who had "something of heaven in her eyes." People smiled and hastened to make room for them, but the charming child was not at all distracted by the admiring glances which followed her. She was all eyes and ears to follow the Divine Office and listen to the preacher. Too young to understand the meaning of the words, she would look at her father, whose attractive face was so expressive. Faith, Hope, and Love were reflected there as in a mirror, and sometimes his eyes filled with tears. Thérèse watched him, admiringly. It was he who initiated his child into the knowledge of the eternal truths. One day, during a sermon on the Passion, she understood for the first time everything the preacher said. She was then five and a half. "After that time," she says, "I was able to understand and appreciate all the sermons."

The Sabbath day, thus sanctified, was later enlivened by a walk, and these little excursions were prolonged as Thérèse grew older. In the fresh country-side of Calvados, somewhat different from that of Orne, the child used to gather large bunches of flowers as in the old days at Alençon.

It was in this way that the happy family spent their radiant Sundays. However, after Compline, the child's happiness would be overshadowed by the thought of the morrow, when the ordinary life of work and lessons would have to begin again. How natural our little Saint was! All the children of the world will find the echo of their sighs in hers!

However, she at once raised her thoughts to the supernatural point of view. This world is a place of exile. Heaven alone, our true fatherland, will be "a never-ending Sunday."

On Monday morning then, she summoned all her courage to face the week; this was made easier by a very pleasant duty, which awaited her that day. Alms were always distributed to the poor on that day, so she left her meditation of heavenly things in order to practise charity.

The poor people of the neighbourhood had quickly found their way to this generous household. With a movement of her little hand, the child imposed silence upon the big white dog, Tom, the companion of her walks, and distributed bread or money to the needy, according to the wants of each. In receiving the alms of the good Monsieur Martin, each one obtained another charming gift — the smile of little Thérèse.

Her child heart was always ready to sympathise with those in distress. One day when she was out with her father, she saw an old man dragging along painfully on crutches, and ran at once to give him an alms. The man, however, fixed the child with a long, sorrowful look, shook his head and refused. The little girl stood still, perplexed. She had wanted to help the poor man, and now she had hurt his feelings; perhaps she had even humiliated him. The thought distressed her greatly. Apparently realising this, the old man turned round and smiled at her. But she remained uneasy and wondered would he accept a cake her father had just bought for her tea. However, she did not dare to run after him, and was on the verge of tears. Suddenly, an idea occurred to her. She had been told that children obtain all the favours they ask on their First Communion Day. Consoled by this thought, she determined to pray for the poor, old man on the day of her First Communion, and five years later she kept her word.

We cannot help admiring her delicacy of feeling and her fidelity in remembering this resolution, even if we regret her oversensitiveness. Her innocent heart always experienced the most generous charity toward the poor — and toward sinners.

One summer's day, she was suffering from the heat, and, on returning from a walk, exclaimed: "Oh Pauline, if you only knew how thirsty I am!" It was a good opportunity for the "little mother" to teach her child the value of self-renunciation through love, which, for God's sake, imposes sacrifices beyond those of strict obligation.

"Would you not deny yourself the drink to save a poor sinner?" she questioned.

The "Yes" came unhesitatingly, but accompanied by a big sigh, for it was, indeed, a big sacrifice that Pauline asked! Satisfied with the generosity of her pupil, the elder sister went to fetch a refreshing drink, but the child feared to accept it lest the sinner would not be saved. Pauline then taught her

that obedience is better than sacrifice and that she would double
her merit by obeying.

On another occasion, she was anxious to know whether all
the elect would be happy in heaven, even the least, even those
who had only just gained entrance to Paradise. Pauline took
Monsieur Martin's big tumbler and Thérèse's tiny thimble, and
filled them both with water. Was one more full than the other?
Both were full to the brim; one drop more would make them
overflow. In a similar way, each soul in heaven will be filled
according to the measure of its own capacity. Envy will never
enter Paradise!

4. *Her Name Writ in Heaven*

In Thérèse's simple life there were not many amusements, but
the child wished for nothing beyond the happy family circle.
Outside her own home, the only company she enjoyed was that
of her kind-hearted uncle and aunt, with whom she was never
shy or unhappy. Every Sunday, the nieces were invited to dinner
in turn. Thérèse was delighted when her day came round, for
Monsieur Guérin was a good talker and had interesting opinions
on all subjects. The kind uncle was very fond of his youngest
niece, whom he called his "little sunbeam," but, when he
perched her on his knee and sang *Bluebeard* in a very deep
voice, she was really somewhat terrified, though she did not let
that be seen. His animated conversation was more to her taste,
and she took the greatest interest in all his remarks.

At eight o'clock her father used to come to fetch her, and they
would walk home together along the dark, deserted streets.
During this long walk home, the child loved to gaze at the stars,
for she never lost an opportunity of admiring nature. One
evening, she noticed a group of golden lights which stood out
in the dark, blue, velvety sky. This was Orion's belt, in which
the reflective child saw a resemblance to the letter T! "Look,
Papa, look," she cried, "my name is written in Heaven." After
that discovery, she wished to see nothing more of this dull earth.
"Lead me, please, Papa," she exclaimed, and then, with her little

hand held firmly in her father's grasp, she walked with head thrown back, lost in delighted contemplation.

How great God was! How good to make the stars so beautiful! How near to the little child whose name was shining in the sky! She yearned to love Him. Already in the heart of the little girl stirrings of immense desires were making themselves felt, immense as the starry sky above.

Monsieur and Madame Guérin spent some weeks every year at the seaside at Trouville. One summer, when Thérèse was six or seven years old, they invited Monsieur Martin and his daughters to join them. In the midst of a fashionable crowd that thronged the famous *Promenade des Planches,* it happened that a lady murmured as she passed Thérèse: "What a pretty little girl!" Monsieur Martin at once made a sign requesting silence on that matter, but the child had heard the remark. The compliment pleased her, for she had not thought that she was pretty. The impression was only a fleeting one, however, and the child soon went to sit down beside Pauline on a rock.

The sun was sinking on the horizon, lighting up the blue immensity of moving water with a golden track of light. Thérèse was silent with admiration. In a few well-chosen words, Pauline commented on the beautiful symbol, explaining that the golden furrow was an image of God's grace, which illumines the path of faithful souls. "Oh," thought Thérèse with enthusiasm, "I shall be like that little boat with the white sail, sailing along in the rays of the sun; I shall never withdraw from our Lord's sight."

Some time later, it was decided that she should make her first confession. She was now six years old and very intelligent for her age. Making a great effort to recall her sins, she remembered one that was bigger than the others. Once, when she had been left at home, because too young to go with her sisters to an evening service during the month of May, she got into a temper with Victoire. The maid had played a trick on her. It was a real temper, for she stamped her foot. Intense shame and contrition followed. It was with this same deep contrition that the child now went to confession. And yet, although usually very impressionable, she was not at all afraid or anxious, for Pauline had told her that it was to God Himself she was going to tell her sins.

When she knelt down in the confessional, she was so small that her curly head did not reach the little hand-rest. The priest was somewhat taken aback at seeing no one there, but presently discovered his small penitent and told her to stand up. Thus Thérèse made her first confession with the greatest confidence and simplicity, standing just in front of the priest who took God's place, and her innocent accusations must have touched his heart. After speaking to her about our Lady, the priest blessed her without giving absolution, for such was the custom in France at that time. Very pleased and quite at ease, the little girl passed her Rosary through the grating so that it could be blessed too, and then came out of the church exceedingly happy and light-hearted. It was getting dusk, as the sisters wended their way home; suddenly Thérèse stopped under a street lamp.

"What are you doing?" asked Pauline.

"I just wanted to see what a blessed Rosary looks like," was the reply.

The elder sisters were greatly amused at this answer, which shows what a delightfully simple child she was.

5. *A Prophetic Apparition*

When the family returned to Lisieux after the happy holiday, Thérèse resumed her everyday life with its childish games and duties. About this time, a strange thing happened — undoubtedly supernatural and certainly prophetic — by which heaven seemed to foreshadow its designs for this little girl. It was nothing less than an astonishing revelation of an unhappy event of the future.

The incident took place at three o'clock in the afternoon on a beautiful summer's day, when everything out-of-doors was bright and pleasant. Monsieur Martin was away on business at Alençon. Thérèse was looking out of the window at the garden bathed in sunshine, when suddenly she saw there, in front of her, a man dressed exactly like her father, with the same walk and of the same height, but bent, aged, and with his head covered by a thick veil.

"He advanced slowly, with measured step, along my little garden," wrote the Carmelite fifteen years later when she had forgotten nothing of the dramatic apparition.

Seized with "supernatural fear," Thérèse called out as loud as she could: "Papa, Papa!" The mysterious personage paid no heed and continued his walk, finally disappearing behind a clump of firs. "He will surely reappear at the other side," thought the child. But there was no sequel; the prophetic vision had vanished.

At the child's cry of terror, Marie and Pauline, who were working in an adjoining room, ran to see what was the matter.

"Why are you calling Papa when he is at Alençon?" asked Marie anxiously.

"I saw a man in the garden exactly like Papa," explained the child.

The unusual incident made an unpleasant impression on the older girls. They knew that their little sister did not tell lies, and they were equally certain that their father was at Alençon. Trying to find an explanation of the matter, they suggested that Victoire had played a trick, covering her head with an apron to frighten the child. Victoire was up in arms at the idea and declared that she had not left the kitchen. So, summoning up their courage, they all went to look behind the clump of trees, where, of course, they found no one. "Think no more about the matter," said Marie and Pauline, trying to persuade the child to forget the incident.

It was easy to give such good advice, but Thérèse found it less easy to put the recommendation into practice. Although always obedient, she could not prevent the vision coming back to her mind; she *knew* that she had not been mistaken and that it was not a question of childishness or hallucination. She felt that is was something supernatural, but could not understand its meaning and wondered why the scene had taken place.

When the Carmelite wrote her *Autobiography* many years later, she had long since understood. Alas, it was indeed her father whom God had shown her, bearing upon his face the symbol of his great trial! Monsieur Martin was, in fact, destined to suffer an illness, which was extremely painful for his daughters' hearts. Stricken with paralysis which affected his intellectual faculties, he had even to be handed over to the care of strangers for three years. One detail is to be noted; during the early stages of his illness, he was often seen to cover his head with a veil.

During this terrible trial, Thérèse's unwavering faith never faltered in adoring the divine plan. She understood that, in a mystic way, her beloved father was participating in the humiliations of Jesus in His Passion, and that the face of the faithful servant was to be veiled as that of the Master. She knew that he was sharing his Master's sufferings in order to have a greater share in the glory of his Divine Lord. "How I admire God's ways in showing us this precious cross beforehand!" the Saint wrote later, in her courageous way. Nevertheless, she could not help asking herself why God gave this light to a child, who would have died of grief if she had understood its meaning.

In her childhood days, Thérèse could not have borne the thought that any harm could befall her father, who was so very dear to her. Once, when her cherished king was standing near the top of a high ladder with his little girl close by as usual, he suddenly called out: "Move away, little Queen, for, if I fall, I shall kill you." The child's heart rebelled at the thought of separation; instead of going further away, she came nearer. "If Papa falls," she thought, "I am certainly not going to have the grief of seeing him die; I shall die with him!"

Her admiration was as great as her love, and she used to listen to her dear father as to an oracle. She felt sure that if the great men of Parliament — of whom Uncle Guérin talked — knew her father, they would take him as their king, and then France would be happier than ever. After reflection, however, she was glad that they did not know him, for two reasons: first of all, because he would be unhappy — "since that is the lot of kings" — and secondly, because he would no longer be just her king alone!

To bear the terrible trial that awaited her, Thérèse would need a very special grace, but at the hour marked by providence that grace would not be denied her, and her heroism should then have attained such heights that she could live through the crucifying years of her poor father's martyrdom with thanksgiving reigning in her heart. "This," she concluded, "is one of those impenetrable mysteries which we shall understand only in heaven, where they will be the subject of our eternal admiration. My God, how good you are! How well you suit the trial to our strength!"

CHAPTER IV

SCHOOL-DAYS

1. *Suffering in Silence*

THE years had passed and Thérèse was now eight and a half. For four years, Pauline had attended to her education and care. Each year, the "little mother" had arranged a festive prize-day — as Marie had done in the old days at Alençon — on which the little girl received her awards and wreaths from the hands of her beloved "King," in the presence of the assembled family. The child's heart used to beat with excitement on these occasions, which seemed to her a picture of the Judgment Day. The verdict had always been favourable, however, for the little pupil worked well at her lessons. Those happy days had now come to an end.

Satisfied with the education given at the Benedictine Abbey, Monsieur Martin decided that his youngest daughter should now have the advantage of that training and take the place of Léonie who had finished her studies.

Fortunately for Thérèse, Céline was not yet ready to leave school, so every morning the two little girls left home together, and met their cousins at the Guérins' chemist shop. At four o'clock in the afternoon, they all returned together accompanied by the maid.

In the strangeness of her new life, this walk with her cousins was a pleasure for Thérèse, for the day spent far from home, in entirely new surroundings, was a great trial to the shy, retiring child, whose oversensitiveness shrank from strangers. Feeling that the time had come to face life bravely, Thérèse strove with all her courage to overcome herself, but did not altogether succeed in conquering her feelings, which gave her many an occasion of meritorious struggle.

The Benedictines of the Abbey of *Notre Dame du Pré* were fervent Religious. Their pupils — by whom they were called Madame — were about sixty in number and belonged to families fairly within the middle-class group. In the Convent atmosphere of piety and kindness, the girls received an excellent and sound education. Monsieur Martin's choice of the Abbey proves the value of this Benedictine education, for he would not have confided his dear little Queen to severe or incapable teachers. However, the little flower never bloomed in the shade of the stern walls of the ancient Abbey. Years later, when writing of that period of her life, the Carmelite spoke of the nuns with gratitude, but, at the same time, revealed sorrows never mentioned until then.

Let us note, in passing, this early evidence of Thérèse's vocation to suffer in silence, for silent suffering was one of the chief characteristics of her sanctity.

Though placed in a class of little girls all older than herself, the new pupil soon attracted attention on account of her quick mind, her careful work, and her obedience; she was nearly always first in the class. As a result, the clever child became the victim of jealousy, that most detestable vice — hitherto unsuspected by her — by which certain natures react toward the obvious superiority of their companions. In the course of time Thérèse was to experience bitterly the painful discomfort caused by this contact with envy. The Saint has not told us everything on this point, but from the disclosures made in her *Autobiography* — written only for her "little mother," who had become her Prioress — we learn the following facts:

A fourteen-year-old companion, who was not very intelligent, was annoyed at her success and made her suffer for it "in a thousand ways." Though not clever, this pupil knew how to influence others and drew them into an underhand petty warfare. We can imagine what suffering that meant for a shy, sensitive child who did not know how to defend herself — and did not wish to do so either. She could not bring herself to answer her disagreeable companion with cross words, and preferred not to make any complaint to others. She believed it was more perfect to keep silence, and so, although she sometimes wept, *she never spoke about her suffering*. "I had not enough virtue to rise above these troubles and my poor little heart suffered greatly," she explained in her *Autobiography*.

Modest as the Saint is regarding her own virtue, we have reason to regard this silence as truly heroic for a child of nine. Céline, "the fearless" as her father called her, would have understood and defended her well. For this a few words on her part would have sufficed. On the walk home when her heart was still smarting from the little pin-pricks of the day, Thérèse could have unburdened herself ever so little — just shown her suffering without naming those who had hurt her. But one word, she felt, might have led to another, and so in the end there might have been a fault against charity. True to her ideal of silent endurance, her lips remained sealed even to her father and "little mother." That was her decision at the time, and at all events her heart was at peace, for she had done the best she knew and had been faithful to her Lord.

Although she found it difficult to learn passages by heart, yet her teachers scarcely noticed this difficulty. At the catechism class, however, the chaplain was amazed at the manner in which she understood the things of God. He humorously referred to her as his "little Doctor of Theology," little thinking that one day she would be the teacher of a spiritual way so sure and so luminous, that theologians themselves would come to learn at her school.

The good Father Domin, in fact, was not inclined to believe too quickly in supreme sanctity, and was always somewhat diffident in her regard. He was told that she was not recollected at Mass and that she did not read her prayer-book. True, she often raised her head, yet she obeyed with charming submission when the nuns made her a sign to go on reading. A minute later, however, her eyes were again gazing into space. No one knew to what intimate union with Himself God had already raised her, and that she was reading "the Book of Life which teaches the science of Love." These holy Benedictine nuns were surprised at her "distractions"; they never quite understood her soul. And so her real worth remained hidden as "by a veil," beneath the extreme sensitiveness which continued to be her trial.

In truth, since her mother's death, Thérèse had been going through a period of darkness and humiliation. "A veil" seemed to have fallen over her eminent qualities, concealing them from others. In the world outside her home, she was often considered incapable and even awkward, in spite of her quick intelligence. It was divine providence that placed this "veil," so that she should remain humble; God wished to preserve her soul from all feeling of self-satisfaction.

In the rectangular playground surrounded by the high seventeenth-century buildings, the pupils played joyously at recreation hours. Little Thérèse Martin did not care much for noisy games; she was not very skilful at them. The other pupils noticed this, and the bigger girls of her class were delighted to take their revenge here for her success at lessons. They made fun of her and laughed at her until they caused her to cry.

In order to dry her tears and escape her tormentors, she used to look for solitary pastimes. Under the limes, she might find a little dead bird, which had fallen from its nest no doubt, and she would bury it "honourably." Often, too, she might say her Rosary quietly, under the shade of the big trees. Yet sometimes she left her solitude to indulge in story-telling, narrating such tales as "The King of the Cats." She told stories well, and the pupils who had just been teasing her would themselves join her audience to listen.

However, school-rules did not allow story-telling at recreation, since that was the time for "exercising the body and not the brain." So Thérèse tried to obey and to shake off the shyness that oppressed her, but she felt that she was "not an agreeable companion." This painful embarrassment lasted until the end of her school-days. We can understand, therefore, her happiness on returning every day to her own dear home, where love reigned supreme.

2. *No Saint by Halves*

Thérèse loved books and could have "spent a whole life reading." Pauline very wisely satisfied this desire by choosing good books which were both instructive and interesting, especially historical narratives. On holidays, the little girl buried herself in her books. In this pastime, however, she found opportunities for "great sacrifices," because her "little mother" limited the period for this favourite recreation. As soon as the time came to shut her book, Thérèse would stop immediately, even in the middle of the most interesting passage. She had already learned to mortify her inclinations.

When she read of heroic actions, her heart beat with enthusiasm, and she longed to imitate the heroines who had accomplished such marvellous deeds. Above all others, Joan of Arc enchanted her. The little girl of Lisieux dreamed of heroism and pictured herself a second Joan of Arc, forgetting perhaps the tragic end of the holy Maid of Orleans. In reality, she dreamed of glory — glory and sanctity together!

"In reading certain tales of chivalry, I did not always understand the reality of life," she admits humbly. Jesus then intervened, for He did not want an overexalted enthusiasm; He wished her to understand clearly the essential side of holiness. "Jesus made me understand that the only true glory is that which lasts forever and that brilliant deeds are not necessary, but rather a life hidden from the eyes of others and even from oneself, so that 'the left hand knoweth not what the right hand doth.' Feeling that I was born for great things and wondering in what my glory would consist, it was made known to me interiorly that my glory would not be seen by the eyes of men, and that I was to strive to become a saint."

This resolution to aim at sanctity so exalted is truly surprising in a child so young. She realised that she had a glorious destiny, but foresaw no less clearly the way of renunciation that lay before her. This austere path she was to follow to the very end, with her entire will intent upon the ideal shown to her, the ideal of holiness.

One day, at Alençon, when Thérèse was still very small, Léonie had come up with a basketful of pretty little trifles, on the top of which lay a doll. Céline and Thérèse looked up wonderingly. "Look, darlings, you may choose," said the generous Léonie. Céline examined the basket and took a ball of braid. Thérèse in her turn put out her hand. "I choose everything," she said and bore off basket and doll without further ceremony. In this childish incident she herself was later to see the summary of her whole life.

"When the way of perfection opened out before me," she writes, "I understood that in order to become a saint, one must suffer greatly, and, renouncing oneself, ever seek to do that which is most perfect. I understood that there are many degrees of holiness and that each soul is free to respond to the voice of our Lord, by doing a great deal or only a little for His sake. Then, as in the days of my childhood, I cried out: 'My God, I choose everything. I will not be a saint by halves, I am not afraid to suffer for Thee.'"

The child, who could utter such a sublime challenge in presence of her God, was indeed of the race of warriors, heroes, and martyrs.

3. *Hoverings of the Divine Eagle*

While these great thoughts were at work in her soul, Thérèse remained outwardly very simple and natural like other little girls of her age. She sought the company of her cousin Marie Guérin, because the latter left her free to choose the games she liked. (In reality, the shy little schoolgirl had the soul of a leader.) At Uncle Guérin's, the two little ones used to play at being hermits. They had only a poor tiny hut, a bit of a corn-field, and a garden in which to grow a few vegetables. One of the hermits used to contemplate while the other worked, and the make-believe continued even during their walks. One day on the way back from the Abbey, the hermit Thérèse said to her cousin:

"Lead me; I am going to shut my eyes."

"So am I," replied hermit Marie.

As neither would give in to the other, the two foolish little girls soon fell over a grocer's stall. The man came rushing out of his shop, storming and threatening, while the two hermits — their eyes now wide open — scampered off as fast as their legs would carry them, followed at a distance by their nurse, as indignant as the grocer.

Thérèse relates the incident with a sprightly pen. In spite of her trials at school, she still had many joys. As soon as she reached home at the end of classes she recovered her good spirits and scrambled on to her father's knee, recounting her marks, which were always good, and usually excellent. Her father's kiss would then make her forget the petty teasing of her companions at school. Her good marks were rewarded by substantial gifts, and many a welcome silver coin found its way into her money-box, which was reserved for the poor.

In truth, life was sweet in Thérèse's home. Through mutual devotedness and loving affection, happiness had been restored to the motherless household. God was loved and served, and the poor were assisted.

"He who has ears to hear, let him hear," said Jesus. God's voice was heard in this faithful family. The great call of Love resounded and the Divine Eagle hovered over the happy, peaceful household. God wanted these hearts for Himself alone; He was to take possession of them all, one by one, but it was Pauline He called first.

As the two elder girls were talking one day about Pauline's approaching entrance at Carmel, their little sister, who was doing her homework in a corner of the room, listened with fast-beating heart. She had once told her "little mother" that she would like to go away with her into the desert, and it had been arranged that they would go together when Thérèse was big enough! And now Pauline was going away alone.

17663

The child's suffering was so great that she thought she would die. The expression is not exaggerated. Her own words were: "I did not yet know the joy of sacrifice. I was so very weak that it was only by a great grace I was able to bear this sorrow without dying; the trial seemed quite beyond my strength."

The "little mother," whose heart must have been wrung with sorrow at seeing the child so grieved, caressed and comforted her, explaining the life at Carmel and its solitude filled with God alone. Somewhat consoled, Thérèse laid up Pauline's words in her heart and reflected on them; then, one evening, our Lord gave her a great light and she understood that the desert for which she longed was Carmel.

There could be no doubt in the matter: it was in Carmel that God wanted her to lead her hidden life. There was an unmistakable certainty in the divine Call, and a great peace filled the sorrowful little heart. The child confided her "light" to Pauline, who, very happy and perhaps not greatly surprised, took her to Carmel one Sunday to see the Mother Prioress. Alone with the Religious, the little girl gravely disclosed her secret: she wished to enter Carmel with Pauline and make her First Communion on her sister's Clothing Day. This naïve and sublime avowal touched the heart of Mother Mary Gonzaga, who replied that she believed in Thérèse's vocation, but that the child would have to wait till she was sixteen to enter, as the rule was inflexible on that point. The "little mother," then, was to go away alone.

On October 2, 1882, Pauline left home forever. Henceforth Thérèse would never see her sister except through the parlour gratings. "Oh, how I suffered in that parlour!" sighed the Saint, after a silence of fifteen years, when, by obedience, she was writing her early Memories. But the suffering of the separation was nothing compared to the impossibility of speaking heart to heart with her own dear Pauline. Accustomed in the past to long, intimate talks with her sister, she now had no more than "two or three minutes" at the end of the short visits allowed to the family. That was all. After spending these few minutes in tears, the heart-broken child used to go away with the thought: "Pauline is lost to me." This sad and bitter refrain never left her mind.

As a general rule, however, she did not show her feelings. She hid her suffering, continuing her school life as best she could and trying to render her interior life ever more intense. She chose, in fact, the name she would like to have when a nun. She knew there was already a Sister Teresa of Jesus in the Carmel, but all the same she wanted to keep her beautiful name. She wondered if she could be named Thérèse of the Child Jesus. The Child Jesus represented humility and recalled God's first appearance among men. The same day in the parlour, Mother Mary Gonzaga said suddenly:

"My dear little girl, when you come to us, you will be called Thérèse of the Child Jesus."

What happiness these words caused her! She felt that it was Jesus Himself who had given her that name, in the person of the Prioress.

4. *The Mysterious Sickness*

Such brief periods of happiness passed quickly, however, and Thérèse's poor little heart, sensitive in the extreme, was over-burdened by sorrow to such an extent that her constitution was shaken. She suffered from headaches and was growing thin, yet no one realised that the little girl was in danger of dying from grief.

At the end of March, Monsieur Martin, Marie, and Léonie went to Paris to assist at the Holy Week Ceremonies in the big churches of the capital. Thérèse was confided to Madame Guérin, with Céline. One day, when her uncle was speaking affectionately about her mother, and recalling souvenirs of the past, the little girl was greatly affected and burst into tears. Her kind uncle, surprised at this outburst, decided that the child needed a change, and, as the Easter holidays were near, he resolved to give her all the distractions likely to bring pleasure to a child of that age.

But that was not to be, for the same evening Thérèse was seized with a strange shivering, and her headache became so acute that she could no longer hide the fact. Madame Guérin nursed her with great devotedness, but, when Monsieur Martin returned from Paris, he found sorrow seated in his home. His grief can easily be imagined. What would he not have done to save his little Queen! Several doctors were consulted, but, alas, medical science was baffled; the illness had no name. In her *Autobiography,* the Saint does not hesitate to attribute this strange malady to the devil. We can easily believe this, for he must have been furious at the harm this family was to do him in the future, a family in which God was so well loved — yet furious, above all, must be have been with the little Thérèse whose singularly high destiny he may to some degree have suspected. He had long been lying in wait for her.

One evening, some months before Thérèse's birth, after reading the life of a saint who had suffered greatly from diabolical persecution, Madame Martin was thinking: "Such things will never happen to me; it is only the saints who need fear to be molested in that way," when, all at once, she felt a grip on her shoulder like the clutch of a tremendously heavy wild beast. The brave woman put the evil one to flight with a prayer. Though he had not attained his object that evening, he did not consider himself defeated, and was ready to bide his time.

When, therefore, in 1883, he saw the child of ten depressed and run down, with shaken nerves, his opportunity seemed to have come. To bring good out of evil, God in His Providence allowed him to have a measure of power over her. For long hours Thérèse lay without a movement. Those around her thought she had fainted, but she heard everything. She seemed to be delirious, but assures us that she did not lose the use of her reason for a single moment. Yet she said things she did not mean, and did things she did not want to do. At times, spasms of suffering seized her; she started up in bed and her sisters had to fight against her to push her back with force. We can imagine their agony at seeing her in such a state!

When the anxious father came in to inquire about his little Queen, she lay prostrate. Her pretty face was so motionless that it seemed deathlike. When she opened her eyes they stood wide open in terror, for the hat in Monsieur Martin's hand seemed to her to have the shape of some horrible monster. The poor father was obliged to leave, sobbing.

Meanwhile, in the convent, the time for Pauline's Clothing was drawing near. God knew what the postulant was capable of enduring. Not only was she unable to nurse Thérèse in this dreadful illness, but she felt that her departure had probably been the cause of the trouble. And now she had to accept the sacrifice of not seeing her little sister on the only day on which she could have held the child clasped to her heart.

But on the part of Thérèse, the sickness she underwent was no mere natural disease. On this all agree. If, then, God had allowed Satan to have a measure of power over her, He could also at any moment withdraw that power. Thérèse had never doubted that God would be merciful. She had felt all the time that she would be allowed to see her charming "little mother" in the white bridal dress of the Clothing Day, and to nestle close to her own dear Pauline as she hid her head under the Carmelite's white veil. And so, against all human possibilities, it happened. Thérèse was not denied the happiness that was heaven to her — and to Pauline.

But on returning from the ceremony at Carmel, the child was put to bed again, with all due prudence. On the following day, her condition was found to be worse than ever. Soon she needed constant attention.

Once, when Léonie was acting as nurse, she was obliged to leave the child alone for a short time. On her return, the little invalid was nowhere to be seen. Amazed, the anxious nurse eventually discovered that she had fallen down between the bed and the wall. Often the little girl fainted and then remained unconscious for a considerable time. She was afraid of everything, especially of the devil, and fancied herself surrounded by frightful precipices.

During this extraordinary trial, the poor little invalid was conscious of the love and tenderness of her dear ones. Marie watched at her bedside like a mother. In fact, the child could not endure to be left without her big sister and expected her to be always present, except when she went to Mass or to the Carmel to see Pauline.

In vain the glad springtime came when the golden-haired child might have joyously romped about in the country gathering the wild flowers she loved. But the baffling malady continued. Céline and Léonie gave up all their Sunday walks to remain with their little sister, for they feared that the hour of her death was fast approaching. They knew also that, if death did not come, something worse might happen. The doctors feared that the child's mind would be affected. What an anxious time it was for the loving hearts of her sisters!

At this period the sick child was transferred to Marie's bright, airy room in the front of the house. At the side of the white-curtained bed, on a pedestal against the wall, was placed the beautiful statue of the Blessed Virgin which Madame Martin had loved so much. In her calmer hours, Thérèse even now made wreaths for our Lady with the daisies and forget-me-nots brought by her sisters. One day during the month of May, Monsieur Martin came into the room in deep distress and gave Marie several gold coins with instructions to send this sum to the shrine of Our Lady of Victories in Paris, asking at the same time for a novena to implore Thérèse's cure. The sick child, who had heard everything, was touched to the depths of her heart at her beloved father's faith and tenderness, but could not even say a word of thanks.

One day during the novena, Léonie remained alone with the little invalid, while Marie went down to the garden for a while. In a low voice, Thérèse began to call "Marie, Marie." Accustomed to her moanings, Léonie paid no attention but continued reading by the window. Then, louder and louder, the child continued to cry out: "Marie, Marie." Hearing her from the garden, the big sister hastened back, but Thérèse did not recognise her.

The child looked at her godmother as if she were a stranger, and continued to call "Marie, Marie." It was indeed a terrible moment.

Marie said a few words in a low voice to Léonie and went away again. Since Thérèse believed her to be in the garden, she would go back there. Léonie then carried the child to the window to let her see Marie, who came toward her with out-stretched arms, calling gently: "Thérèse, darling Thérèse!" Still the child failed to recognise her.

5. *The Statue Comes to Life*

That was more than Marie could bear. Returning to the room, she threw herself on her knees before the statue of our Lady. With touching fervour, she begged the cure of her little sister, her god-child, her child. With irresistible perseverance, she continued to entreat the Blessed Virgin to obtain this cure. Léonie and Céline, who were both present, implored the same favour with an equally suppliant prayer, and the united pleading of the three sisters "was a cry of faith which forced heaven's gates."

Somewhat calmer, the sick child turned toward the statue and implored her heavenly Mother to have pity on her. Her prayer was heard. She herself has related what then took place:

"Suddenly, the statue came to life. The Blessed Virgin became so exceedingly beautiful that I could never find words to describe that heavenly beauty. Her face was ineffably sweet, tender, and compassionate; but what touched me to the very depths of my soul was her wonderful smile. Then all my troubles vanished. Two big tears started to my eyes and fell silently; they were tears of true, heavenly joy. Our Lady came toward me and smiled at me. 'How happy I am,' I thought, 'but I shall not tell anyone or my happiness will cease.' Then I lowered my eyes and recognised by beloved Marie immediately. She looked at me lovingly, with deep emotion, and seemed to guess that I had just received a great grace."

Marie had, indeed, seen the heavenly reflection on Thérèse's face, which had become transparent and radiant. She had had a glimpse of the ecstasy. Heaven had descended to that room and the devil had been put to flight forever.

Thérèse was cured.

What joyous thanksgiving reigned in the hearts of the four sisters as they kissed one another with tears of gratitude.

However, the silent child said nothing about the mysterious vision. When they were alone together, Marie questioned her lovingly but persistently, for she felt sure something extraordinary had taken place. Had she not the right to know, since her prayer had obtained the miracle? At length, Thérèse yielded to her godmother's request, and, in spite of her instinct to keep silence, related all that had happened.

Thrilled with the account, Marie asked permission to repeat the story at Carmel. The child could not refuse. At her next visit, not a few of the nuns gathered in the parlour; Mother Mary Gonzaga showed special affection for the little girl who had been miraculously cured, and eager questions were asked: "Was the Child Jesus with the Blessed Virgin? Did angels accompany her?" Thérèse was troubled by these childish and indiscreet inquiries. She had not seen as much as that. The sincere child could only repeat one thing:

"Our Lady seemed to me very beautiful. I saw her come toward me and smile at me."

The nuns were disappointed. Fearing that she had not given a good account of her "grace," Thérèse was troubled. She wondered if she had been guilty of an untruth, and this distressing scruple became a source of intense humiliation for her. Jesus knew quite well that she had told the exact truth, but He allowed this torturing doubt for the good of her soul, as the Saint explains in her lucid way: "But for that suffering, vanity might have crept into my heart. As it was, humiliation became my lot and I looked on myself with feelings of the deepest contempt. My God, you alone know what I suffered."

Four years later, our Lady herself reassured her privileged child, and peace was restored to the troubled conscience.

CHAPTER V

SPIRITUAL JOYS AND DARKNESS

THÉRÈSE had, indeed, been cured by the Queen of heaven. Notwithstanding the secret anxiety that tortured her mind, she soon regained strength, while the elder girls vied with each other in showing their tender love for their little sister so unexpectedly restored to health.

Three months later, in the month of August, Monsieur Martin took his little Queen to visit friends and relatives, beginning with Alençon, where the child's exceptionally good memory recalled reminiscences of her early childhood. She was delighted with the fortnight's tour, during which she visited many famous places, including the Château of Saint Denis and the Château of Grogny. The fine estates with their well-kept gardens and parks, the charming fashionable visitors who petted and admired her, and all her new surroundings appealed to the child of ten and attracted her greatly. The Saint admits this, quite candidly. It was the first time she had come into contact with this happy, easy-going life of legitimate pleasures. She quite realised that one could live that life without offending God and that she could choose that easy life if she wished, but she knew that her soul would not be satisfied, for her heart sought a more sublime ideal.

In later years, when a Carmelite, Thérèse wrote: "Perhaps Jesus wished me to know something of the charm of this world before His first visit to my soul, so that I could choose my future path with greater certainty." It was divine providence that allowed this temptation, due perhaps to the cunning of the devil, trying to catch by "the enchantment of trifles" the prey that had escaped him. At all events, notwithstanding the attraction she felt, Thérèse remained strong and faithful to grace.

1. *Thérèse's First Communion*

After six months' absence from school, she returned to the Abbey of *Notre Dame du Pré* in October; the new school year was to prepare her for her First Communion. What joy that thought brought her! For many years the devout child had been longing for that great day.

It was long before the time of Pius X, and the decree concerning children's Communion at an early age had not yet been promulgated. In Thérèse's day, children were allowed to make their First Communion only in the year of their eleventh birthday. As Thérèse was born on January 2, 1873, she had to wait till the year 1884; even for her there was no exemption from the existing law.

Once, on Christmas Eve, when only seven years of age, she had begged Marie to take her to Midnight Mass; in her clever little way, she had conceived a very simple plan, which she explained to her sister: "I shall slip in among the people who are going to receive Jesus, quite close to you, Marie, and no one will notice me, being so small."

Indeed, why should she not have received Holy Communion at that early age, since her heart was pure and she longed for Jesus? However, she did not succeed in obtaining her request. On another occasion, if her sisters had not prevented her, she would have stopped the Bishop of the diocese in the streets of Lisieux to ask for the permission, so ardently desired, to make her First Communion before the accustomed age.

Céline's First Communion had brought great happiness to Thérèse, for the latter had joined in her sister's preparation as if it were for her own great day, listening very earnestly to Pauline's instructions and noting carefully that "from the day of her First Communion, Céline should live an entirely new life." Thérèse eagerly longed to begin that "new life" also and begged for no further delay. But alas! four years were to pass before she could have the happiness of receiving her Lord and her God in Holy Communion.

Now, however, that great joy was near at hand, and she was preparing with great fervour for that happy hour. God's agents were zealously instructing the innocent, little soul. The kind priest, Father Domin, taught her catechism at the Benedictine Convent, and Marie — who had taken Pauline's place — had long talks with her little god-child every evening. The noble, generous heart of the elder sister, who was to enter Carmel two years later, communicated its zealous ardour to Thérèse's soul. Many years after, the latter wrote: "As the ancient warriors taught their children the art of warfare, so she taught me the combat of life and showed me the glorious palm of victory."

Marie's words fell into the child's soul as the good seed into fertile soil. It seemed to the innocent child that the most hardened sinners would be converted by her sister's eloquence, if they could but hear her.

To appreciate to the full the spiritual treasures given to her, the child wished to have time for "mental prayer," but Marie refused this request, fearing that such serious concentration of thought was beyond her little sister's powers. Thérèse accepted this decision with humble obedience, but frequently hid behind the curtains of her bed in order to "think."

"What do you think about?" one of the nuns asked her.

"About God . . . about the shortness of this life . . . about eternity," was the shy reply.

Without meaning to disobey, the little child had given herself up to contemplative prayer.

In her cloistered convent, Pauline prayed for her little sister and helped the child's fervent preparation by compiling a little book of devotional thoughts and quotations. Her symbolism was mainly drawn from flowers, since Thérèse had such a love of nature. Roses, violets, primroses, daisies — symbols of love, of humility, of gentleness, of simplicity — were foremost among the mystical flowers which the fervent child was to gather, within the next seventy days, to form a cradle of flowers for Jesus when He came to her heart. Aspirations and sacrifices were to accompany the gathering of the flowers. When adding a daisy to her bouquet, for instance, she was to say: "Dear little Jesus, grant me your simplicity." During the nine days preceding her First Communion, however, she was to gather nothing but lilies.

For her retreat, Thérèse was a boarder at the Abbey. It was the first time she lived under a strange roof, but this fact made no impression on her, for she was indifferent to everything but the great reality of her approaching First Communion. Her soul soared toward her God, on the wings of love and praise.

One little incident may be noted. Every evening, the head mistress went round the dormitory, with a lantern in her hand. Drawing aside the white curtains around Thérèse's bed, she used to kiss the child on the forehead in a very motherly way. Touched to the depths of her heart, the little girl responded one night by a spontaneous disclosure of her great secret. "Oh, Madame, I am so fond of you, I shall tell you a great secret," she exclaimed, and, drawing from under her pillow the precious little book received from Carmel, she showed it to the nun, while her eyes sparkled with joy.

The retreat for the first communicants was preached by Father Domin. Thérèse listened attentively to the sermons and summed up the instructions in a note-book, but she would not write anything about her impressions, saying that she would remember them quite well.

At recreation time, the other boarders noticed the large crucifix, a present from her sister Léonie, worn ostensibly at her belt by the little girl, and thought that she wished thereby to imitate her Carmelite sister. In truth, Thérèse often thought of Pauline, whose Profession, by a charming coincidence, was to take place on the date of her First Communion. To the one, Jesus was going to give Himself; from the other, He was going to receive the gift of complete oblation.

The morning of May 8, 1884, dawned at last. The Saint has given us in detail a touching account of this radiantly beautiful day, "the happiest day in life." She tells us of the joyous awakening at dawn, the affectionate, respectful kisses of the nuns and the older girls, the snow-white wreaths, the white, symbolic dresses, and the procession into the chapel while the little ones sang, in their clear, sweet voices, the traditional hymn:

"O Sacred Altar, which angels surround . . ."

Then her pen hesitates . . . she cannot tell us all, she does not wish to reveal all . . . she is afraid of spoiling the exquisite memory of that day by putting her thoughts into words . . . at last, she allows her heart to speak, but we must remember that she is writing for Pauline alone.

"Ah! How sweet was that first embrace of Jesus in my soul. I felt that He loved me and I said to Him, 'I love You; I give myself to You forever.' "

Jesus had no request to make and no sacrifice to ask from the child to whom He came for the first time sacramentally, because her heart was already His, irrevocably. "On that day," she says, "our meeting was not a mere glance; it was 'union.' "

As a drop of water is lost in the mighty ocean, so Thérèse disappeared entirely in the presence of Jesus. He alone remained. He was Lord: He was King. Had she not asked Him to take away from her that liberty which she feared to retain? She was so conscious of her weakness and frailty that she wished to be united forever to His Divine Strength.

"I love You and I give myself to You forever."

She had been told to imitate the simplicity of the daisy. What simplicity there is here in the glowing heat of the divine flame! Theologians, who have studied the soul of the little Saint, tell us that her union with God was already very great. What words can human language find more expressive than that simple phrase "I love You!"

The child's happiness was so intense and so complete that it betrayed itself in tears — a flood of happy tears that her companions could not understand. "Why is she crying? Has she anything on her conscience? Does she regret the absence of her mother or her Carmelite sister?" they asked, in their misunderstanding way. Oh no, there was only joy, ineffable, overwhelming joy. The feeling of separation had gone; heaven dwelt in her soul, and all those she loved were in her soul with Jesus. In a beautiful description of overflowing joy, the Saint expresses her feelings by these profound words:

"No one understood that when all the joy of heaven comes into a human heart, that poor, weak, exiled heart cannot contain such happiness without shedding tears."

In the Convent chapel, the little girls were separated from the faithful by the cloister grating. Monsieur Martin, Marie, Léonie, and Céline — with the relatives of the other children — prayed fervently in the outer church. It is most probable that they did not recognise their darling amidst those twenty little girls, veiled in white and carrying lighted candles, for it would have been difficult to distinguish faces behind the bars of the grating, but, very likely they caught a glimpse of the sweet face, lit up with happiness, when the child knelt at the altar rails and raised her veil to receive the Sacred Host. A young Benedictine nun, whose eyes were fixed on Thérèse during the greater part of the ceremony, never forgot that vision of Paradise.

In the afternoon, in the name of all her companions, Thérèse Martin recited the Act of Consecration to the Blessed Virgin. This honour was due to her, for she was an exemplary pupil, but, with the exception of her godmother, no one in the congregation knew that this little girl had been miraculously cured the previous year by a smile from the Queen of heaven.

Toward evening, the people of Lisieux might have noticed in their streets the ideal First Communicant with her father, on their way to the Carmelite convent, where Pauline was waiting for them, adorned also with a white veil and a crown of roses. On this wonderful day, when all was sweetness, the parlour grating seemed to disappear for Thérèse; her soul was united to that of her "little mother" in one single act of thanksgiving.

At home in the evening, at *les Buisseonnets,* there was a family gathering for a festive dinner, at which Thérèse received presents including a beautiful watch from her father. The child was very pleased and very grateful, but her happiness was calm and peaceful, quite beyond this mortal world.

2. Confirmation and Combats

In the little book in which she took notes from the sermons of the Retreat, preparatory for her First Communion, we find no allusion to the wonderful favours of her Communion morning, but three resolutions, clear and concise, were written that evening:

"I shall never let myself be discouraged."

"Every day I shall say a *Memorare.*"

"I shall try to humiliate my pride."

The next day was tinged with sadness. The little first communicant yearned to receive Jesus again in the Sacred Host, but she had to wait until May 22, Feast of the Ascension, when her second Communion renewed the intense happiness of the first. Kneeling between her father and Marie, and weeping for joy, the happy child repeated those words of St. Paul: "It is now no longer I that live, but Christ lives in me."[1]

The Rev. Father Bernadot, a Dominican, considers that Thérèse was already raised to "the mystic prayer of union."[2]

Marie used to prepare her god-child for those wonderful eucharistic meetings, which, alas, were limited to the principal feasts, since the piety of the time was still tinged with Jansenism. Seeing the unutterable joy of the little communicant, her god-mother thought it wise to explain that there are other ways which lead to God. Thérèse mentions this later: "I remember once she spoke to me about suffering, telling me that God would probably always carry me like a little child instead of making me walk in the path of suffering."

The meditative child pondered over Marie's words, which came back to her mind at her communion the next day. Quite a new feeling took possession of her: "My heart was inflamed with an intense desire for suffering and with an intimate conviction that a great many crosses were reserved for me." This austere revelation was accompanied by a wonderful sweetness. Thérèse was

[1] Gal. 2:20.
[2] M. V. Bernadot. *Vie Spirituelle*, May, 1924.

lost in an ocean of happiness, such as she had never experienced at any other moment of her life. It was the time of Mount Tabor, prelude to Calvary. All the saints have known these flights to Paradise, the souvenir of which strengthens their souls during the trials of the spiritual life.

Our Lord was preparing His little Victim of Love. The question might be asked: "Was Thérèse's desire for suffering not contrary to the instincts of human nature?" St. Thomas Aquinas says: "Man, created for happiness, must necessarily wish to be happy." It is impossible to wish for suffering for its own sake. How then can we explain the child's desire? Was it not contrary to nature? We need have no fear on this point. There was nothing exaggerated or unbalanced in the clear-sighted soul of the child-saint. It was not for its own sake that she loved suffering, which is the consequence and punishment of sin. She longed for union with God, the Supreme Good, who had captivated her soul forever in the sacrament of His love; suffering seemed to her an incomparable means of calling forth God's love and of responding to it. In this way she was able to say: "Suffering attracted me; I found it had a charm which delighted me, although I had not yet experienced that charm." In the ineffable recollection which followed her communions, like a child repeating words suggested by a friend, she quoted, quite naturally, that saying of the *Imitation:* "O Jesus, ineffable sweetness, change all the consolations of this world into bitterness for me." The Divine Person of the Word, sacramentally present in her soul, inspired her with fitting words for her thanksgivings.

The year of her First Communion brought another gift from God: the sacrament of confirmation. During the retreat given at the Benedictine Abbey in preparation for that sacrament, Thérèse awaited the coming of the Comforter promised by Jesus, and she understood — in a way that was quite extraordinary for a child eleven years of age — the role of the Holy Spirit in the supernatural life. With great earnestness and exceeding joy, she prepared for His coming, making a careful study of the gifts which are given to us in that sacrament. A holy enthusiasm and an enraptured happiness took possession of her whole being at the approach of that Feast of Pentecost. Céline remarked this and questioned her. Thérèse then let her soul overflow; for a moment, the Lord raised the veil with which He had covered His chosen one.

When giving evidence in view of the Beatification of her sister, Céline declared: "She explained what she understood by the Spirit of Love taking possession of her whole being. There was such a strong conviction in her words, and such a glowing light in her eyes, that I was quite penetrated with a feeling of the supernatural and went away in deep emotion. This fact made such an impression on me that I can still see her gesture, her attitude, and the place where she was; the memory of this scene will never be effaced from my mind."[3]

After this demonstration of sacred enthusiasm, the veil fell back, and Thérèse was again the calm, silent child whose exceptional sanctity passed unnoticed. She was confirmed on June 14 and never forgot the radiant happiness of that day on which she became a perfect Christian. She has summed up her impressions in the following words: "I did not feel the impetuous wind of the first Pentecost, but rather that gentle breeze whose murmuring the prophet Elias heard on Mount Horeb."

In the caressing of that light breeze was concealed the gift of strength. Thérèse recognised that fact, for she wrote: "It was on this day that I received strength to suffer."

The earlier intimation given to her on this subject was now to be realised. Having drunk from the chalice of spiritual joys, the child was now ready for suffering. The "martyrdom" of her soul began during a retreat which she made some time later, when the serene sky of her soul became overshadowed.

Accustomed to raise her soul to God unceasingly, quite simply, by an irresistible impulse. Thérèse now experienced the agony caused by a troubled conscience. Notwithstanding her habitual determination never to offend God, she feared to sin at every moment and was incapable of discerning whether her fears were

[3] Deposition of Sister Genevieve of the Holy Face (Céline Martin).

founded or not. This anguish of mind can be realised only by those who have experienced similar torture. Thérèse was suffering from scruples, a spiritual malady which is exceedingly subtle and tenacious. To get out of its clutches, there is only one remedy. The soul must be given the guidance of a director, accepting his judgment completely and with full obedience.

Thérèse had no director, so she confessed her constant worries to Marie, who always insisted on hearing the whole story. The godmother had the grace to listen and to advise, and, after each avowal, Thérèse's troubled mind enjoyed a little peace, but soon other fears would rise, ridiculous and humiliating. This anguish, like unto the torment of purgatory, was purifying the soul already so pure.

That summer, Madame Guérin took her nieces to *Villa Colombe* at Deauville, for a fortnight at the sea-side with its healthy pleasures: shrimp-fishing, donkey-rides, the delight of inhaling the pure air from the ocean, and the charm of admiring the ever changing beauty of the sea. All these amusements should have proved a healthy diversion for the little soul too self-centred in her suffering and worry, but the anguish of scruples did not open its clutch.

The child received from her kind aunt some pretty, sky-blue ribbon for her hair. The effect of the blue in the fair curls was charming, and Thérèse felt a childish joy which, suddenly, changed to doubt: was it not wrong to be pleased at having pretty ribbons to tie one's hair? Her mind knew no peace until she had confessed that childish pleasure which seemed to her a sin.

3. Some New Experiences

During these holidays, Thérèse had a trying experience which was very profitable to her soul. Her cousin, Marie Guérin, suffered from headaches and took care to let others know. "I have a headache," she would exclaim, and Madame Guérin would pet her tearful little daughter. Thérèse also had frequent headaches, but bore her suffering in silence. However, one evening, tempted to imitate her cousin and wishing to receive a little petting herself, she sat down in an armchair in the drawing-room, leaning her head against the back of the chair in a very dejected attitude and moaned "I have a headache," just as Marie used to do. Far from having the desired effect, her lamenting only evoked reproaches.

"Evidently it did not suit me to complain," she tells us humorously, and makes fun of herself by quoting the fable of the ass and the lap-dog. Like the poor ass, she had wished to have a share of the caressing reserved for the lap-dog, but only got into trouble instead. No one believed that she was crying on account of a headache, so she was scolded for not wanting to acknowledge the real reason of her tears.

The extraordinary thing is that this little incident was enough to cure her forever of the desire to attract attention. The keenness of her intelligence and the uprightness of her will were strong enough to enable her to take definite resolutions from this one incident, where others would scarcely have seen a passing lesson.

The return to Lisieux brought no relief to Thérèse's state of mental anguish. The child worked bravely during the first term of the school year, but soon her health began to fail and she was unable to continue. Anxious about his little Queen, Monsieur Martin took her away from school at Christmas. She then studied at home, under her godmother's guidance, and her father took her several times a week to a lady who gave her "excellent lessons."

The pupil's description of these lessons gives us an amusing little picture of provincial life. They took place in a drawing-room, quaintly furnished, where the one, solitary pupil overheard many a conversation of the good ladies of the town. The teacher gave her lessons at one end of the room, while her mother received visitors at the other end, and the child's quick hearing lost nothing of the conversation. "With my head in my book, I heard all that was going on, even when it would have been better for me not to hear the remarks," she tells us.

"One lady said I had beautiful hair; another inquired who was that very pretty little girl. Such remarks, all the more flattering because they were not said to me personally, gave me such pleasure that I could clearly see I was full of self-love."

Thérèse began to worry at this feeling of pleasure, which made her realise the dangers of vanity. Was she not just at the age when the desire to be attractive awakens in young hearts? As a wise little virgin, she decided to consecrate herself to the Queen of Virgins under the title of Child of Mary.

The Benedictine nuns had under their direction a large Association of Children of Mary, but only enrolled their own pupils as members. To be admitted, Thérèse was therefore obliged to return to the Abbey. So she went twice a week for needlework lessons, though she had to make a great effort to overcome her shyness. It is really an extraordinary fact that a girl so charming, affectionate, and gifted in every way, should have had no friends at the Abbey, no intimate friends. She had tried to form friendships, but without success. She had shown special affection for two little girls of her own age, but one of them at least caused her keen disappointment. When Thérèse showed her joy at seeing this little friend again after some months of absence, the latter showed that she was completely indifferent, Thérèse was bitterly disappointed, but was too proud to beg for affection from one who was so changeable. However, she never forgot her fickle, little friend.

"God has given me such a faithful heart," she writes, "that when I give my affection to anyone, I never take it back. So I always pray for this little school-companion and I am still fond of her."

Following the example of other girls, she had tried to have an enthusiastic admiration for one of her teachers, but there again she did not succeed. Later on she realised, with great thanksgiving, that these sentimental little trials were in reality great graces sent by divine providence, though they were bitter experiences at the time. "A heart like mine would have been so easily captivated by human affection. If my wings had been

cut, how could I have taken my flight to rest in God?" She
gives vent to her feelings by an exclamation of loving thanksgiving which reveals the beauty of her soul:

"He has loved me with an ineffable, far-seeing love, so that
I should love Him now, with the folly of the saints."

At the age of thirteen, however, it is hard to feel alone among
so many little girls, chatting gaily and confiding childish secrets
to one another, in their unending conversations. As Thérèse
bent attentively over her needlework, the gold of her hair was
like the halo of a young saint in a stained-glass window; her lips
remained closed because no one spoke to her; her companions
considered her pretty and pious, but thought no more about her.

The young nun, who had watched her so attentively on the
morning of her First Communion, did indeed notice the very
pure charm of her ways, the sudden ardour that would enkindle
its flame in the habitual calm of her large grey-blue eyes, the
delightfully witty but unoffending smile that often animated
the expression of her face, the exceptional care she took not
to hurt anyone's feelings, and her exquisite courtesy in wishing
to give pleasure, but the mystery of her soul was a sealed book
to all around her. All this incomprehension was decreed by Him
whose thoughts and ways infinitely surpass our limited human
understanding.

After the needlework lesson, the pupils used to go down to the
recreation grounds. As her once habitual companion, Céline, had
finished her school-days, and as no one else paid any attention
to her, Thérèse used to be more embarrassed than ever at this
hour, wondering what she would do till her father came to fetch
her. She used to take refuge in a corner of the chapel, quite
unnoticed. There the solitary child forgot her isolation, feeling
that in that spot she was understood and loved. The Benedictine
chapel in its cloistered walls keeps secret the aspirations of that
child for whom Jesus wished to be "the only Friend."

Her contemplative vocation was growing ever more manifest
and her visits to Jesus would continue for over an hour, and
even sometimes for two hours. One day this sweet colloquy was

disturbed. Thérèse Martin was wanted; the portress searched high and low for her — in the garden, in the classrooms, even in the chapel. She was nowhere to be found! Sister Josephine grew anxious and called her name at every corner. Every one in the convent was getting alarmed, when someone suddenly thought of the little tribune on the first floor. The portress hastened upstairs. What a relief it was when she discovered the little pupil who had the knack of disappearing, unnoticed by all around!

At length the time came for Thérèse to leave the Benedictine Abbey forever. Her heart always retained a "profound gratitude" toward her kind teachers, through whom her childhood had been placed in most charming and pious surroundings. The souvenirs of the intense happiness of her First Communion and the mysterious graces of her confirmation were linked with the memories of the Benedictine Abbey, and the monastic atmosphere of this convent was a distant preparation for her cloistered life.

4. *She Gains Peace and Strength*

In the autumn of that year, 1886, Marie joined her sister Pauline at Carmel. What heart-rending sorrow this departure caused their little sister! The tender affections, which had surrounded her childhood with such sweetness, were being dispersed; the human support of those on whom she counted was being removed. First, her "little mother" had left her; now her godmother had said good-bye. "Since Pauline's departure, Marie was my only oracle, and I was so fond of her that I could not live away from her sweet companionship," Thérèse tells us.

However, the grace received in confirmation was strong in her soul. Through her tears, she could see the austere path pointed out to her by God. "I resolved to take no further pleasure in anything here below," she writes in her *Autobiography*.

But there was also the question of her scruples. How was she to overcome the anguish caused by her troubled conscience now that she could no longer confide in Marie? In a few well-chosen words, the elder sister had always been able to restore facts to their proper proportions and to dispel the trouble. Who would replace her?

Thérèse's lively faith solved the problem. In heaven, she had four powerful protectors in her two little brothers and two little sisters, who had died young. To them she now appealed for help. This is the first time we notice in her prayer that striking confidence — simple, unhesitating, undaunted — which was to become one of the characteristics of her piety.

The Saint has given us a detailed account of this conversation with the inhabitants of the other world.

"I spoke to them with a child's simplicity, drawing their attention to the fact that I had always been the best loved and the most petted by my parents and sisters, because I was the youngest of the family, and that, if they had remained on earth, they would no doubt have given me the same proof of their affection. The fact that they were already in heaven did not seem to me a reason for them to forget me, but rather a reason for helping me and loving me still more."

She then asked her little brothers and sisters to obtain the gift of peace for her from the divine treasury. This was the pledge she asked from them to show that, in heaven, they still could love her. Her confident trust must have caused a smile among the heavenly inhabitants; the answer to her prayer soon came in the way she had asked. Peace, with its ineffable joy, took possession of her soul, thus proving that she was loved in heaven as on earth. This family intercourse with the other world enkindled still more her ardent desire for heavenly beatitude.

Looking back on this hour of her life, the Saint pronounced a harsh judgement on herself when she wrote: "Though heaven enriched me with graces, there was really no merit on my part. I always had an intense desire for acquiring virtue, but what imperfections remained in my actions! My exceeding sensitiveness made me quite unbearable."

The word "unbearable" is unduly harsh; for once in her life, the truthful Saint seems to have exaggerated, but it was through her exceeding humility. All those who had the happiness of coming in contact with her during the few years of her earthly life are unanimous in praising her charming character. The aged servant, Victoire, whom Thérèse mentions in the *Autobiography,* called her "a little angel of sweetness." Another servant, Felicity, who succeeded Victoire, says: "Our dear little Saint was very gentle and sweet-tempered, and took great care never to hurt anyone's feelings."[4] Humble testimonies of this kind are very convincing. But Thérèse felt that an extraordinary fidelity was due to the wonderful graces which had been given to her. She longed to attain her sublime ideal, but, notwithstanding her constant efforts, she would sometimes fall into the same imperfections.

Her pen narrates this fact relentlessly: "I never did anything myself. Céline did our bedroom, and I took no interest in any form of house work. However, occasionally, *in order to please God,* I did make a bed, or, if Céline were not at home, I brought in her flower-pots or seedlings in the evening. But, later, if Céline did not show her surprise and delight at my little services, I was displeased and showed this by weeping."

If Thérèse happened to offend anyone — quite unintentionally of course — her tears flowed again. "Instead of making the best of the misfortune, I was so miserable that I nearly made myself ill on account of the misunderstanding, which only made matters worse; and when I began to feel consoled, I wept at the thought of all my useless tears; I worried and cried about everything."

With this habit of constant weeping, there was little hope of entering Carmel at an early age. Thérèse was wise enough to know that she must control her tears if she would face the trials of the Novitiate. She prayed and trusted in God, awaiting from Him the miraculous grace that would cure her. The change was wrought by a very simple incident. On returning from Midnight Mass early on Christmas Morning, in the year 1886, Monsieur Martin showed his displeasure at the sight of Thérèse's

[4] Letters quoted in *Les Annales de Sainte Thérèse de Lisieux*, April, 1934.

shoes,[5] filled with Christmas presents, placed in the dining-room fireplace. The elder sisters were accustomed to play "Santa Claus" in this way for the youngest member of the family. "It is really too babyish to give surprises of that kind to a big girl like Thérèse," said Monsieur Martin; "I hope it will be the last time." Thérèse overheard these words on her way upstairs. Céline, too, heard the remark, and whispered to her oversensitive little sister: "Don't go down yet; you would cry too much in looking at your presents before Papa."

But Thérèse was no longer the same person, for Jesus had changed her heart. "Keeping back my tears," she says, "I ran down to the dining-room, and, in spite of the violent beating of my heart, I took hold of the shoes, gaily drawing forth the various presents, apparently as happy as a queen."

Céline's amazement can be imagined. She could not believe her eyes. Her surprise was gradually turned into joy as she watched the little scene. It was no dream, but a consoling reality. Thérèse had just recovered her strength of character, lost at the age of four and a half. Giving all the glory to God, the Saint says: "Jesus, accepting my desire, had wrought in a moment the work that I had been powerless to accomplish by years of effort."

The Holy Child, whose birth had just been celebrated, had given a special grace to this privileged little soul. From this "luminous night," Thérèse dates the third period of her life — her happiest years filled to overflowing with God's grace.

[5] Instead of hanging up their stockings on Christmas Eve, children in France put their shoes on the fender of the fireplace.

CHAPTER VI

THE CALL TO CARMEL

1. *The Voice of the Bridegroom*

"JESUS had made me strong and courageous. He gave me His own weapons for the combat, and ever since then I have passed from one victory to another, beginning, so to speak, *to run as a giant*,"[1] wrote the Carmelite, long after, in referring to this period of her life.

Even among the most perfect Christians, how many have to fight against their faults to the end of their days, without ever really conquering them! That is the common lot of human nature wounded by original sin.

To Thérèse of the Child Jesus, who was destined to become a model of spiritual perfection to all the world, God gave a very special grace by restoring to her in a moment that perfect balance of the faculties by which the will victoriously governs its interior kingdom.

"Charity took possession of my heart," says the Saint, "and with it came the spirit of self-forgetfulness. Ever since then I have been happy."

Those questing for happiness might well take this statement for lengthy meditation.

Thérèse's virtue was witnessed by all in her home, where her smiling unselfishness bestowed on others something of the mysterious joy that reigned in her heart. Serenity, amiability, gentleness, kindness, and constant thoughtfulness for others, all these virtues were practised so naturally "that no one would have thought she had to make any effort in her continual self-abnegation."[2]

---

[1] Cf. Ps. 18:5, "as a giant to run the way."
[2] Deposition of Léonie Martin at the Apostolic Process.

This treasure was not to be confined merely to the home circle. Freed from love of self and mistress of her emotions, Thérèse spread out her wings for her flight into the heights, from which she never again descended. She soared beyond the "narrow circle" in which she had previously lived, and gazed into the realm of souls. The entire world was beneath her and drew forth her ardent zeal.

For a while, she hesitated in her choice between the active vocation of a missionary and the contemplative life of Carmel; she felt a very strong attraction for the distant missions, but the voice of Jesus called her to a more hidden and more intimate life with Himself.

Céline, the only one with whom she used to discuss this matter, has given us in striking terms an account of this vocation:

"The religious life seemed to Thérèse above all a means of saving souls. For that reason, she thought of joining the foreign missions, but the hope of saving a greater number of souls by mortification and self-sacrifice made her decide to become a Carmelite. She considered that it is harder for our nature to work without ever seeing the fruit of its labour, without encouragement, and without any kind of diversion, and that the most trying work of all is self-conquest; she chose 'this living death' because it is the surest way of gaining souls."

This sublime ideal shows us the purity of intention that guided Thérèse's decision. Its radiant light shone on the path to Carmel and directed her footsteps to the home chosen for her by her Divine Spouse.

"What a lesson for those so-called Christians, who consider that the world has no need of the contemplative life!" remarks Father Petitot.

Thérèse, therefore, wished to become a Carmelite, but no one yet knew her secret. At this important moment of her life, her exceptionally well-balanced mind weighed all the arguments for or against such a decision; she examined her own feelings and awaited the decisive impulse of the Holy Spirit before taking the final step.

Freed from her scruples and from the habit of weeping, Thérèse's keen intelligence now sought intellectual food. She studied certain subjects alone. Her mind was developing and in a few months acquired more knowledge than in all the preceding years. In relating this fact, the Saint asks the question: "Was not this ardour for learning really 'vanity and vexation of spirit'?"[3] We venture to reply in the negative. Since she was destined by the Divine Will, by means of her *Autobiography*, to become the teacher of a new "Way," was it not part of providence's plan for her that her intellectual faculties should be trained and developed by study? But the Saint realised that her thirst for knowledge might have led her astray. "With my ardent nature," she says, "I was just at the most dangerous time of my life."

Thérèse's life was developing into a charming girlhood. Like all rich natures, she was capable of strong passions, but Jesus watched over the heart that He wished to keep entirely for Himself. In an outburst of gratitude, she has noted the numberless graces which adorned her soul at that time, and with exquisite modesty, she allows us to penetrate the secrets of her interior life. In the language of Scripture, she compares the graces received by her to "glittering robes" and "precious perfumes." "He saw that the time had come for me to be loved; He entered into a covenant with me and I became His."[4] Her expression of love here reminds one of the gentle martyr, St. Agnes, who in her love for Christ proclaimed: "When I love Him, I am chaste; when I touch Him, I am pure; when I possess Him, I am a Virgin." Her vocation is above all a vocation of love.

With zealous care, she kindled the hidden fire of her love by nourishing her soul with meditations and reading, in harmony with her aspirations. The *Imitation of Christ,* which she knew by heart, was her favourite book. Madame Guérin used to take pleasure in opening the little volume at any page and in making

[3] Eccles. 1:14.
[4] Cf. Ezech. 16:8.

her niece recite by heart the first passage on which her eyes happened to fall.

After the Gospel, the *Imitation* is the book best known to Christian readers, and it is interesting to note that the girl of fourteen had nourished her soul on the spiritual food of the doctrine contained therein.

A book called *The Mysteries of the World to Come* is mentioned by her, from which she drew a foretaste of the happiness of Heaven. The future Carmelite meditated on this book "with a joy which was not of this world." How short this life seemed to her and how she longed to love Jesus with all the passionate love of her heart!

Without revealing the great object she had in view, Thérèse now found in Céline an intimate companion worthy of understanding her aspirations. The playmate of her early days had developed into a deeply religious girl whom the Lord had already chosen to be His spouse one day. The two sisters had become "sisters in spirit" also. In the quiet of the evening, from the turret window, together they beheld the stars twinkling in the immensity of the heavens and thought of that other heaven which is **God Himself.**

The great Teresa of Avila, who was to be their spiritual Mother, once wrote: "Before I was twenty years of age, I already held the world enchained at my feet." The Child of Lisieux was not yet fifteen, but she also had soared above the world.

All these yearning desires bore fruit. "The practice of virtue became sweet and natural to me . . . gradually self-sacrifice became easy; I accepted mortifications spontaneously." She was advancing toward the great end she had in view, and each grace faithfully received brought many others in its train.

The parishioners of St. Peter's Cathedral remember the pretty child who came each day to an early Mass. "When she prayed," said one of them, "I felt that nothing could disturb her recollection." The child heard Mass in the Blessed Virgin's Chapel, an exquisite gem of fifteenth-century architecture. The apse, so beautiful when lit up by the sun's rays, is adorned in bas-relief with representations of the life of the Child-God. Under the high arches of this Chapel, then, Thérèse gave herself up to her sublime dream.

She did not go to Holy Communion every day, but as often as her confessor allowed her. Her simple faith saw Jesus so clearly in His representative that she accepted the priest's decision without comment. Fortunately he allowed her to communicate several times a week, and this permission filled her soul with joy, as it "came directly from God."

However, at this decisive hour of her life, she did not otherwise seek the support of priestly advice. She compared directors to faithful mirrors, but the path by which the Lord made her walk was so straight and luminous that she thought God did not wish any intermediary in her case. Jesus Himself became her Director. The future was to prove the reality of this wonderful privilege.

In referring to this grace, Thérèse stopped her narrative once more to proclaim her thanksgiving: "He wished to show forth His Mercy in me. . . . As I was small and weak, He stooped down to me and taught me sweetly."

The child did not hesitate in her love; all these favours called for a generous response. She felt grace urging her to follow her Carmelite vocation in order to give herself to Jesus and to souls. The offering of the flower of her youth and the renouncing of all human joy cost her nothing. He who captivated her heart forever was the Son of God and the Son of Mary, the most beautiful of the children of men, the Eternal Word, Jesus Christ.

Like the Apostles, she heard His call. "Abandoning their nets and their father, they left all things to follow Him." The "nets," which Teresa left, represent her happy life with its agreeable, self-imposed occupations. She did not have to earn her living, and her future was assured by her family dowry. But she disdained all earthly advantages; her childish hands had weighed the world and found it light in the balance. However, there was the sacrifice of her father, her kind, dearly loved father, who had given his two eldest daughters to God. How could his little Queen speak to him of another separation! Besides, he was not in good health. He had suffered an attack of paralysis, and, though now recovered, there was fear of another stroke. To so loving a daughter the struggle was heart rending, but the divine call became more and more insistent.

"Had it been necessary to pass through fire, I would have thrown myself into the flames to follow my Divine Master," she proclaimed.

2. *A Little White Flower for Carmel*

The courageous child began making her plans. She thought of entering the convent on the anniversary of the miraculous grace received at Christmas; that would be ten days before her fifteenth birthday.

She consulted her two Carmelite sisters, who gave different opinions. Marie thought her god-child was too young, but Pauline, who saw that this was an exceptional vocation, seconded her little sister's decision and encouraged her not to delay. When Céline was told the secret, she was most generous in her sacrifice. Though she herself wished to become a nun, she was willing to let her younger sister go before her.

It was the month of May and the Child of Mary prayed earnestly to the Blessed Virgin. The Feast of the Ascension came and went. During the Novena made to prepare for the Coming of the Holy Spirit, Thérèse's fervour increased. On that day, she felt sure, she would receive the gift of Strength to disclose her great secret to her father.

At last Pentecost dawned. In spirit, the child was in the Cenacle, penetrated by the mystery of light and fire. She went to Holy Communion beside her father. Together they heard High Mass with its splendid words of love and triumph: "The Spirit of the Lord hath filled the whole earth. . . . Confirm, O God, what Thou hast wrought in us. . . . Come, O Holy Spirit, fill the hearts of Thy faithful; and kindle in them the fire of Thy Love!"

With her heart strengthened and her soul uplifted by the
grace of the Holy Spirit, Thérèse returned from Vespers.
Monsieur Martin went into the garden to enjoy the evening
air, and his soul was filled to overflowing with peaceful happiness. In the splendour of the liturgical office from which he had
just come, this true Christian felt that God was near to him;
and in his flowering garden, too, he felt God's presence.

The trees, with their fresh foliage, stood out clearly in the
splendour of the early summer; the rays of the setting sun
gilded the tender leaves where hidden birds were singing. It was
one of those calm and splendorous days on which nature seems
to clothe herself again with the beauty of the earthly Paradise.

Six o'clock had just struck. On the watch for the right moment
to make her petition, Thérèse saw her father sit down on the
bench where the path turned. She stopped an instant to send
forth a last prayer to heaven, and then came near. Monsieur
Martin heard the step he knew so well. What sweetness there
was for him in the presence of his youngest daughter, grown
into such a charming and such a pious girl! Soon she would
be "grown-up." He felt sure she would give her life entirely to
God; in five or six years, no doubt, she would leave him as her
sisters had done, but in the interval he loved to be with his
delightful little Queen, who was so pretty and so clever. She
was the joy of his old age, for the years were passing and he was
now sixty-four.

But the call of God brooks no delay. Thérèse sat down on
the bench beside her father. She did not speak, but Monsieur
Martin saw that her eyes were filled with tears. She herself has
described the scene for us.

"He looked at me with an ineffable tenderness, pressed me
to his heart and said: 'What is the matter, little Queen? Confide
your sorrow to me.' Then rising, in order to hide his own
emotion, he walked on slowly, holding me close all the time."

Thus, with her head resting on her father's heart, Thérèse
succeeded in making her holy, though heart-rending, avowal.
"Through my tears, I spoke of Carmel and of my desire to enter

soon, then he wept too." The first blow, the hardest, had been given; the tears of father and daughter mingled in their mutual, heart-raking sorrow.

"However, he said nothing to turn me from my vocation," the Saint tells us. "He merely pointed out that I was still very young to make such a serious decision. But as I insisted and explained my reasons, my incomparable father, so upright and generous, was soon convinced that I was right."

This child, the chosen spouse of God, was no doubt very eloquent, but how admirable is that father, from whom God could ask such a sacrifice and obtain it without hesitation! The paternal authority could easily have protested, in the name of human prudence, and insisted on a delay. But instead, by his immediate and magnanimous consent to his daughter's vocation, he cooperated efficaciously in the speedy blossoming of this flower of perfect sanctity, now known to us as St. Thérèse of the Child Jesus.

Continuing his walk, Monsieur Martin gathered a little flower, resembling a tiny lily, which was growing on a low wall.

"God made that fragile little flower blossom and grow, though any trifling accident could have broken it," he said.

In this charming parable Thérèse recognised the story of her own life. The souls of father and daughter were united in their sublime sacrifice. Monsieur Martin gave his daughter the floweret, gathered so gently by his hand that even its tiny roots were not broken. So, too, was the life of Thérèse to be transplanted from her home to Carmel. Carefully fastened to a picture of Our Lady of Victories, this symbolic flower accompanied her through all her religious life. When Pauline became Prioress and bade her to set down her early memories, the young nun wrote on the first page of her manuscript the simple title: "The Story of the Springtime of a Little White Flower." The symbol may seem childish to some people, but it expresses very exactly the grace of the manifold favours God accorded to Thérèse Martin and the virility of her character in corresponding to that grace.

The days to be spent in her home circle were now numbered,

for the future Saint was being drawn on to her high destiny by the Spirit who guided her. But the project had still to be explained to Monsieur Guérin, who was her guardian, and so Thérèse chose the Wednesday after Pentecost, the first of June, to speak to him of her vocation.

His youngest niece — such was his comment — little more than a child, not yet finished with her education, wanted to enter the Carmelite Convent, and that immediately! He considered this decision an act of pure folly, an act of imprudence which might even harm the interests of religion itself. Greatly distressed at his attitude, Thérèse tried to make him understand that hers was an exceptional case, but in vain. He declared that he would oppose her vocation at that early age, that he would never yield, and that nothing but a miracle would change his mind. Nothing daunted at the condition he laid down, Thérèse determined to obtain the miracle.

It was raining as she returned from her uncle's house, and, for three days, the gloomy rain from the grey Norman skies covered with its misty mantle the bitter disappointment of her heart. Her sorrow was increased by an interior trial, and her desolation of spirit might be compared to life in a frightful desert. Jesus seemed to have abandoned her, and she knew not where to find Him. She sought Him anxiously, as Mary and Joseph had done in the streets of Jerusalem. She herself has compared the darkness of this spiritual night to the desolation of spirit of our Saviour in the Garden of Olives. That is all the Saint has told us of the agony of those three days during which she proved the fidelity of her virtue.

On the fourth day, a Saturday, in the steady downpour, she returned to her uncle's house to make another attack. What a surprise awaited her! His attitude had completely changed! After reproaching her affectionately for having been a little constrained in her attitude toward him, Monsieur Guérin told her, with emotion, that he had just received from God the sign he had asked for, "a simple inclination of his heart." He then embraced his niece with fatherly affection and consented to her vocation in words which remind us of Monsieur Martin's own comparison:

"Go in peace, my dear child; you are a privileged little flower that God wishes to gather for Himself. I shall put no obstacle in the way."

What a wonderful change had been wrought in her uncle's feelings! Then Jesus allowed His presence to be felt again in Thérèse's soul, and the sun shone in a clear, blue sky. During her visit to her uncle, *the clouds had completely disappeared.*

The Saint draws our attention to these last words. She had begun to notice an extraordinary phenomenon, namely, that nature associated itself with her intimate feelings.

"In all the important events of my life, when I wept, the skies wept with me; when I rejoiced, no cloud darkened the blue of the heavens."

Thérèse, though so humble, does not fear to state the truth. She was under no illusion. We have every right to think that this great miracle-worker, who was to receive such exceptional glory after her death, obtained even in this life a miraculous homage from nature through the loving power of almighty God.

3. *Carmel Gates Inexorable*

Having obtained the consent of her family, Thérèse now thought of approaching the religious Superiors, from whom she expected no opposition whatever. From Sister Agnes of Jesus,[5] however, she learned that Father Delatroëtte, who was parish priest of the Church of St. James and superior of the Carmelites, had declared to the Prioress that he would not listen to any talk of the little Martin girl entering before she was twenty-one. This unforeseen opposition seemed insurmountable, but Thérèse's courage was undaunted. Accompanied by her father, she went to visit Father Delatroëtte. The worthy priest, a man of strong

[5] Pauline had taken the name of Sister Agnes of Jesus.

faith and inflexible character, listened politely but coldly to the reasons given by this little girl, who thought she could overturn religious rules which had been established on the soundest principles of prudence. Considering that his little visitor was deluding herself by a misguided fervour, the ecclesiastical superior of the Carmelites wished to save her from an imprudent action. He therefore remained invincible and to all her entreaties he replied by a repeated "No." His very decided refusal was indeed excusable, for he considered it to be sheer folly to allow a postulant to enter Carmel at the age of fifteen. God had enlightened her father and her uncle, but He did not move this priest to realise that he had to deal with an exceptional vocation. However, at the end of the interview, Father Delatroëtte remarked: "I am only the bishop's delegate; if he allows you to enter so young, I shall have nothing further to say." This was his final decision.

When the visitors left the Presbytery, it was, of course, *raining in torrents*. Monsieur Martin did not know how to console his daughter, so he suggested: "If you wish, little Queen, I shall take you to Bayeux to see the bishop." Touched at her father's heroic conduct, Thérèse accepted his offer with gratitude. Recourse to the bishop was her last hope.

However, several months elapsed before the visit to Bayeux; indeed, the whole summer passed by, that of 1887, the last that she was to spend in her home. Although the weeks dragged slowly and wearily for the child, whose gaze was fixed on the heroic object she had in view, still she loved the sweetness of all the things she was leaving. As she beheld the June roses in bloom, she knew she would not see them flower the following year. Later on, when a Carmelite, she wrote these simple lines which recall the sweetness of her life at home:

> O Memory, what peace you bring,
> You waken thoughts of many a thing:
> Of sunset meals, perfumes that roses fling,
> And summer joys at Buissonnets!

During these months of uncertainty, Jesus sustained His chosen one. Exteriorly, she seemed to be the same little Thérèse Martin continuing her education, for she studied zealously and with success, and assisted at the meetings of the Children of Mary. Physically, too, she was developing into a tall, beautiful girl. But her interior development was far greater, though unnoticed by those around her. Her soul rejoiced in her increasing love and soared to God under the impulse of Divine Charity, experiencing at times "a very rapture of love."

One evening, wishing to tell our Lord how much she longed to see Him served and glorified everywhere, and thinking sorrowfully that from the depths of hell there would never arise one single act of love to Him, she cried out: "Willingly would I consent to be cast into that place of torment and blasphemy that He might be loved there eternally." The Saint explained her meaning, for her theology was never in fault. She knew quite well that God would not wish this to take place, since He desires only our happiness, but she explains quite simply: "When a soul loves God, it proclaims its love in a thousand foolish ways."

Thérèse's heaven was love, and nothing would ever be able to separate her from the God of Love who had captivated her heart. She would have brought love everywhere, even into hell, if that had been possible. These expressions of love recall the ardent exclamations of the great St. Teresa whose daughter she wished to be.

The reality of her love was proved by acts of charity. Divine providence wished that, before entering the cloister, Thérèse of the Child Jesus should have the joy of practising charitable work, by taking an active interest in several poor families, and especially in two little girls whose mother was ill. This short experience brought her a store of useful knowledge. In particular she noticed the extraordinary facility with which children receive the truths impressed on their minds and how easily they understand supernatural doctrine. "Baptism must indeed implant deeply in our souls the theological virtues," she says, "since from early childhood the hope of heavenly reward is sufficient to make us accept sacrifices."

She did not think, however, of telling us how very persuasive her instructions must have been. In her teaching, she displayed all the energy of her faith and the charm of her character. The scene of the youthful Saint teaching these two poor little girls and acting as a mother to them makes a charming picture.

Thérèse possessed indeed the finest and most attractive qualities to be found in women, those qualities which make fiancées of ideal character, wives of undaunted courage, and mothers who possess their sons' entire affection. The little Queen would have been Queen in any surroundings, but it was in the Heart of Jesus that she was to reign, in the suite of the Virgin Mary. "After her shall virgins be brought to the king."[6] But while on earth, she was to be a hidden Queen.

4. *Thérèse's First Sinner*

Once more a grace was given to her to understand the mystical form of her great apostolic calling. One Sunday in July, as she closed her book at the end of Mass, a picture of our Lord on the cross slipped partly out between the leaves, showing just one of His Sacred Hands. An unutterable feeling of sorrow, such as she had never previously experienced, penetrated her heart at the sight of this adorable Hand, pierced and bleeding, which seemed to plead for love that should be given the abandoned Saviour. Instantly came her loving response, for she tells us: "I resolved to remain ever at the foot of the cross, in order that I might receive His Precious Blood and pour It down upon souls."

This zeal for the salvation of souls grew ever more intense, and, in her mind, there echoed the words of the dying Saviour *I thirst*, enkindling "a hitherto-unknown and very ardent fire" of love in her heart. She longed to quench the thirst of her Beloved; she shared His burning thirst for souls, and her apostolic zeal counted on miracles such as were accorded to the Apostles after Pentecost.

[6] Ps. 44:14.

A hard-hearted bandit, seducer, and murderer, named Pranzini, was the first to benefit by her consuming zeal. All the newspapers of the time recounted a threefold shocking murder committed by this miserable criminal, who had been condemned to the scaffold and deserved it on many counts. The news penetrated even to Thérèse's quiet home circle. The little Queen, who now became an ardent "fisher of souls," at once determined to "cast her net to capture this enormous fish." In other words, she was bent on converting that most depraved and impenitent of men, and for that purpose employed all the spiritual means in her power, deciding at once on the surest means of gaining the victory, as she herself tells us:

"Knowing that of myself I could do nothing, I offered for his ransom the infinite merits of our Redeemer and the treasures of holy Church."

Her faith did not falter, but, in order to gain courage in her quest for souls, she turned to heaven and prayed in her characteristically simple and confident way:

"My God, I am quite sure Thou wilt pardon this miserable Pranzini; I should believe this even if he did not confess his sins nor give any sign of contrition, because I have confidence in Thy unbounded Mercy. *But as he is my first sinner, I beg for a sign of repentance for my own consolation.*"

Although she did not usually read the newspapers, Thérèse now eagerly scanned the pages of *La Croix,* just to learn about Pranzini. The day after his execution, she hastily opened the paper to get final news of the unhappy murderer, and this is what she read:

"On the threshold of the prison, the assassin looked deadly pale. The chaplain went before him, to hide the hideous guillotine from view; others were helping him along. He pushed aside the priest and the executioners. When he came to the block, Diebler pushed him down. But before that, his conscience was evidently touched by sudden repentance, for he asked the chaplain for his crucifix, which he kissed three times."

And the Catholic paper commented: "If human justice was

satisfied by his death, perhaps this last kiss of the crucifix satisfied Divine Justice, which asks only for repentance."[7]

Thérèse's tears betrayed her emotion on reading this account. She ran out of the room, for she wished to be alone with God. What a sign had been given her! What a response to her prayers! It was in looking at the Wounds of Jesus that the thirst for souls had taken possession of her, and the final act of her "first sinner" had been "to place his confidence in these Sacred Wounds by kissing the crucifix three times." The Saint never forgot this criminal, who was her "first-born" from the ranks of sinners; for the remainder of her life she prayed for him and had Masses offered for the repose of his soul.

5. Audience With Bishop Hugonin

Autumn had begun, the chrysanthemums had replaced the roses, and the paths of their garden were covered with reddish-brown leaves, when, on October 31, Monsieur Martin and his daughter set out for Bayeux, where an interview had at last been arranged with the bishop. This was a great undertaking for a shy girl, who had been accustomed to leave everything to her elder sisters. By virtue as much as by natural inclination, she had got into the habit of speaking only when spoken to. Now she would have to do the talking herself and explain her vocation — and all that to a bishop!

Eight years later, when writing her *Autobiography,* the Carmelite still remembered the intense emotion of that day and the great effort it cost her to overcome her shyness.

As they set out on the Eve of All Saints, the sky was clouded and the beautiful Calvados countryside was damp and depressing. When the travellers reached the bishop's house, the rain was falling in torrents. Thérèse draws our attention to the fact, for she knew it was a very bad sign for her.

The vicar-general, Father Révérony, awaited them. He was "a priest of great piety and wholehearted devotedness to his many duties," as Monsignor Laveille tells us. Though he wel-

[7] *La Croix,* September 1, 1887.

comed them kindly, there was a look of surprise in his eyes. The would-be Carmelite noticed this, and the tears which came to her eyes betrayed her emotion. "Oh, those diamonds must not be shown to His Lordship," the priest said smilingly, speaking with the kindly condescension one shows to a nice little child. He wished to put her at her ease but she felt exceedingly embarrassed, and, as they passed through a suite of large reception rooms, she felt "like a little worm."

When depicting the scene many years later, the Carmelite remembered all the details of this interview with the aged bishop. There were three enormous armchairs in front of the fireplace, where a bright fire blazed because of the chilly autumn day. Father Révérony offered her the armchair in the middle; she did not wish to accept it, but, as he insisted, she found herself installed like a true little Queen between the bishop and her father, while, to her dismay, the vicar-general took an ordinary chair. All this was very disconcerting. To make matters worse, her father told her to explain the object of their visit herself and then lapsed into silence.

With the courage of a soldier ready for the assault, Thérèse began an eloquent explanation of her vocation. The three elderly men, bent toward the child, listened in silence, somewhat as the Ancients and the Doctors had listened long before to the Child of Nazareth in the Temple of Jerusalem. Heaven listened too, for the destiny of a great Saint was in the balance. When she stopped speaking, His Lordship, Bishop Hugonin, asked how long she had been thinking of becoming a Carmelite.

"A very long time, my Lord," she replied.

"Come now," said Father Révérony laughingly, "it cannot be as long as fifteen years."

"That is true," replied Thérèse gravely, with the utmost assurance, "but it is not much less, for I have wished to give myself to God since I was three years old."

"This little girl takes matters seriously," thought the bishop and his vicar-general, though they were by no means convinced of the reality of such an early vocation. The bishop was kind and did not wish to hurt her feelings, but he considered it right to make certain objections. Thus he suggested that it would be well to remain some time longer with her father, who would surely be very happy to have her near him. The prelate had not foreseen that the father was a saint.

Monsieur Martin now joined in the conversation to take his child's part, adding quietly that they were going to Rome with the diocesan pilgrimage and that his daughter would not hesitate to speak to the Pope, if her request were not granted by the bishop. The two priests had never witnessed such a scene — a father as eager to give his daughter to God as she was to make her sacrifice. However, though greatly edified, they did not give their consent.

As the ecclesiastical superior of the Carmelites had taken shelter behind the bishop's decision; so the bishop now maintained that he could decide nothing without seeing the superior. And this superior was the unassailable Father Delatroëtte! Thérèse's tears began to fall. . . . The bishop was distressed at the sight of the tears, but not conquered. The child's simplicity had touched his fatherly heart; he tried to console her by saying that she must not consider her cause lost, as the final decision had not yet been made. He told her to think of the beautiful pilgrimage to Rome with her father and to rejoice instead of weeping. In reality, he was talking to her as to a little girl who does not really know what she wants, and she had to take her departure without being able to prove that hers was an exceptional vocation.

Wishing to honour his visitors, the bishop accompanied them to the door of the palace. On the way, Monsieur Martin mentioned the fact that his little daughter had put her hair up for the first time that very morning to make herself look older. The little incident amused His Lordship, who often repeated the story to others. It was indeed the first time that the mass of Thérèse's fair hair had been gathered up under the hat with its two white seagull's wings.

As Thérèse walked down the straight paths of the episcopal

garden, the rain was falling in a steady downpour. Bishop Hugonin may have watched her for a while, but he never thought for a moment that the visit which had just taken place would bring him greater fame than all the years of his episcopate.

Monsieur Martin and his daughter took the return train; the melancholy, rainy day was in unison with the bitter disappointment in the child's heart. For a while, she felt as if her future were shattered forever. How could a mere child strive against all these high dignitaries! And yet, notwithstanding her great sorrow, she felt deep down in her heart an assured haven of peace which the will of man could not take from her. This wondrous peace was the recompense for the purity of intention with which she had acted. In truth, she sought nothing but the Will of her Lord and her God.

CHAPTER VII

A PILGRIMAGE TO ROME

1. *A Last Look at the World*

"WHAT an interesting study it is to look on the world around us when we are on the eve of saying good-by to it forever!" exclaimed the Carmelite when writing an account of her pilgrimage to Rome.

Thérèse Martin's unusual gift of observation enabled her to store up a rich harvest of experience during her visit to Italy in November, 1887. The pilgrimage had been organised by the dioceses of Coutances and Bayeux to celebrate the Golden Jubilee of Leo XIII's ordination. "This act of filial piety toward the 'Prisoner of the Vatican' was at the same time a most enjoyable and interesting holiday," says Monsignor Laveille, who was one of the party. The agents, Messrs. Lubin, saw to all arrangements of trains, hotels, and conveyances.

Monsieur Martin loved travelling; some years before, he had been to Vienna and Constantinople with a friend, and had returned via Italy. This time he was taking his two youngest daughters with him on his journey.[1] Most of the pilgrims belonged to aristocratic or well-to-do circles of the Norman province and all were pious Catholics. "We found ourselves in the company of many distinguished people," Thérèse tells us. The child's observant gaze, however, soon noted — with the severity of innocence — the little weaknesses of poor human vanity.

---

[1] Readers may wonder why Monsieur Martin's third daughter is not mentioned. Léonie had entered a convent of the Poor Clares. This Order, however, proved too severe for her health and she was later obliged to return home. She did not therefore accompany the pilgrimage to Rome in November, 1887, but was at home when Thérèse entered in April, 1888. Some years later, in August, 1893, she entered the Visitation Convent at Caen, and received the name of Sister Frances Teresa. (Note by the Translator.)

"All these titles seemed to us a vapour of smoke," she wrote. "In heaven we shall know our real titles of nobility; those who choose on earth to be the poorest and the least known for love of our Saviour will be the first, the noblest, and the richest in the other world."

These serious thoughts occupied the mind of the little girl who sat upright and silent in the corner of a second-class compartment. But a more useful experience followed in the knowledge she gained of priests. She had often been surprised at the earnest exhortations of St. Teresa of Avila to her daughters, recommending them to consider the sanctification of priests as the principal object of their prayers and penances. The apostolic zeal of the future Carmelite easily understood the ardent appeal of her great patron imploring prayers for sinners, but she was indeed astonished at the idea of praying for priests, whose souls seemed to her purer than crystal. Her pilgrimage brought light on that point, as she tells us in a discreet but eloquent remark:

"I understood my vocation in Italy; even such a long journey was a small price to pay for such valuable knowledge."

During that month, she met several "holy priests"; yet, notwithstanding the profound respect she had for their virtue and for their priestly dignity, she noticed that they were but "weak and imperfect men." She does not mention any definite imperfections in any priest, but her impressions convinced her of the urgent need of the great Carmelite work: prayer for the priesthood.

These deep thoughts and reflections did not prevent her in the least from enjoying the charms of her journey. Like all artistic and ardent natures, her whole being responded to the beauty of all she saw, and the account of her one long journey is full of enthusiastic admiration.

2. *Paris, Lucerne, the Alps, Milan, Venice*

At three o'clock in the morning on November 4, Monsieur Martin and his two youngest daughters drove through the silent streets of Lisieux in order to take the train that was to reach

Paris — *Gare St. Lazare* — at seven a.m. Thérèse was thoughtful and recollected on the journey. As she did not know Paris, her father showed her the most interesting sights during the three days spent there. The future Saint of Lisieux trod the wide avenues of the French capital, saw the *Arc de Triomphe,* and probably visited the *Louvre, les Invalides,* and the Cathedral of Notre Dame. But the happiest time for her was the visit to the church of Our Lady of Victories, where she received a special grace. The Virgin Mary, who had cured Thérèse during the novena made in this sanctuary, now made her presence felt, and, speaking heart to heart to the happy child, assured her that it was really she herself, the Mother of God, who had smiled on her and cured her miraculously. At that moment, there disappeared forever the oppressive doubt on that point which had troubled the child's mind for the past four years.

With a feeling of happiness comparable to that of her First Communion, Thérèse consecrated herself and commended her future to the gentle Queen, before whom burned numberless candles here, forming a glowing pedestal of entreaty and prayer.

Preserved from evil in her quiet provincial life, Thérèse felt that on this journey she would come across things that might well trouble her and perhaps even unsettle her vocation. Later on, looking back upon her experiences, she wrote:

"I understand the people who presumed that my father had undertaken this journey in the hope of making me change my mind about the religious life; it might indeed have shaken a vocation that was not very strong."

Thérèse's vocation, however, was of a different kind. Taking refuge under the virginal mantle of Mary, she seemed to receive an assurance that our Lady would protect her, and this conviction filled her with joy. Later she learned that "to the pure all things are pure." Among the many deep sayings which surprise us in her *Autobiography,* we find the following: "Evil exists only in impure hearts and not in inanimate objects." She invoked also the most pure St. Joseph and felt that she was well protected by heaven for the coming journey.

The pilgrims met at the Basilica of *Montmartre* to consecrate themselves to the Sacred Heart before leaving for Italy on November 7. They took the train at the *Gare de l'Est*. Each compartment of the train was named after a saint, that of Monsieur Martin and his daughters bearing the name St. Martin. This was an act of kind consideration on the part of the organisers of the pilgrimage, but the thoughtful little attention was well deserved by the humble, sincere father. "True greatness is not in titles but in the soul," as the Saint tells us.

As the train rushed along, Thérèse gazed with admiring eyes at the beautiful country of the Eastern provinces. She did not foresee that twenty-seven years later those same counties — and the surrounding ones — would witness the merciless bloodshed of her countrymen in barbarous warfare, nor did she foresee that the soldiers of the Great War, during their long heroic struggle, would invoke as their heavenly protectress the little pilgrim of 1887, transformed into the most powerful of wonder-workers.

At night, the train stopped some hours at Basle and then set off through Switzerland. Thérèse was lost in admiration before the wonderful Swiss landscapes which are perhaps the most beautiful in Europe: Lucerne and the emerald lake with its indented margin, the banks of the Reuss, the precipices, the smiling valleys, and the snowy peaks of the majestic Alps. The only "mountains" she had ever seen before were the little hills of the district of *Caux*.

These magnificent landscapes passed by almost as quickly as the pictures of a movie, but they left a lasting impression on her soul, absorbed as it was in adoration of Him who had created these immense and varied scenes of grandeur. Visible beauty always raised her mind to heaven and made her think of the unfailing splendours of Paradise. Before reaching these, however, she was to live the life predestined by God for her on earth. That life was at Carmel.

What a contrast between the vast stretches of country, through which the train was speeding, and the walls of the narrow monastery wherein she would see little more than a tiny bit of sky, the bare cloisters, and her cold cell! The child traveller wisely thought of the reality of her austere future. She understood clearly what awaited her and prepared herself for her cloistered life. She realised that one might easily become self-centred in that life of daily hidden sacrifices and little duties, which might be performed through mere routine if the sublime end of one's vocation were forgotten. She resolved that, if the hour of trial came, she would think of the power and grandeur of almighty God; she would not be so foolish as to attach any importance to the fleeting trifles of this world; she would ever remain in the heights like the great eagles winging their flight to the tops of the snow-capped peaks before her.

After passing through the St. Gothard tunnel, the pilgrims found themselves in Italy. Indeed, to the travellers from Normandy it appeared as if summer had returned. Floods of bright sunshine bathed the whole countryside with indescribable charm and light. They passed by Lugano and Como, then stopped at Milan in the evening. After a night of well-deserved rest, Monsieur Martin and his daughters heard Mass in the wonderful cathedral, that rose magnificent with its façade of white marble and its myriad tapering spires. With the enthusiasm of girls in their teens, Thérèse and Céline went directly up into the dome, high enough to discourage the less adventurous.

"When we came down from this lofty pedestal," the Saint writes gaily, "we began our sight-seeing which lasted a month, but the constant driving about cured me forever of the desire to be always in carriages."

Thérèse took a real delight in all that God's providence displayed before her wondering eyes. While she and Céline were expressing their enthusiastic admiration at the statues of the *Campo Santo*,[2] a bad-tempered old gentleman muttered between his teeth: "Oh, what enthusiasts these French people are!"

"And yet," remarks Thérèse, "he was French himself." With that she frankly gives her own opinion in the matter: "This poor old gentleman would have done better to have stayed at

[2] Cemetery.

home. He grumbled at the cities, the hotels, the people, and at everything." In vain did Monsieur Martin employ his patient charity in trying to interest his discontented neighbour.

After passing straight across to the east of the Peninsula, they reached Venice, the city of wonders, whose palaces are reflected in the rippling waters of the dark green canals.

The silence of the water-ways was broken only by the sound of the oars and the cries of the gondoliers. Yet Thérèse found Venice a melancholy city. She thought of the prisoners of former days who were left to languish in the dungeons of those splendid palaces that she was then visiting. "It is a city full of charm but full of sadness," was her comment.

At the Hotel *della luna,* no one suspected that the fair-haired girl of fourteen was in the presence of her future historian, Monsignor Laveille. This eminent priest did not even notice her among so many pilgrims, though many others were attracted by the pretty child. One young pilgrim was even too attentive. Thérèse noticed his attitude and showed him only a marked reserve. To Céline she mentioned her desire to be hidden behind the beloved gratings of Carmel, "for I am no stronger than others," she said humbly.

At Bologna they venerated St. Catherine, the Poor Clare who was kissed by the Child Jesus. In this town, she had an unpleasant experience. A group of Italian students entered the station. One of them gazed at her in a bold-faced way and wanted to catch hold of her, but she faced him with such a look that he slunk away abashed. The Virgin Mary was watching over her child.

3. *Loreto, Coliseum, Catacombs*

The next stop was Loreto, and what a happy visit that was for the child who was soon to be called Thérèse of the Child Jesus! Impressions of Nazareth invaded her heart. Jesus, Mary, and Joseph formed the happy earthly trinity whose humble, hidden life the Carmelite would imitate.

With Céline again, she succeeded in hearing Mass in the *Santa*

Casa, the Holy House, and the remembrance of that morning
was ever one of her happiest recollections.[3]

Too soon came the hour to leave Loreto. The travellers then
crossed Umbria, bathed in transparent light, where the fair
white villages are half hidden by the pines and evergreens on
the rounded hills. Then quickly they reached the Sabine district.
When night came, Thérèse fell asleep in the train, till she was
awakened by the cry *"Roma, Roma!"* At last she was in Rome!

Of the many wondrous sights she saw during her short stay
in the Eternal City, the places which thrilled her most and left
a lasting impression on her mind were the spots where the
martyrs had shed their blood for Christ. Her first visits were
to the Coliseum and the Catacombs.

As she gazed on the gigantic Flavian amphitheatre, her heart
beat with emotion and with the desire for martyrdom. She did
not think it enough to look on the immense arena; she wanted
to go down there to touch the sacred ground. The guide told
them that would be dangerous and even impossible as the real
soil of the early centuries was now buried at a depth of about
twenty-six feet. But Thérèse did not listen to him.

Glancing round the arena, she saw a wide opening, closed by
a thick barrier. "Come along," she called out to Céline, "follow
me, we shall be able to get through." With the swiftness of deer,
the two sisters scrambled down over the crumbling ruins to the
spot pointed out by the guide as being the authentic soil of
the martyrs' combats. There they threw themselves on their knees
and kissed the stone marked with a cross which denoted the place
where the Martyrs had laid down their lives. A desire for
martyrdom filled her soul as she pressed her lips to the
sacred soil:

"I asked for the grace to be a martyr too for Jesus and in
the depths of my heart I felt that my prayer had been heard."

[3] As a matter of fact, Thérèse and Céline even received Holy Communion
in that spot. As they were the only two members of the pilgrimage who
received our Lord in His own House, instead of in the Basilica surrounding
the Holy House, the fact is worth noting. Thérèse says: "No words can
describe the ecstatic happiness of that communion." (Note by the Translator.)

The grace of that moment marked a new stage in the spiritual life of the Saint; henceforth, she longed for martyrdom.

The two girls then hastened back; Monsieur Martin, surprised at their boldness but inwardly proud of their courage, did not attempt to scold them.

Their next visit was to the catacombs of St. Callistus. There they saw the tomb where the Virgin Martyr, Cecilia, had been buried for several centuries. From that day, an intimate friendship was formed between the little French girl of the nineteenth century and the noble Roman virgin of the early Christian ages. They were kindred souls. The boundless confidence of Cecilia, as she sang a hymn in her heart to Christ her Spouse whilst pagan rites were uniting her in public to an earthly lord, delighted the dauntless faith of Thérèse, who felt herself called to practise the same total abandonment to God. Filled with admiration of this incident she was later to allude to it again in her poem, "The Melody of St. Cecilia":

> O dove, within the rock of God's strong heart concealed,
>   No fear hadst thou, that night, of subtle fowler's snare:
> The Face of Jesus, then, its light to thee revealed,
>   His sacred Gospels lay upon thy bosom fair.[4]

As the patrician lady had done in her rich palace, so also the Carmelite in her humble convent would carry upon her heart, day and night, the holy book of the Gospels.

In the ancient Basilica of St. Agnes Without-the-Walls, which stands in the Roman Campagna, Thérèse felt as if she were meeting a friend of childhood's days. She wanted very much to bring Sister Agnes of Jesus a relic of her holy patron, and, although she could obtain nothing, she hoped against hope that her desire would be fulfilled. "Men refused me, but God came to my aid," she tells us. A little piece of red marble from a mosaic dating back to the time of the saint fell down at her feet. She quickly picked it up as a present from St. Agnes herself. One of the most beautiful of her poems was later to be written in honor of this saint.[5]

---

[4] Translated by Susan L. Emery.   [5] "Canticle of St. Agnes."

While at Rome, Thérèse looked on herself as a child in her father's house and felt that for her there were no restrictions. At the Church of the Holy Cross of Jerusalem, she obtained permission to put her finger through the opening of a reliquary and in that way touched one of the nails which had pierced our Saviour's hands or feet.

Thérèse has told us nothing of the remaining sights visited during her short stay of six days in Rome; she does not even mention her prayers at the Vatican Basilica, St. Peter's, where the Catholic Church proclaims the glory of her saints, but, undoubtedly, the future St. Thérèse of the Child Jesus knelt at the altar of the Confession of St. Peter, at that altar where Pope Pius XI would celebrate the Mass of her canonisation thirty-eight years later.

4. *Thérèse Pleads With Pope Leo XIII*

On the Sunday morning, the day for the papal audience, Thérèse set off for the Vatican, with mingled feelings of hope and fear. The sky was hidden by dark clouds; and the rain, which was pelting down on cupolas and basilicas, was most distressing for the pilgrims. Thérèse was soon to know the reason of this downpour.

When St. Joan of Arc went to meet Charles VII at Chinon, she did not hesitate to proclaim before the entire Court the warrior's mission which had been given to her by the King of heaven. It was not to an earthly king that Thérèse Martin wished to speak, but to the representative of the King of kings. Almighty God wished her to be a warrior also; her mission was to do valiant combat in the invisible world of souls.

She was going to speak to the Pope, in the presence of bishops, prelates, and all those who form the papal court. It needed all the graces that had been bestowed on her and all the enthusiasm that had filled her heart in the past few days to stimulate her courage. At eight o'clock, she assisted at the Holy Father's Mass in one of the chapels of the Vatican. His fervent piety made her declare that he was in truth the "Holy Father." She was delighted to find that the Gospel of the day contained these words: "Fear not, little flock, for it hath pleased your Father to give you a kingdom."[6] In her case, was it not Carmel that would be the kingdom given by God? During the Mass of thanksgiving, she sang in her heart a hymn of confidence, like unto the trustful confidence of St. Celicia.

Then the Audience began. Leo XIII was robed in white and seated on a throne which raised him above the respectful throng of pilgrims. Around the Pope were grouped princes of the Church and other high ecclesiastical dignitaries. Each pilgrim knelt in turn and kissed first the foot and then the hand of the Holy Father. No one uttered a word. It was almost Thérèse's turn, when the Vicar-General of Bayeux proclaimed in a loud voice that he strictly forbade anyone to speak to the Holy Father. Father Révérony had been watching Thérèse and did not want her to disturb the ceremony by any inopportune action. What was she to do? Would she obey him or would she disregard his orders? With a look of consternation, she turned toward her sister, who was just behind her.

"Speak," said Céline.

The next moment, the child was on her knees; she kissed the Pope's slipper, then raised her head and said:

"Most Holy Father, I have a great favour to ask from you."

A painting by Céline has portrayed for us this never-to-be-forgotten scene. The child-saint was wearing a dress of black velvet; her fair curls shone through the black lace veil; her sweet face was upraised suppliantly toward the Pope whose frail, white countenance was bent down toward the little girl entreating him. In that pale, thin, ascetic face, the piercing black eyes lit up and looked long into the child's beautiful eyes which were glistening with tears. With a charming movement of filial confidence, Thérèse had joined her hands and placed them on the Pontiff's knee.

"Most Holy Father," she implored, "in honour of your Jubilee, will you allow me to enter Carmel when I am fifteen?"

[6] Luke 7:32.

Thérèse had said what she meant to say, but, before the Pope could reply, Father Révérony interrupted, showing his displeasure.

"Holy Father, this is a child who wants to be a Carmelite, but the superiors of Carmel are examining the question."

"Well, my child," said Leo XIII, "do whatever the superiors decide."

The superiors! How well she knew their opposition! Notwithstanding her emotion, she had enough presence of mind to add:

"Oh, Holy Father, if only you would say 'Yes,' everyone else would agree."

One wonders what the Pope thought of her daring courage! The Saint tells us that he looked at her fixedly and replied in an impressive tone of voice, emphasizing each syllable:

"Well, indeed, you will enter if it is God's Will."

By placing Thérèse Martin's destiny in the hands of the diocesan authority and in God's good pleasure, the Sovereign Pontiff showed his prudence and his faith. He had not closed the door of Carmel, but Thérèse wanted a definite consent and was going to speak again, when the Pope gently placed his hand on her lips. Two of the Noble Guard, assisted by the Vicar-General, drew her away whilst the Holy Father gazed after her for some time.

Did the Sovereign Pontiff foresee the sanctity of this child? His successors would one day kneel before the image of the little girl who had just been prostrate at his feet. He himself, thirteen years later, would hold in his hands the wonderful book in which she recounts her short life.

Thérèse left the Vatican in tears and returned to her hotel, *Via Capo le Case,* in a deluge of rain. *"The sun did not venture to shine that day,"* she tells us. The little pilgrim seemed very unhappy, but in spite of all her tears a deep peace reigned in her heart. She had done everything in her power to attain her object; now she abandoned herself and her future completely to her Divine Master. If He really wished her for Himself, He would take her at the hour He willed. It was for Him to arrange everything. All she had to do now was to unite her will to His, with complete abandonment. She gave herself up to the divine good pleasure, even though she did not understand.

Some time previously, she had offered herself to the Child Jesus to be His plaything, to be like "a little ball" that He would throw about as He wished.

By this offering of herself, which she purposely expressed in this naïve way, Thérèse entered on the royal road of abandonment to God's Will, which was to lead her on to the heights of perfection.

At the actual moment, however, her disappointment was great. The grand pilgrimage had lost all its charm, since she had not obtained the consent for which she had come.

5. *Sunshine and Clouds*

Notwithstanding her grief, Thérèse had to do like the other travellers. The day after the papal audience, they left early in the morning for Pompeii. Beholding the devastated city, the contemplative little traveller would have liked to meditate on the instability of human things, but there was no time for that. The coach was waiting to take them to Naples. The wonderful Bay stretched out at her feet, but she only glanced at it without enthusiasm; nothing that day could capture her attention. "Joy is not found in the objects that surround us; it resides in the depths of the soul," she exclaimed long after, at the remembrance of that marvellous sight which had left her indifferent.

A few days later, divine providence sent her a little gleam of hope. When the pilgrims left Assisi, the land of St. Francis was bathed in the glowing rays of the *radiant sunshine*.

Just as they were leaving the Franciscan monastery, Thérèse noticed that she had lost the buckle of her belt. It took some time to find the missing object and in the interval the carriage set off without her. Only one carriage remained, that of the Vicar-General of Bayeux! Fearing to miss the train, she had to come forward and explain matters. She tried to hide her embarrassment, but felt extremely ill at ease. One of the gentlemen of the party immediately offered her his seat and went to sit beside the coachman. She felt like a squirrel caught in a snare, for she was face to face with the "formidable" ecclesiastical personage, whom she had disobeyed a few days previously by speaking to the Pope. She feared that he would reproach her.

Father Révérony, who was really a very enlightened priest and an experienced director of souls, had been studying Thérèse Martin from the beginning of the pilgrimage. She had, indeed, noticed the fact, for she mentioned later: "Even at table, he would lean forward to look at me and listen to me." But saints, unlike ordinary people, show up to advantage when closely studied. The conclusions drawn from this study by the Vicar-General of Bayeux were in her favour and his good opinion of her did not change. He was therefore very kind and affable, and promised to do all in his power to obtain for her the permission to enter Carmel at the age of fifteen. This meeting was like balm to her wounds, but all her recent experiences had taught this exceptional child to trust in God alone.

"I had lost confidence in creatures and could count only on God Himself," she exclaims.

However, her youthful enthusiasm returned for the beautiful sights which remained to be seen. On November 25, she visited Florence and venerated the tomb of St. Mary Magdalen of Pazzi in the Carmelite church there. Then came the return to France via Pisa and Genoa. The blue waters of the Mediterranean enchanted her. Her eyes admired, her memory stored up these last scenes of Nature's beauty. On the second of December, the train reached Paris and the pilgrims disbanded. The glorious pilgrimage had come to an end.

Monsieur Martin soon proposed taking his daughter on another pilgrimage, this time to Jerusalem, and we may imagine that Thérèse was tempted by such a project. She would indeed have liked to visit the land sanctified by our Lord's footsteps, but she felt that she had seen all she was destined to see of this world. Her only desire was for Carmel.

She had scarcely reached home when she went to visit the

convent. Eagerly she questioned: "Has His Lordship not said anything . . . nor written anything?" Alas, there was no word for her on the subject nearest to her heart. On the advice of Sister Agnes of Jesus, she wrote to the bishop herself, renewing her request for the permission to enter at Christmas, but that great feast came and went without any reply from the bishop. Thérèse lived in a spirit of abandonment in the hands of the Child Jesus, but the waiting was a sore trial. It was so hard to understand why Jesus allowed such obstacles to come in her way, considering that He Himself had made His call felt so persistently in her heart.

On January 1, 1888, she received the grandest of New Year gifts. Mother Mary Gonzaga wrote to tell her that the bishop's reply had come, granting the necessary permission for her entering at once. What joy filled Thérèse's heart! But another disappointment followed immediately. Out of a prudent consideration for the child's health, and perhaps to appease Father Delatroëtte who had not withdrawn his opposition, the Prioress had decided she would not receive her till after Lent. Another three months waiting! What a long delay it seemed to the heart of the child who in spirit had severed all ties with the world.

The temptation did come to her to take things rather easy in those few months, but she did not yield to it. God's grace urged her on and she resolved to give herself up to a life "more serious and mortified" than ever. Thérèse's mortifications were always practical and thorough. She did not practise extraordinary bodily disciplines, but little acts of virtue which often passed unnoticed and which were almost continuous. Her mortifications consisted in keeping back an impatient answer, in going against her natural inclinations, in doing little services to those around her without drawing attention to the fact. From her early childhood, Thérèse had practised these "moral disciplines," which are excellent for overcoming self-love. As Father Petitot says: "If people only knew what deep self-knowledge and above all what great self-command we learn through this form of mortification, they would esteem it far more."

"By the practise of these trifling mortifications," exclaimed the Saint, "I prepared myself to become the spouse of Jesus and I could never express in words how this prolonged period of waiting increased my abandonment, my humility, and my other virtues."

There remains one little anecdote to be told of the last days spent in her home. Returning from a walk, Monsieur Martin brought an unexpected present to his little Queen: "A little lamb, one day old, all white and curly," as she described it to her sister Marie, now Sister Mary of the Sacred Heart. The gift gave the greatest pleasure to Thérèse and Céline, but the charming creature did not delight them long, for "Alas! the pretty little animal died that afternoon. Poor, tiny thing, scarcely was it born than it suffered and died! But it was to receive all due honors. It was buried by the hands of Monsieur Martin; Céline sketched its portrait, and Thérèse covered it with a shroud made of pure white snow. She could draw from it another lesson of the perishableness of the things that she was leaving.

PART TWO

CHAPTER VIII

CARMEL AT LAST

1. *Entering on the Great Adventure*

SILENT cloisters, bare cells, white walls adorned only with severe admonitions from Scripture — such is Carmel!

Thérèse did not yet know what the interior of the convent was like, but her visits to the parlour had given her some idea of the aspect of austerity she would find within the convent walls, and she had already experienced the eloquent significance of the grating studded with sharp points, which had caused such suffering to her affectionate, childish heart. Moreover, her cloistered sisters had taught her not only the letter but also the spirit of the Carmelite life; and she was ready to face hardships. Like a valiant knight, her heart glowed with longing "to enter the lists."

Her entrance was fixed for the Feast of the Annunciation. In the year 1888 — on account of Holy Week — this feast had been transferred to Monday, April 9. The day before her departure, she assisted for the last time at Mass in the beautiful parish church of St. Peter, and in the evening there was a family gathering, for Monsieur Martin had invited the Guérins to dinner. Though all were heroic in their sacrifice, their hearts were too full of sorrow to prolong the farewell party.

"I do not understand saints who do not love their family," the Saint once exclaimed.

Thérèse has told us nothing of the last night spent in her father's house. Early next day, she was ready. In the freshness of that spring morning, she cast a last look round the familiar rooms and on the garden still wet with dew, as she said good-bye forever to her happy home, *les Buissonnets.*

There was only a short distance from her home to Carmel. Passers-by, who may have looked admiringly at the attractive girl, did not know that she was passing there for the last time, nor did they think that this day would be an historic day for the town of Lisieux.

After Mass in the Carmelite chapel, at which she assisted with all her family and where they all received Holy Communion, came the solemn moment of separation. Stifled sobs were heard on all sides, yet Thérèse did not shed a tear. But as she walked to the cloister door her heart beat so violently that she wondered if she were going to die.

Teresa of Avila experienced the same agony of suffering when she entered the Convent of the Incarnation, but she had been obliged to leave home secretly, as her father would not consent to the departure of his favourite child. Thérèse of Lisieux was more fortunate in that respect, but it is interesting to compare the two saints of the same name — the Mother and her spiritual daughter — on the threshold of the convents where they were to bury their youthful charm.

In bidding good-bye to the world, Teresa y Ahumada[1] chose no doubt the dress described by the nuns of the convent of the Incarnation — a pretty orange-coloured gown trimmed with black velvet, which showed off to such advantage her dark Spanish beauty. Thérèse Martin wore a soft blue woolen costume, which matched the blue of her eyes and harmonised with her golden hair and delicate Norman complexion.

Unlike, they yet resembled each other, and with three and a half centuries between them, their hearts were enkindled by the same heroic ardour.

2. *The Cloistered Life of Carmel*

Through the large cloister door just opened, dark-veiled figures could be seen. Before going to join them, Thérèse embraced all whom she was leaving and then knelt for her father's blessing. But, in order to bless her, Monsieur Martin

[1] This is the family name of Teresa of Avila.

went down on his knees himself. Kneeling, he gave to God the jewel of his heart.

But before Thérèse now lay steeper paths to climb.

"From the very beginning," she tells us, "my way was strewn with thorns rather than with roses." One of the thorns, and that a sharp one, must have pierced her most unexpectedly at the very moment of entering the Carmel.

"Well, Reverend Mothers," stiffly said Father Delatroëtte, who presided at the ceremony, "you may sing a *Te Deum*. As the bishop's delegate, I present you this child of fifteen whose entrance you have requested. I hope she will not disappoint your expectations, but I must remind you that, if it should be so, you alone must bear the responsibility."

And this in the very presence of Monsieur Martin! Then the cloister door closed and Thérèse was welcomed by all the nuns who now became her sisters. She thus entered "a new family," is she affectionately remarked, "whose devotedness and love are not dreamt of by the outside world."

There had been, it is true, a little opposition by some of the nuns. They wondered how such a young postulant would act, for they looked on her in truth as a mere child, with her hair still hanging down in curls. These, in fact, had been put up on only two occasions — one when she visited His Lordship Bishop Hugonin, and the other when her photograph was taken before she entered the Convent.

This picture presents us Thérèse at the age of fifteen. Her beautiful hair, gathered on the crown of her head, seems almost too heavy for her youthful face with its sweet but energetic expression. The forehead is broad; the mouth is firm but gentle, arched by a slight smile which reminds us of the three-year-old little mite whom her eldest sister described as "gay and mischievous." The words still aptly apply to her bright intelligent countenance, but an ardour of soul and a new strength of character now accompany those charming features, while an interior fire glows behind the sweetness of those eyes. Her head is erect with a quiet dignity that commands respect.

That was the impression made on the Carmelite nuns in presence of the modest, dignified bearing of the little Queen. Noting her decided and earnest manner, they felt that this girl of fifteen was no ordinary character. Years later, when the Mistress of Novices spoke of Thérèse's early days at Carmel, she did not hesitate to use the word "majesty" in describing the general impression caused by the young postulant.

The little ceremony of reception over, Thérèse was taken along the white corridors to her cell. The complete silence reigning everywhere delighted her.

After the intense sorrow of the morning, she was at last alone . . . in Carmel! With a full heart, she gazed round this little room, three yards wide, in which she was to live henceforth. The furniture was of the simplest. Apart from the bed, which consisted of a plank on trestles with a straw-mattress and heavy common blankets, there were only a jug of water, a little wooden bench, and a stand to hold writing materials or a work-basket.

On the white wall hung a wooden cross without the figure of our Saviour. Thérèse already understood the eloquent language of the bare cross. We can imagine that she knelt down, lost in adoration, stretching forth her arms to her invisible Redeemer, to whom she offered her youth to be nailed, in His place, to the redeeming cross.

A deep peace filled her soul, a peace so sweet that she could not express its serenity in words. In the many hard trials that God sent her afterward, she ever retained this peace of soul as her treasure and her greatest security; it proved to her that her call was really from on high.

Thérèse felt that she was now where God wished her to be. In a transport of joy, she kept saying: "Now I am here forever."

This "ever" was to last but nine and a half years — years of wondrous merit and love, of which the following chapters will give some idea. The child who had just entered Carmel had no illusions. Her well-balanced mind had foreseen the austerity of the religious life, and the daily sacrifices caused her no surprise.

Every form of religious life is a means offered to souls to help them to reach their final and supreme end: God. This chief and supreme object is achieved in ways which differ in each spiritual family. The Carmelite rule is austere, though broad-minded. It assists the soul in its flight toward God by a life of penance and contemplation.

Early rising, hours of mental prayer, recitations of the Divine Office in choir, fasting during nearly seven months of the year, perpetual abstinence, complete silence except for the two hours of recreation daily, corporal penance, heavy garments made of coarse rough material, manual work that is wearying for delicate arms unaccustomed to such labour, strict poverty, unhesitating obedience: all these form the daily life of a Carmelite in the unchanging surroundings of her cloistered convent of about twenty nuns.

The life based on these strong, monastic principles is able to attract souls for one reason only, because of the spirit which animates it: the love of God. It is that love which impels them to accomplish, as most perfectly they can, the first great commandment: "Thou shalt love the Lord thy God with thy whole heart, and with thy whole soul, and with thy whole strength." To advance in that love is the purpose of a Carmelite's mortifications and her long hours of prayer. It is the life of the Blessed, a life of adoration and praise already begun here upon earth.

The second commandment is like unto the first: "Thou shalt love thy neighbour as thyself." To love one's neighbour means "to wish the same good to him as to oneself and to procure that good as far as it is in one's power to do so."

The supreme good is God Himself. The Carmelite therefore desires God for her neighbour and tries to bring her neighbour to God by the same means as she uses for herself: prayer and penance. The Carmelite order is essentially devoted to the practice of mortification.

Teresa of Avila had witnessed, with intense anguish, the heresy of Protestantism devastating Christianity. For that reason, she put more austerity into her Rule than she had intended at first.

The high ideals put before the Daughters of St. Teresa are

prayer and mortification, practised in order to save sinners; in order to open the gates of heaven for the many who are ignorant, for the many who are sinful, for the many who have strayed from the straight path; and above all, in order to help priests, "the salt of the earth," who are to convince, convert, and instruct souls.

Every Carmelite, according to her temperament and the grace she receives, strives to ascend the Holy Mountain of Carmel, the summit of which is perfect love. To help her in the ascent, she has the enlightened teachings, precise and life-giving, of the illustrious Reformer of her Order, St. Teresa of Jesus,[2] and the books of mystical theology of its great Doctor, St. John of the Cross.

Complete liberty is given to each soul, for Carmelites are not all expected to be formed after the same model. Each soul is free to keep her own personality, her own special form of interior life. The wide breadth of view that distinguishes the great Saint of Avila would not allow any undue interference in the intimate cultivation of souls, where the Holy Ghost is the divine Gardener. No soil, therefore, could have been better chosen for the development of the "entirely new Little Way"[3] which Thérèse of the Child Jesus was first to live perfectly herself, and then to expound to other souls.

3. *Three Personalities Meet*

In her cloistered home, the postulant had exchanged her blue costume for a simple black dress; a black bonnet covered her fair silky hair. With an even, unhurried step, she passed through the silent corridors. This firm, quiet manner of walking was always characteristic of her and caused her to be recognised by all, even when her veil concealed her face. It might indeed be taken as a symbol of her manner of advancing in her "Little Way" and of the perfection that she was to give to all things, even to seemingly insignificant actions. Father Petitot states: "We do not hesitate to affirm that of all the saints, with the

[2] The name in religion of St. Teresa of Avila.
[3] For an explanation of the expression *"entirely new* Little Way" see Preface by the General Editor, pp. ix, x; text, pp. 154, 158.

exception of the Blessed Virgin and St. Joseph, St. Thérèse of the Child Jesus was the most faithful *in minimo*."[4]

However, there was nothing unnatural or constrained in her manner. "She set about her new duties with charming graciousness," declared her Novice Mistress, Mother Mary of the Angels. This experienced nun was very fond of Thérèse whom she had known since childhood, but in the Noviciate she learned to appreciate the postulant still more and was often silently amazed at this child, who was growing "in wisdom and in grace" under her attentive eye. Unfortunately, in her zeal, the good Novice Mistress gave her postulant long exhortations, "the piety of which did not atone for their monotony," says Monsignor Laveille.

Thérèse listened with great respect. "I scarcely left her side because she taught me how to work," wrote the Saint. Yet her soul was really somewhat weary of these lengthy discourses, for her vocation was that of "interior silence."[5] Writing later of these early days in the religious life, the Saint remarked: "I did not know how to express in words what was taking place in my soul; the time of spiritual direction was, therefore, a veritable martyrdom for me." This difficulty of opening her heart to her Mother Mistress was a hard trial for a postulant beginning her monastic life. Yet Thérèse appreciated fully the excellence of the saintly Mistress of Novices, for she wrote these words of high praise: "Our Mistress was a real saint; she was the perfect type of the early Carmelites. . . . I was very fond of her . . . her kindness to me was beyond expression."

Notwithstanding her affection and her admiration, Thérèse's soul, however, did not expand. She felt more drawn to talk of her interior life to her Prioress, Mother Mary Gonzaga, whose attitude had always been so kind and so understanding in listening to her childish secrets, and who had always believed in her youthful vocation.

Eager and trustful, she went to her superior to talk of her inner life, little suspecting the bitter disappointment which

---

[4] At all events she was the Saint who concentrated on charming Christ by "trifles," and it was that which was to make her so imitable by all little souls.
[5] Monsignor Laveille.

awaited her. In her perfect charity, the Saint does little more than allude to this matter.

Mother Mary Gonzaga thought it her duty, we are told, to test in a very special way this unusual vocation, which providence had confided to her care, and to give this soul many an occasion of practising humility. It was precisely because she recognised Thérèse's "unusual strength of character" that she changed her attitude. The kindly welcome which had formerly led to intimate conversation was now changed for a systematic air of indifference and even of harsh severity.

We shall see how the postulant, still a mere child, acted under the guidance "of this truly severe hand."[6] She herself, let it be repeated, has told us very little on the subject, saying simply that many pages of her monastic life "will never be read on earth." It has been generally admitted by those around her that the Prioress' attitude was one of Thérèse's hardest trials. But let us not be overharsh in our judgement.

Mother Mary Gonzaga was in reality an instrument used by God in the formation of a soul of exceptional value. Monsignor Laveille describes her as strong, well-educated, and generous, having a rich active nature with regrettable limitations. "Very impressionable, easily offended, and inclined to melancholy," she tended to be inconsistent and lacked judgement.[7]

This description will suffice for those who know what tact, discrimination, prudence, and gentleness are needed in a superior, if she is to rule her Convent with success. Mother Gonzaga had been chosen as Prioress on account of her many good qualities and the material services she had rendered to the Community, and also on account of her charming manner due to her early training.[8] This charm of personality must have been real, since Thérèse, so sensitive and refined, loved her. The motherless postulant felt a humble affection for the superior

[6] Monsignor Laveille's designation.
[7] The translator wishes to state that she does not necessarily associate herself with certain remarks concerning the character and attitude of Mother Mary Gonzaga, nor with certain expressions concerning Father Delatroëtte.
[8] She belonged to a noble family of Calvados.

whom she could call her Mother. After so many years, she was able to say the word "Mother" again! It was surely not unreasonable to rejoice in the prospect of that intimate affection.

4. *The Waters of Bitterness*

With all due recollection, the postulant used to sweep the cloister, offering this humble occupation in union with the household tasks of the Virgin Mary in the little house of Nazareth.

Was it her contemplation that made her overlook a detail? She had not seen a spider's web in the corner! Mother Mary Gonzaga, passing by, noticed this. In presence of the whole community, the Prioress called up the negligent postulant, proclaiming:

"It is easy to see that our cloisters are swept by a child of fifteen. It is really too bad. Go and sweep away that cobweb and be more careful in the future." The effect of this humiliation on the shy, sensitive child can be imagined!

At half-past four every afternoon, the tall[9] postulant used to pass down the corridors with lowered eyes; the Mistress of Novices used to send her to weed the garden, for she thought it absolutely necessary that a growing girl, who had entered an enclosed order so young, should have air and exercise. This little expedition out-of-doors, being an exception to the Rule, was a real penance for Thérèse, especially as she was almost sure to meet her Prioress on the way. Once the latter remarked with a dissatisfied air: "Really! This child does absolutely nothing. What are we to think of a novice who needs a walk every day?"

"She treated me constantly in this way," wrote Thérèse, who felt keenly this frequent upbraiding about slowness at work, want of generosity in the discharge of duties, and similar faults. "On the rare occasions when I spent an hour with her for spiritual direction, I was scolded nearly all the time."

Dismayed, the postulant wondered how she could correct her

[9] Thérèse was taller than the average height and grew even after she entered Carmel.

faults and satisfy her Prioress. It was hard to correct faults she did not possess, for Mother Mary Gonzaga's criticisms were hardly justifiable. In all humility and hoping to please her superior, Thérèse decided to spend her free time in sewing instead of in prayer as was her custom, but she spoke to no one of this, as she wished to be "faithful in acting solely for Jesus, doing things for Him alone."

In the midst of these daily vexations, the postulant said nothing though she suffered keenly. The gift of fortitude helped her to bear this trial, but did not make her heart insensible. When blamed too unjustly, she would go to talk things over with the kind Mistress of Novices. She did not complain, but her loyal nature needed to unburden itself. Then the light of grace strengthened her at once. "I can see her still as she came to open her heart to me," said Mother Mary of the Angels.

If it had not been for these rebuffs coming from her Prioress, Thérèse's heart, which had been so carefully guarded in the world, might have become attached to creatures in the convent, and that would have been a real misfortune for a soul called to such a pure love of God.

"She recognised the fact that it was God who allowed these difficulties and she smiled in spite of her suffering," said Mother Mary of the Angels. How well that sweet smile concealed her interior struggles!

Pauline and Marie — her "little Mother" and her god-mother — were near at hand behind those closed doors. It would have been so consoling to tell them of her troubles, but in that desire she recognised a temptation. She had not come to Carmel to continue the sweet joys of family life and to have her heart comforted; she had come to seek Jesus alone. Wishing to mortify her yearning for affection, she resolved never to act according to nature. At recreation, she never sought the company of her sisters, but took any vacant place, preferably beside the nuns for whom she felt the least attraction. Sister Agnes of Jesus and Sister Mary of the Sacred Heart did not understand and were sometimes hurt at their little sister's attitude, for the child whom they had brought up seemed to be withdrawing from their sisterly affection, but the angels saw the heroism of her generous conduct. The efforts she made to overcome the inclinations of her affectionate heart may be numbered, no doubt, among those trials "more bitterly felt even than the others," which she mentions without going into details.

All these sufferings, which came to her from creatures, would have seemed light to her generous soul, if He, for whom she had entered Carmel and whom alone she sought, had granted her the joy of His presence. But that was not to be. In the semidarkness of the early morning, the postulant would kneel — or sit on her heels in the Carmelite manner — trying to meditate or pray, but, in spite of all her efforts to be recollected and to keep guard over her faculties in order to think of God alone, her imagination would wander and her heart remain cold. With all her courage, her tenacity of purpose, and her spirit of faith, she struggled against distractions and dryness, against weariness from the uncomfortable position, and drowsiness caused by the unusually early rising, but in vain.

The suffering of her soul at that time is a well-known spiritual state. It is called spiritual dryness. "The daily food of my soul was bitter dryness," she tells us.

Unceasingly, she whispered to her Divine Master that she loved Him and desired to love Him ever more and more; she offered herself to His divine good pleasure, abandoning herself to Him as a little child, but her Divine Spouse remained invisible and silent, not making His presence felt in any way.

Her courage was not daunted by this terrible period of desolation. Her first letter to Céline, written just a month after her entrance, reveals her thoughts and feelings. It is dated May 8, 1888, the anniversary of her First Communion.

". . . Yes, as you say, life is often bitter and wearisome; it is hard to begin a day of toil, especially if Jesus hides Himself from our love. What is this sweet Friend doing? Does He not see our anguish and the burden that weighs us down? Where is He? . . . Why does He not come and comfort us?"

To these agonising questions, Thérèse herself hastens to reply:

"Do not be afraid, Céline; He is there, close at hand. He is watching us . . . He begs of us to offer Him these sufferings which cause our tears, for He needs them for the good of souls, for the good of our own souls. He wishes to prepare a glorious recompense for us. Ah! I assure you He does not like to give us to drink of the waters of bitterness, but He knows that is the only way to prepare us to know Him as He knows Himself, and to participate in the Divine Nature. . . . Let us rise above all earthly things. Higher up, the air is so pure. Jesus may hide Himself, but we feel that He is there. . . ."

One is amazed at the thought that these lines were written by a girl of fifteen! There is not a word of complaint or regret that her Beloved should try her thus. She was persuaded that it was all for the good of her soul and took care to point out that He "does not like" to impose suffering on His loved ones. Thus, true to her resolution taken the previous year while gazing upon the grandeur of the snow-capped Alps, this young postulant took her flight far beyond the average heights.

"Higher up the air is so pure. . . ." It was indeed the highest summits that she proposed for Céline's ascent, and her own.

With humble thanksgiving, she realised that we are called to participate in the Divinity of Him who deigned to clothe Himself with our humanity, that is in the Divinity of Jesus Christ.[10] How well she understood the meaning of that admirable prayer which rises from earth to heaven at every Mass which is celebrated throughout the world!

God became man so that man might participate in the Divinity! Thérèse's heart thrilled with enthusiasm at the thought. What mattered trials, great or small, in comparison with such a splendid destiny! By what means is that sublime destiny attained? With deepest conviction, Thérèse declared that there was "only one means": Love.

Even as a child, during the solemn moments of Holy Communion, she had received intimations of the necessity of suffer-

[10] Offertory of the Mass.

ing and she found that it had an attraction for her, though her trials as yet had been few. But now the hour had come when she was to experience its relentless "charm." In the silence of Carmel, suffering, as a messenger sent from God, stood before Thérèse **Martin.**

"Suffering stretched forth her arms to me from the first and I clasped her hand with love."

With love! These two words explain the whole life of Saint Thérèse of **Lisieux.**

CHAPTER IX

TRIALS OF THE NOVICE

1. *The Foot-Hills of Carmel*

"HOLINESS," it has been said, "is acquired in the drama of daily life."[1] The details of that drama no one will ever know except the soul that is the theatre itself wherein the scenes are enacted.

The walls of Thérèse's cell do not reveal the secret of her hardest struggles. Alone with her God, whose Presence it was not granted her senses to apprehend, the postulant felt as if walking in dark and ice-bound paths. She wished indeed to suffer, to suffer with love, to suffer in order to reach holiness and to save souls, for that was her object in coming to Carmel, but the solitude was intolerable, and bitter was her desolation of spirit. How sweet, now, the remembrance of her home life, with its pleasant affection and tender happiness!

Even as we, the saints have felt a shuddering of nature at certain self-abnegations demanded of them, but where we perhaps failed they carried off the victory by their heroic courage.

"When I was a postulant," wrote the Saint in that part of her *Autobiography* which is addressed to Mother Mary Gonzaga, "I was grievously tempted to give in to nature and to seek some little joy for self. The longing to talk to you made me think of a list of permissions that I might ask; I had to pass your door quickly and to hold on to the banisters, so as not to give in to my desire to turn back to your cell."

The lively imagination of the young postulant at once summoned up a host of plausible pretexts for going in to her Prioress' room. For though very severe, Mother Mary Gonzaga

---

[1] *Le Carmel,* by Marie Madeleine Vaussard.

was nonetheless now her "Mother," and the solitude at times seemed almost unbearable. But grace, with its relentless light, which never failed to shine upon her soul even in the darkest hours, made her aware of the subtle temptation. Nature was seeking self-satisfaction, whereas her soul sought God alone. In silent combat, she conquered self and passed on.

The Retreat of Father Pichon, a saintly Jesuit who always urged souls toward love and confidence in God, afforded Thérèse a welcome respite in the loneliness of her ascent up the mountain of perfection. She knew this worthy priest already, for on her sisters' advice she had consulted him the previous year about her vocation. He had encouraged her in her decision, and now once again his presence was helpful.

Although she had extreme difficulty in opening her heart, the little she said showed him the abyss of suffering in which she had spent the first two months at Carmel. He was amazed indeed, for he had expected to find in her only a childlike piety exempt from difficulties, but now he perceived very clearly that God wished her to become a great saint. Deeply impressed by this conviction, he spoke solemnly to reassure her in her anxiety about her early life.

"The fear of having stained the white robe of my baptism had caused me great suffering," Thérèse tells us. She therefore made a general confession to this good Father, going over the faults of her whole life. Hearing such an innocent avowal, he did not hesitate to dispel all her fears by the solemn affirmation: "Before God, the Blessed Virgin, the angels, and all the saints, I declare that you have never committed one mortal sin. Thank God for the favour He has bestowed on you without any merit on your part."

What inexpressible joy these words brought her! She could be certain that her soul had always been pure, that she had never for a moment been separated from her God, and that the grace of her baptism was intact! Cherishing, too, those final words, "without any merit on your part," she joined humility to her thanksgiving.

Father Pichon was one of those priests, uniting "wisdom with holiness," whom St. Teresa of Avila wished to have for her spiritual daughters. Since Thérèse had never had a director, she asked if he would undertake to guide her.

"My child," he answered, as if directly inspired by the Spirit of God, "may our Lord be always your Superior and your Novice Master!"

"Such He ever was, and my Director also," wrote the Saint.

Soon after, Father Pichon returned to Canada and Thérèse found herself again without a guide. All she could hope to receive from her so-called director was one letter a year. Once again Jesus had shown that He wished to be sole Master, and Thérèse quietly abandoned herself more and more to the guidance of Him whom she called "The true Director of all directors."

Thus passed the summer of 1888, and in October, after six months spent at Carmel, the postulant wrote her second letter to Céline:

". . . When at the beginning of our day we feel no courage or strength for the practice of virtue, this is really a grace; it is the time to lay the axe to the root of the tree, relying on Jesus alone."

We marvel at the self-control of the little Carmelite, at her clear-sighted, far-seeing vision, and telling expression. It was a peculiar gift she possessed for the guidance of others. Her superiors were soon to take notice of this fact. It is experience that helps us to know our weakness and to rely on God's strength alone. As St. Paul says: "When I am weak, then I am strong."[2]

After this lesson on humility, she encouraged her sister's efforts in her own charming manner: "If we fall, an act of love will set all right, and Jesus will smile again."

Love! That word will be ever on her lips.

The postulant who found it so difficult to speak to her superiors of the workings of grace in her soul, was at ease with her sister, for she did not write to talk of herself. Her

[2] II Cor. 12:10.

only desire was to help Céline, so lonely at home without her, but her words at the same time reveal the state of her own soul. The whole letter, indeed, is worth citing, but suffice it here to quote the advice given at its close where she displays the bold courage of her own desires:

"You wish to become a saint. I shall not tell you to aim at the seraphic sanctity of the most privileged souls, but rather to be perfect as your heavenly Father is perfect."

She once expressed this same thought to a Jesuit, Father Blino, who happened to be at the Convent:

"O Father," she said, in the generosity of her heart, "I want to become a saint; I want to love God as much as St. Teresa did."

"What pride and what presumption!" was the surprised comment of the Father, obviously unacquainted with her, "Confine your efforts to overcoming your faults . . . and restrain your rash desires."

"But, Father," answered Thérèse, not in the least troubled, "I do not consider that a rash desire, since our Lord has said: 'You therefore are to be perfect, even as your heavenly Father is perfect.'"

The good Father was not convinced, but, had he been able to observe her in all the actions of her daily life, he would have changed his mind. The virtue of this child was indeed exceptional and was growing daily stronger on its firm foundation of love and sacrifice. Overcoming all the inclinations of her sensitive, ardent nature, she made herself the humble servant of the whole community.

Mother Mary Gonzaga herself, notwithstanding her affected indifference, could not help admiring her virtuous postulant and confided to those around her that Thérèse was "the best among her best, a real angel."

Father Delatroëtte, however, who did not see her in the round of daily life, remained of the same opinion as Father Blino and did not change his attitude. It was no doubt due to him that the time of her postulancy was prolonged three months.

Thérèse waited humbly. When Céline and Léonie visited the convent, she always received them with a smile on her lips and peace in her heart.

Having recovered from a second attack of paralysis, Monsieur Martin, who was now sixty-six years of age, went to Alençon for a brief stay, which was to be his last. During a visit to the convent shortly after, the saintly old man confided to his daughters that he had received such great graces and such intense consolation in the church of Our Lady at Alençon that he had cried out:

"My God, it is too much, I am too happy; I shall not get to heaven like this, I wish to suffer something for Thee."

In adding that "he had offered himself," his humility prevented him from pronouncing the last words "as a Victim," but Thérèse guessed his meaning. God was soon to accept the offering of His faithful servant.

The three extra months of Thérèse's postulancy were winter months during which she underwent a hard apprenticeship to penance. She had always felt the cold very much, and had never spent the winter without a fire. Now the icy dampness penetrated her cell where she suffered from cold; the nights were the hardest of all to bear, and she sometimes shivered until morning without being able to get warm. The rule could easily have been mitigated a little in her favour, but she would not ask for that. Jesus made her feel that the enduring of this suffering would be a proof of her love. No one ever knew to what extent she had suffered from the cold until she was dying, when she admitted the fact in reply to obedience: "I thought I would have died from cold." The words need no commentary. Even from saints not specially noted for penance God sometimes asks these heroic sacrifices, which would be want of prudence in less exalted souls. At the end of her life, Thérèse herself said that it was a sin against prudence not to take into account differences of climate in the application of religious rules.

At length, the weary months of waiting came to an end, and it was decided that the postulant would be allowed to receive the religious habit on January 10. At Carmel, the Clothing ceremony is preceded by a week's retreat, during which the postulant examines, before God, in silence and in prayer, the sincerity of her motives and the proof of the divine call. Thérèse never wrote intimate notes for herself, so we should not have known anything of the state of her soul during these days of recollection, if it had not been for the letter written to Sister Agnes of Jesus, in which she says with poignant sincerity:

". . . In my intercourse with Jesus, there is nothing but dryness and weariness . . . I am happy, very happy, to suffer. . . . All the beauties of creation matter little to me. . . . How good He is to me, my Jesus who will soon be my Spouse. . . . He knows well that if He sent me but a shadow of earthly happiness, I would cling to it with the intense ardour of my heart, and so He refuses me even this shadow. . . . He prefers to leave me in darkness rather than to give me a false glimmer which would not be Himself. . . ."

The severity of this mysterious despoiling of self appals us. In this desert of spiritual aridity, there was no oasis of consolation. But God knew what strength and fortitude He had given to this child; He had prepared the upward paths of this great soul. The letter continues:

"I do not wish to bestow the smallest degree of my love on creatures. I wish to give all to Jesus, since He has made me understand that He alone is perfect happiness. All — all will be for Him! And even when I have nothing to offer as is the case to-night, I shall give Him this nothing."

Unflinchingly, Thérèse determined to continue her course in the path she had chosen; nothing would hinder her in her ascent to the very summit of Mount Carmel.

2. Clothing and "Miracle of the Snow"

On January 10, the day fixed for her Clothing, Thérèse wore a bridal dress of white velvet, trimmed with swansdown and Alençon lace, for her father wished her to look her best. A long veil of tulle covered the fair curls which hung down her back for the last time, and she wore a wreath of lilies. Thus adorned, she passed through the cloister door in her own charming and dignified manner.

In the outer court, her family watched her approach, a picture of youth, purity, and grace. Though his eyes were filled with tears, Monsieur Martin exclaimed: "Ah, there is my little Queen," and, giving her his arm, with a holy pride, he led her to the altar where she was to hear Mass.

When the holy Sacrifice was ended, the postulant came down the nave of the Chapel with a lighted candle in her hand and knelt before her father as on the day of her entrance. The bishop watched the scene with emotion. Instead of the *Magnificat,* he intoned the *Te Deum,* which is sung at Professions but not at Clothing ceremonies. The mistake seemed to Thérèse to be a special mark of attention from heaven, for this happy day was the supreme triumph for her saintly and dearly loved father, whose sacrifices were now all made: pure, living sacrifices. His five daughters belonged to God, since Léonie and Céline had told him of their desire to enter the convent too.

Jesus was pleased to give another little mark of His favour to this child who had left all for His sake. Thérèse had wished to see the earth clad in white like herself on this day, but the simple, childlike desire seemed doomed to disappointment, as the weather was very mild and almost like spring. On returning to the enclosure, however, she beheld an immense white carpet — the quadrangle covered with snow! Everyone was amazed and some people whispered the word "miracle." With charming simplicity, Thérèse rejoiced in this gift from her Divine Spouse.

When she reappeared behind the grating, the bishop put the usual question:

"What do you desire?"

"The Mercy of God, the Poverty of the Order, and the Society of the Sisters," came the reply.

The slender figure, clad in white, then retired, and the ritual ceremony took place within the convent; the child's beautiful curls, which reflected the tints of pale gold with the deeper tints of burnished gold, were subjected to the merciless scissors. The hair was carefully preserved and is now venerated as a precious relic by pilgrims from all over the world.

Henceforth her head would be adorned only by the monastic veil. Clothed in her heavy, coarse habit, she felt that she was truly a Carmelite! Her happiness is portrayed in the two photographs taken, a few days after the Clothing, at the foot of the large crucifix in the quadrangle. In one picture, the novice is seen, radiantly happy, in her white choir mantle, with one hand round the bottom of the crucifix and the other holding lilies. In the second, she is taken in her brown habit and the short white veil. In both photographs, this child-novice of sixteen is charming in the austere Carmelite habit. She ever retained this charm and the beauty which God had given her, while accomplishing her mission, which was to impress on souls the merciful love of God for poor, human creatures.

3. *Prophetic Vision Fulfilled*

These days of mystic joy were followed almost immediately by the saddest trials. A month after the Clothing, Monsieur Martin had a third attack of paralysis and this time his intellect was affected. We can understand how intense was the sorrow of his daughters in seeing him so suddenly reduced to helplessness, "his fine intellect clouded," as Monsignor Laveille expresses it, "and his tender affection reduced to indifference." On February 12, 1889, he left Lisieux for a private asylum where he could receive the necessary care. Thérèse's prophetic vision was accomplished.[3] A willing victim, her venerable father was to ascend the most humiliating Calvary, accompanied by his sorrowing daughters. In this suffering, the most heart-rending that can touch a child's heart, Thérèse showed her great strength of character.

In her letters to Céline, she soared to heights hitherto unexplored by her. In January, when the fear of the coming trial overshadowed them, she wrote: ". . . Now we have nothing

[3] See pages 41, 42.

more to hope for on earth, 'the cool mornings have passed away.' "[4] All the happy past is summed up in these words. She longed to see the companion of that sweet childhood rise above earthly things and tried to draw her upward with her in her own amazing flight. "Suffering alone remains for us. Ours is an enviable lot and the Seraphim in heaven envy our happiness."

The young novice wanted her sister to be more than merely resigned; she wished her to be *happy,* to be *united* to God, by the joyful acceptance of their terrible cross. She quoted and underlined that beautiful saying of Madame Swetchine:

"Resignation is something apart from God's Will; there is the same difference as that which exists between union and unity; in union there are still two, in unity there is but one."

In her letter of February 28, she continued her sublime lesson of love: "Our Father must indeed be loved by God since he has so much to suffer. It is a joy for us to be humiliated with him." She accepted the heart-breaking emotion and humiliation — which her heroism ventured to call "joy" — as true spiritual riches, as "a gold-mine" given by God to be turned to account. But she does not always speak figuratively, as the following sentence shows: "I know that saints are made only by humiliation."

But March 12, she soared to the heights that are verily dazzling: "Céline, I want to forget this world. . . . I find only one joy, that of suffering; and this joy, which is above that of the senses, is beyond all happiness."

Only saints understand the language of saints! Suffering is habitual joy for them because it is the obstacle to be overcome if they would remain happy in their love; the habitual joy in which they live consists in transforming suffering into love. This is the mysterious alchemy wrought by grace in those hearts freed from all self-seeking.

Wishing to see Céline rise to the heights which she herself had reached, Thérèse continued:

"Let us suffer in peace. Peace is not necessarily joy, at least not

[4] St. John of the Cross.

sensible joy. In order to suffer in peace, it is enough to will, with our whole heart, all that our Lord wills."

She admitted frankly that her nature had had a hard struggle to reach and to remain in those heights:

"Do not think we can find love without suffering. Our nature remains and must be taken into account, but it enables us to amass spiritual riches."

A deep, trustful humility characterised all her remarks:

"We should like to suffer generously and nobly. What an illusion! Why should I be discouraged even if I fall at every moment! In that way I realise my weakness and I gain thereby. My God, you see what I am capable of, if you do not carry me in your arms. . . ."

Then followed this unexpected remark:

"If you are willing to bear in peace the trial of not being pleased with yourself, you will be offering the Divine Master a home in your heart . . . the poorer you are, the more Jesus will love you."

The saintly novice, enlightened by heavenly wisdom, understood the meaning of the beatitude: "Blessed are the poor in spirit, for theirs is the Kingdom of heaven." The verb is in the present tense, for it is now that the humble begin to receive their reward. The treasures of faith, hope, and charity are theirs. What riches the humble Carmelite novice of Lisieux possessed!

4. *Inspiration From the Holy Face*

About this time, her soul felt drawn to a devotion which had a special link with her father's great trial. This was the devotion to the Holy Face of Jesus, which devotion subsequently went out of favor with the faithful and is less frequently referred to at present.

"The words of Isaias: 'Who hath believed our report. . . . There is no beauty in him, nor comeliness'[5] constituted the foundation of my devotion to the Holy Face or rather the very foundation of all my piety."

[5] Isa. 53:2.

Speaking of the great importance of this devotion in the life of St. Thérèse of Lisieux, Father Petitot remarks that "the piety of St. Thérèse of the Child Jesus was according to tradition," since "its strongest and most distant roots spread through the Gospel right to the most vital prophecies of the Old Testament."

By daily contemplation of the authentic portrait of her humiliated Saviour, the young Carmelite fed the flame of her love, and the words of the prophet were ever in her mind:

"His look was as it were hidden and despised. Whereupon we esteemed him not. . . . He was offered because it was his own will and he opened not his mouth; he shall be led as a sheep to the slaughter and shall be dumb as a lamb before his shearer; he did not open his mouth to complain."[6]

Nor did Thérèse complain. Like her Beloved, she wished "to be unknown and esteemed as naught"; she longed "to suffer and to be forgotten."

Father de Foucauld, so like Thérèse in humility of heart and simplicity of love, became a gardener at the convent of the Poor Clares at Nazareth and, later on, a hermit in the Sahara. In his thirst for humiliations, he sought the humblest life, but the very excess of his humility attracted the attention of the whole world.

The young novice in Normandy, with her keen common sense and her clear-sighted logic, concealed her holiness under the guise of simple, everyday, commonplace actions; she seemed quite *ordinary*. The child, who had dreamed of glory and who had wished to be a second Joan of Arc, never sought esteem. She felt that her special call was to be despised and unknown, and the year of her noviciate was passed in the exercise of humble and unnoticed acts of self-abasement.

5. "I Prefer Sacrifice to All Ecstasies"

The spirit of poverty was another virtue zealously cultivated by Thérèse from the beginning of her religious life. One evening, the little lamp she used was not on the shelf where it usually

[6] *Ibid.,* 3, 7.

stood. As it was the time of the "Great Silence," she could not inquire about it and had to spend the ensuing hour in the dark. "If I had not had the interior light of grace, I should have complained," she confessed. Reflecting that true poverty consists in being deprived of even necessary things, she rejoiced at this little mishap, and in the exterior darkness she found true light.

As a postulant, the careful, well-brought-up child was pleased to have convenient and attractive things for her own use, such as a pretty little jug in her cell. This was soon replaced by a large chipped jug, which caused her equal joy, for she had now taken a great liking for plain and inconvenient things. Her heavy habit of coarse material was badly made, but she showed no displeasure, and her sandals were worn until they fell to pieces. In the refectory, one jug of water was placed on the table for her and the nun who sat next to her; being often very thirsty, this sister took the greater part of the contents of the jug, so Thérèse largely refrained from drinking. As she never complained about anything, no one knew what her tastes were, and the sisters in the kitchen got into the habit of serving her with the remains. One can imagine what "the remains" were like in a Carmelite convent. "Little Sister Thérèse is satisfied with anything; she is quite indifferent to what she is given to eat," they said. It is true that her nature sometimes resisted, but her will had the upper hand; she had made up her mind to endure everything.

We do not continue this subject, lest the narration of these details should grow monotonous — as wearisome as the little difficulties of daily life.

When in the world, Thérèse's virtue might have been compared to the work of a great artist; in the cloister, it reached the perfection of an incomparable masterpiece. But this wonderful skill was not acquired without incessant practice. Some of the nuns tried her patience exceedingly and she was sometimes tempted to insist on her "rights," but, when the interior combat became too fierce, she saved herself by taking to flight "like a deserter," as she humbly remarked.

There are many occasions of acquiring merit, when one lives in the narrow space of a convent enclosure without any kind of diversion, meeting the same commonplace causes of annoyance every day and living with the same people, who are not always kindly disposed and not always congenial. Thérèse felt this great mortification of community life more keenly than any other form of penance.

She admitted frankly that she had a natural antipathy for one of the nuns, who seemed to have "a real talent" for displeasing her in every way. The young novice was well-armed, however, for the spiritual combat. "I decided to do for this sister the things I would have done for the person I loved most," she tells us. Her resolution was kept so well that no one guessed the real state of her feelings. The nun in question said to her one day with a radiant air: "Sister Thérèse of the Child Jesus, would you tell me what attraction you find in me? Every time I meet you, you greet me with a most gracious smile." We do not know what reply she received. When Thérèse wrote the account in her *Autobiography,* she probably did so with an amused smile at the corner of her mouth, such as the Benedictine nun had noticed in her school-days. Her pen then wrote the reply she could not give to her interlocutor: "What attracted me was Jesus hidden in the depths of her soul, for He changes the bitter into sweet."

A change of occupation from the linen-room to the refectory, after her Clothing, brought Thérèse another opportunity for sacrifice. One after the other, the nuns receive this humble task of sweeping, filling water-jugs, fetching beer from the cellar, and similar domestic duties. Thérèse did this work with Sister Agnes of Jesus. How she longed to talk to her "little mother," especially at this time of sorrow when their hearts were overwhelmed with grief at their father's illness! If they had asked for the permission to speak, the Prioress would surely have accorded it, but Thérèse would not ask for any concession. An exclamation in her *Autobiography* shows what this silence cost her:

"Oh, my little Mother, how I suffered at that time . . . I could not open my heart to you and I thought you no longer knew what was taking place in my soul!"

It was perhaps as a reward for her heroic silence that, in the following month of July, at the grotto of St. Mary Magdalen in the garden, a wonderful feeling of joy took possession of her heart, carrying her above all suffering.

"All the things of earth seemed covered with a veil . . . I was entirely hidden under the Blessed Virgin's mantle . . . I was no longer on earth; I did all my work in the refectory and elsewhere as if my body did not belong to me." This state lasted for a whole week.

Notwithstanding her humility, Thérèse did not hesitate to admit — when narrating this fact toward the end of her life to Mother Agnes, the then Prioress — that this grace was a mystic state such as described by St. Teresa of Avila. She summed the matter up quite simply by saying: "It was a supernatural state, such as God alone can bestow. This grace is sometimes sufficient in itself to detach a soul forever from this earth."

After a week of this intense happiness, the novice returned to the state of spiritual dryness and interior suffering which were almost habitual to her. It was a battlefield to which she was accustomed. She did not regret the change, for she felt that she could show the maximum of love to her Lord Jesus in this stern warfare. In a letter addressed to Sister Agnes of Jesus at this time, 1889, we find these words: "I prefer sacrifice to all ecstasies."

The sacrifice, which was her portion, was the most hidden form of suffering, the daily "pin-pricks" and the heartaches that cause so much pain. What blood of heroes flowed in her veins, or rather what power of love glowed in her heart!

Notwithstanding her own sufferings, she continued to comfort her beloved Céline, so sad and lonely. In October, she sent her a picture of the Holy Face and exhorted her to become a true Veronica. By a strange coincidence, Céline was one day to be called Sister Genevieve of the Holy Face, and her pencil was destined to give the world a most faithful reproduction of the Divine Face of our crucified Saviour according to the holy Winding Sheet of Turin.

Another source of trial and of consequent spiritual blessing to Thérèse was again Father Delatroëtte, who only later was to be convinced of her sanctity.

According to their Rule, Sister Thérèse should have been allowed to make her vows one year after her Clothing, that is in January, 1890, but Father Delatroëtte intervened, putting his unjust veto to the Prioress' request for her novice's profession. At first, Thérèse's sorrow was great. She could not understand this refusal on the part of their Ecclesiastical Superior, and her sense of right and justice protested against this enforced delay. Soon, however, her trustful humility came to her assistance and she set about preparing her mystical wedding-dress, enriching it with "precious stones," for thus she termed the numberless acts of virtue with which she adorned her soul in preparation for the great day of her religious vows.

Then, with that engaging frankness of which our Lord Himself had taught her the secret, she said to Him with humble confidence:

"When you find it rich enough, I am sure that nothing will keep you from accepting me as your spouse."

In the meantime her zeal for acts of virtue and corporal mortifications increased and she humbly asked for permission to do extra acts of penance, but the only mortification allowed her was that of humiliation.

The Blessed Virgin, too, was watching over her child. "She helped me to prepare my spiritual wedding-dress," proclaimed Thérèse.

As soon as this mystical robe was ready, the obstacles vanished. Our Lady of Mount Carmel made human wills bend before the Divine good pleasure. The date for the profession of Sister Thérèse of the Child Jesus and of the Holy Face — for she wished henceforth to bear this second title in honour of the devotion so dear to her heart — was fixed to take place on September 8, 1890, the Feast of Our Lady's Nativity.

CHAPTER X

ASCENT OF THE MYSTIC MOUNT

1. *The Underground Passage*

IN CARMELITE convents, the Profession takes place in the Chapter Room, in the presence of the community alone. The farewell to the world is said on the Clothing Day; at the Profession, the soul binds herself to God by the three religious vows of poverty, chastity, and obedience. During the ten days' retreat which precedes this great undertaking, the novice lives in profound solitude, renewing her fervour by increased prayer and penance.

As we have seen, Thérèse did not write retreat notes, but fortunately she wrote to Sister Agnes of Jesus before her Profession as she had done before her Clothing. The following passage describes in symbolic terms the state of her soul, for symbolism alone could translate the invisible into human language.

". . . My Beloved asked me in what land I wished to travel and what road I wished to take. I told Him that I had only one desire, that of reaching the summit of the Mountain of Love. . . . And our Lord took me by the hand and led me to *an underground passage* where it is neither hot nor cold, where the sun does not shine, and where neither wind nor rain can enter; it is an underground place where I see nothing but a half-veiled light, the light that gleams from the downcast eyes of the Face of Jesus. My Beloved speaks no word, and I say nothing save that I love Him more than myself; in the depths of my heart, I feel that this is true, for I belong to Him more than to myself. I cannot see that we are advancing toward our journey's goal, since we are travelling by a subterranean way; and yet — I know not how — it seems to me that we are nearing the summit of the mountain."

Some years later, the Saint wrote in her *Autobiography:* "The retreat before my profession, like those of later years, was a time of great aridity. However, the means to be employed for pleasing God were clearly shown to me, although I did not notice how."

This aridity of the emotions, accompanied by these mysterious lights of grace, was the sign that her love was being purified, as she realised herself, and, at the end of her letter to Sister Agnes of Jesus, she cried out in thanksgiving:

"I give thanks to my Jesus for making me walk in this darkness, in which I enjoy profound peace. I am pleased, very pleased, to be without any consolation . . . Thérèse, the little spouse of Jesus, loves Him for Himself alone . . . *Jesus! I wish so much to love Him! I wish to love Him as He has never yet been loved!*"

These last words are underlined. Though the boldness of her language may be disconcerting, the young novice meant exactly what she said. May we not be allowed to think that the saints, especially those who are destined to become the heads of a spiritual lineage, are like *new* manifestations of God, and are therefore called to love God *in a way* that He has never been loved before?

The work of grace in the saints is always new and always different. Yet though it varies, it is always *one* in its essence, because it is the same Love which bestows abundant favours on the elect to unite them all in *one*. Praying to His heavenly Father on the eve of His Passion, Jesus asked "that they all may be one, as Thou, Father, in me, and I in Thee; that they also may be one in us."

To attempt to contrast — in a spirit of rivalry — the sanctity of one saint with the sanctity of another saint would be like comparing the relative value of God's graces. The Church admonishes us not to discuss relative merits of the saints.

The humble Thérèse of the Child Jesus never felt the temptation of restless rivalry that sometimes disturbs less exalted souls, but she exulted with enthusiasm as she realised that the Holy Spirit was forming a "new creation" in the depths of her soul.

Had she a presentiment that her life on earth would be a short one? ". . . Love can make up for the shortness of one's life," she wrote to her sister. "Jesus does not consider time, since He is eternal. He only considers our love." Then comes that cry of a soul purified of all self-love:

"I do not desire love of which I can feel the sweetness; it is enough for me if Jesus feels its sweetness."

Love! For Thérèse, at all times, there is question only of love! What is love? How can it be defined? To love means to tend toward happiness. To love our Lord means that we have received from Him a spiritual light which draws us out of ourselves and draws us to Him, the eternal joy of the elect.

Therein lies the secret of the happiness of the saints. Their souls tend unceasingly toward the Object of their love, with complete self-forgetfulness. The *Imitation of Christ*, on whose words Thérèse had so often meditated, tells us that "the moment we seek self, at that very moment we cease to love [God]."

2. *A Carmelite Profession*

On the eve of the great day on which Thérèse was to become in very truth the spouse of Jesus, the Son of God, the Community decorated in a befitting way the Chapter Room where the novice was to make her vows. She herself adorned with flowers and candles the statue of her dearly loved Child-Jesus, but, instead of the new rose-coloured candles offered to her, she preferred to keep the half-used and somewhat discoloured candles of her Clothing day.

Sister Mary of the Sacred Heart expressed her surprise. "The old ones mean more to me," explained her god-child. "They were lighted for the first time on my Clothing day. . . . Papa had given them to me and he was there . . ." The child-novice, whose affections were ever strong and deep rooted, was being crucified in her filial love and could no longer delight in any earthly joys, in those "rose-coloured" joys of youth such as she had formerly experienced. The symbolism of her present action associated the mourning of her heart with the spiritual happiness of her mystical wedding-day. The discoloured candles were the symbol of the past which had gone forever; henceforth for her — to use her own expressive words — there were only joys "where created fleeting things give place to the uncreated reality."

In this spirit of complete detachment, the saintly novice went like a valiant knight of old "to keep her vigil" before the Tabernacle, in loving adoration and devout meditation on the vows which would bind her soul to God and be for her the armour of light.

Suddenly there arose a spiritual tempest, "the most dreadful storm" she ever experienced. It was far worse than her customary aridity. The devil was making a final assault on the little novice who was to save so many souls. "My vocation seemed to me like a dream and sheer folly," she wrote later when narrating the darkness of that hour. She wondered why she had come to Carmel; she felt she had made a mistake, that she had no vocation, that she had unwittingly deceived her superiors, and that the only thing for her to do now was to return home.

Profoundly humiliated and troubled, the poor novice called Mother Mary of the Angels out of choir and told her of her fears. The wise Mistress of Novices began to laugh, for it was so obvious that the devil was making an attempt to ensnare this holy soul. Her attitude at once reassured the novice, and the devil was put to flight. "What he wanted was to prevent me from confessing my troubles," said Thérèse, "but it was now my turn to ensnare him." To make her humiliation more complete, she told the whole story to her Prioress, whose consoling words dispelled her remaining fears. This victory over the devil was rewarded by God in a supremely fitting manner, for, on the morning of September 8, a "river of peace"[1] flooded her soul. Peace, which has been defined as "the tranquility of order,"[2] is a state in which all combat has ceased. Jesus gave this blessing

[1] Isa. 66:12.
[2] St. Augustine.

to His disciples, saying "peace I leave with you; My peace I give to you." The peace of Jesus is Jesus Himself.

Thus, with serenity of soul and strength of will, as a bride adorned for the bridegroom, the young novice went forward, with that peace "which surpasseth all understanding," to make her vows. She felt herself "truly a queen" that day and took advantage of that title to ask numberless favours from her King and Lord. She wished "that all sinners would be converted on that day and that purgatory would set all its captives free." For her dear ones, too, she asked graces, making her intentions very detailed. For Léonie, who had been obliged by delicate health to leave the Poor Clare Convent where she had tried her religious vocation, she prayed with bold confidence:

"Grant that it be Your Will for Léonie that she should become a Visitation nun. If she has no vocation, I beg You to give her that grace; You cannot refuse me this favour."

Did she not ask for her father's cure on this great day when she felt herself so powerful? Mother Mary Gonzaga suggested this, overlooking the fact that Thérèse had long before understood that her father's trial was part of the divine plan for him: The little Carmelite, therefore, prayed with due reservation: "Oh my God, since Mother Prioress has told me to ask You, grant that Papa be cured *if it be indeed Your Will.*"

Her desires for herself were contained in a letter which she bore upon her heart. There was no need for her to make any further petition for herself, since Jesus could read all her desires in this letter of love.

As her theology was always practical, she began by begging for the grace never to commit any deliberate fault, and then asked for complete detachment. "May creatures be nothing to me, and I nothing to them!" After this austere petition, she prayed for peace of soul . . . that peace which Jesus had given her on this day of her espousals as the infallible sign of His presence and of His dominion in her heart. "I ask but peace . . . peace, and above all love, boundless and without limit."

The burning ardour of her soul then broke forth, like the

piercing flame mentioned in the *Imitation of Christ,* reaching to the heights of oblation:

"Oh Jesus, for Your sake may I die a martyr; grant me martyrdom of soul or body, or rather give me both!"

It is God Himself who inspires such supernatural desires, for it is always in response to His grace that our souls are thus raised on high. Divine Love had already decreed the intense suffering which would complete the sanctification of His little spouse.

Her last request was for humiliation: "May no one think of me; may I be trodden underfoot, as a little grain of sand."

The sun was shining in a glorious sky and a flight of swallows flew low over the convent while Thérèse of the Child Jesus and of the Holy Face lay prostrate, face downward, with her arms stretched out in the form of a cross. The oblation made that day was one of the most complete sacrifices ever afforded. The triumphal words of the *Te Deum* soared aloft, while the motionless figure of the newly professed Carmelite recalled the names of the young martyrs whose palm of victory she wished to share.

Profession days are always great feasts in convents. In the Refectory, Sister Thérèse was seated next to the Prioress and her place was decked with flowers. When evening came, she took off her crown of roses and laid it at the feet of our Lady's statue, but she felt no regret that the great day was over, for she knew that time could not lessen her happiness. Gazing up into the star-lit September sky, she thought of the eternal joy that awaited her. Indeed, that joy came sooner than she expected, for in seven years' time her soul took its flight to heaven.

Mother Mary Gonzaga was really very proud of her newly professed daughter. In a letter of September 9, to the Carmel of Tours, she speaks as follows of the nun who had taken her vows on the previous day:

"This angelic child is only seventeen and a half, but she is as mature as a nun of thirty. . . . She is a perfect religious."

A newly professed nun continues her religious formation in

the noviciate for some time, so Sister Thérèse lived her humble life among the novices until September 24, when the ceremony of the reception of the black veil took place. This feast was truly "veiled" in tears, for it brought Thérèse a great sorrow. Her father had been a little better, and she had hoped — vain day-dream — that he would be able to assist at this solemn ceremony, which terminates the rites of a Carmelite Profession. However, at the last moment, Monsieur Martin's nurses thought it wiser not to allow him any great emotion. The young Carmelite was bitterly disappointed. Possibly she foresaw then that she would never again see her father here below. A few days later, he sank down into a state from which there was no hope of recovery. In tears, she wrote to Céline: "Jesus wishes me to be an orphan." This was the last exclamation which she allowed her human sensibility to utter.

She did indeed accept God's Will without hesitation, but found it difficult to understand the trial. She knew that God wished her to be alone, so that He could bring her to more intimate union with Himself, but her sorrow was so great that she could not restrain her tears. This link with the happy past broke forever just when she had hoped that the chain of loving affections was to be renewed. The Community was surprised to see her in tears and considered her attitude childish. Jesus seemed to leave her to herself that day. "I soon showed my weakness," she admits humbly, "and my tears were misunderstood."

At the canonical examination which preceded her profession, Sister Thérèse of the Child Jesus and of the Holy Face pronounced her apostolic zeal: "I came to pray for souls and especially for priests." On the day she received the black veil, September 24, 1890, Feast of Our Lady of Ransom (the Virgin Mother who delivers captives and converts pagans) she received a new "call" to suffer for the salvation of souls.

3. Love Repaid by Love Alone

The indignation caused by the entrance at Carmel of a postulant aged fifteen had gradually subsided. Her early entrance

— the only extraordinary action in this uneventful life — had been blamed even by priests, but, now that she was hidden in her cloistered home, she attracted very little interest and rarely received a visit except from near relatives. Even Father Domin, who had taught her catechism, seemed to lose all interest in the "little Doctor" of former days, who had amazed him by her clear understanding of the things of God. When he heard the convent chaplain praise her, he merely thought such praise exaggerated. This absence of interest on all sides was clearly the work of divine providence.

In the convent, too, very little attention was paid to the young nun. Her amiability and unselfishness, her gentleness and good humour, made her an agreeable companion in community life. On account of her youth and her childlike serenity, it had become a custom in the convent to speak of her as "Our little Sister Thérèse," although she was really tall. The word "little" was just what she wanted; it typified her special form of sanctity.

Shortly after her profession, Sister Thérèse received a visit from her cousin, Jeanne Guérin, who had just married Doctor la Néele. The young wife naturally spoke about her new duties and her loving devotedness to her husband. The young nun of seventeen listened, while her elders kept up the conversation. It was probably the first time she had listened to such expressions of human love, but, hearing of the little attentions and loving tenderness bestowed by her cousin on a simple creature, she resolved, with an eager heart and a more animated faith, to treat her Lord Jesus with an even greater delicacy of love.

The announcement of her cousin's marriage had given her the idea of writing for the novices in similar terms, an invitation to her mystic espousals. By this ingenuous amusement, she took care to proclaim the predominant thought in her mind, which made her soul overflow with grateful enthusiasm, namely, that the glory of the grandest earthly union is as nothing compared to the title of a Spouse of Jesus.

At this period of her life, Sister Thérèse of the Child Jesus was studying the lessons of pure love and of perfect detachment as taught by St. John of the Cross. "What supernatural light I found in the works of St. John of the Cross! His writings were my only spiritual food when I was seventeen and eighteen," she wrote later. These few words are of the greatest importance, as they show clearly the state of her soul. The young Carmelite, who seemed so simple and childlike, was in reality a great mystic; grace urged her to find the spiritual nourishment she needed in the writings of the prince of mystical teaching. She read and meditated deeply on his celebrated works: *The Ascent of Mount Carmel, The Night of the Soul, The Spiritual Canticle,* and *The Living Flame of Love.* Her clear-sighted intelligence, which excelled in seeing essential points, did not delay over the obscure style in which the holy Spanish writer often veils his thought. The point which attracted her most was his direct appeal to love.

The daughters of the noble Teresa of Avila sometimes adopt a mystic coat-of-arms, portraying some intimate devotion of the soul. The motto inscribed on her armorial bearings by Sister Thérèse of the Child Jesus and of the Holy Face was this saying of St. John of the Cross, "Love Is Repaid by Love Alone."

Another saying of this great mystic, "The least act of pure love is of more value to the Church than all other works together," seemed to her a confirmation of her spiritual "Way."

The young Carmelite accepted, wholeheartedly, the insistent appeal to perfect abnegation and to "pure, naked faith," which her holy Father, St. John of the Cross, addresses to souls who aspire to pure love. At his school, she learned with absolute certainty that, although the aridity of the desert she was traversing was an intense trial, it was in reality the surest and most excellent means for her soul to reach perfect union with God.

"The just man *lives* by faith," says St. Paul. Faith is not merely a formula proposed to us; it is a life that is given to us. This hidden nourishment, which guided and strengthened her

without any appeal to the senses, and this light, which was un-
accompanied by any sweetness, proved that Sister Thérèse was
now living by pure faith.

The aspirations of Thérèse's soul were quite in harmony with
the teaching that on earth God can only be attained by faith
and not by visions. Her courageous faith did not delay over
shadows or figures which sometimes impede the soul's upward
flight. She was so impressed with this truth that she was able
to say: "Few souls have desired to have ecstasies and revelations
as much as I have desired *not* to have any."

Has not our Lord Himself said: "Blessed are they who have
not seen and have believed"? To St. Thérèse of the Child Jesus
it was given to understand the deep meaning of that austere
beatitude.

From St. John of the Cross she learned that the soul, living
by pure faith, should remain passive under God's action, allowing Him to do what He will and accepting His conduct even in
the most trying ordeals, since He alone can make us saints.
"Action belongs to God; passive acceptance of God's action
belongs to the soul," which does not exclude, but rather supposes
immense energy on the part of the creature under His guidance.

Nourished by this exalted teaching, the youthful saint knew
how to clothe this doctrine with sweetness in order to help other
souls. Writing to Céline, in October, 1890, shortly after receiving the veil, she quoted a gracious passage from a poem by
the holy Doctor, rather than one of his austere sayings.

> I continued in oblivion lost,
> My head was resting on my love;
> Lost to all things and myself,
> And, amid the lilies forgotten,
> Threw all my cares away.[3]

4. *Asceticism in Little Things*

Although each day of her religious life seemed outwardly the
same, Thérèse's every action was animated by her ardent love.

---

[3] *The Night of the Soul.* The translation of these lines of St. John of the
Cross is taken from the English version by David Lewis.

She was ever ascending the mystical mountain, but her wonderful growth in holiness was unnoticed, for she remained simple, growing more and more childlike and unassuming. Peacefully, with a smile on her lips, she practised her holy Rule perfectly and was careful never to offend against the virtue of Charity, but by this time she had lost her earlier attraction for the practice of extraordinary penances. She had once obtained permission to wear a little cross surrounded with pointed spikes, but as it caused an open wound she understood that this was a sign from divine providence, showing that her combats were to be interior. She had noticed, too, that those who practised additional mortifications were not always the holiest. As self-seeking finds a certain amount of satisfaction in the practice of extraordinary penances, she felt that the common Rule of the religious life was the wisest. What perfection she put into that community life!

Constant mortification in one's daily actions, or "Asceticism in little things" as Father Petitot calls it, is perhaps harder than any other form of penance for poor human nature, so inclined to impatience. Taking on oneself the most troublesome work as if it were one's due; offering one's services in winter for washing with cold water in the garden when a person's hands are chapped and bleeding; offering one's services in summer for washing with hot water in the stifling laundry; exclaiming "What a God-send" instead of frowning when a sister — unwittingly — splashes dirty water into one's face, and even returning the next time to that same place where such treasures are freely bestowed; passing slowly by the doors of those who are apt to ask one's services, so that they may importune if they wish — such little sacrifices are excellent for overcoming self.

One of the nuns was a trial to the Community on account of her tendency to exceeding pessimism, so Sister Thérèse of the Child Jesus, under the guidance of divine grace, asked for permission to help her in her work!

At recreations, she was both good humoured and witty, putting into practice the charming advice of St. Teresa of Avila, who did not like "scowling" saints and begged her daughters, in the name of charity, not to stifle the little wit they had received from God. The young nun entertained the Sisters by her witty sayings and her gift of mimicry; she had a real talent for imitating others, though she was always tactful and charitable, and refrained from all hurtful remarks. If, for any reason, she was not at recreation, the other nuns would exclaim: "Sister Thérèse of the Child Jesus is not here to-day, so we shall have no laughing." None of her sisters knew that her constant cheerfulness was accompanied by great desolation of soul!

Sometimes, however, a little sweetness came into this life of continual abnegation. Flowers, which had always been her delight, were sent to Carmel for the altars by friends and benefactors in such abundance that she mentions the fact in her *Autobiography* as something quite providential. She received flowers of all kinds, cultivated and wild, and the latter were not the least welcome. She delighted in arranging them for the various statues, but even in this matter her wishes were sometimes opposed. One of the nuns could not bear odours of any kind, not even the perfume of a rose, so Thérèse had to sacrifice the pleasure she would have felt in putting flowers in the hermitage, which had to be adorned in some other way. On one occasion, she had just placed an artificial rose in the hermitage, when the sister in question, from afar, made a sign to her to take it away. If St. Thérèse had not been well exercised in the virtue of perfect charity, this would have been a fine opportunity for her to ridicule the poor Sister's mistake! She took up the rose, however, with a smile, saying: "Just look, Mother, what good imitations are made now-a-days; one would think this rose was natural." It is possible that St. Thérèse of the Child Jesus deserved her title of Saint of the Roses on that day more than at any other time.

Shortly after her profession, she was appointed assistant sacristan. Her happiness was great indeed in being allowed to touch the sacred vessels and prepare the altar linen on which our Lord was to be laid. She took a childlike pleasure in watching the reflection of her face at the bottom of the golden chalices. Was not her Beloved entirely hers and she entirely His?

All the while, however, the state of interior dryness continued, though the annual retreat in September, 1891, was a source of light and comfort to her. The brief remark, "I was enduring all kinds of interior trials," shows that God was accomplishing His grand work in her soul. As a rule, the sermons of these retreats were trying for this contemplative soul, who was taught inwardly by her own heavenly Director, but this year the words of Father Alexis, a Recollect of Caens, brought her great consolation and light. She felt unable to explain her trouble to anyone, but the good Religious at once saw the exceptional value of this child-like soul. She tells us that he understood her in a marvellous way:

"He launched me full sail on that ocean of confidence and love which attracted me so strongly but on which I had not dared to advance. He told me that my faults did not offend the good God."

Thérèse was surprised and delighted at this last affirmation, for she had never heard anyone say that some faults did not offend God. Father Pichon had assured her that she had kept her baptismal innocence; Father Alexis now taught her that there is no sin in small thoughtless faults which are not deliberate. With this assurance, she was able to bear the exile of this life more patiently.

In truth, the priest's words were only the echo of her own inmost thoughts, for she had long known that our Lord is more tender than a mother, and that a mother is always ready to pardon her child's little involuntary "peccadilloes," but she was greatly encouraged by the fact that this good Father fully approved of her "Way" of confidence. This providential meeting brought her the advice she needed and enabled her soul to advance swiftly in the way of perfection. However, notwithstanding her desire to remain in touch with this holy Religious, she never saw him again. The help she received from creatures was always given in this detached, austere way.

5. *"To You I Leave My Heart"*

Two months later, the Foundress of the Carmel of Lisieux, Mother Genevieve of St. Teresa, departed this life. Age and infirmity had obliged this gentle, holy nun to lead a life of solitude, while the commanding character of Mother Mary Gonzaga took the place of her pious, kindly influence. The young Saint had immediately realised the sanctity of this humble soul, who once brought great consolation to her troubled mind. With her habitual smile on her lips but with intense anguish in her heart — for she no longer knew if she were beloved of God — Sister Thérèse went one day to the infirmary to visit an aged nun, who said to her, with something of inspiration in her manner: "Serve the Lord in peace and joy. Remember, my child, that our God is the God of peace." The words seemed to Thérèse a reply from Jesus Himself and her heart was filled with exceeding joy. She wondered if God had revealed the state of her soul to Mother Genevieve; the latter, however, assured her the following Sunday that this was not the case. This negative reply did not trouble Thérèse's faith, but made her think that God had united that soul to Himself very intimately, directing her words and actions, and she concluded: "That form of sanctity seemed to me the truest and the holiest; it is the holiness I desire, for it is free from all illusion."

Mother Genevieve, it is true, had not always understood her youngest spiritual daughter and feared that there was presumption in her unlimited confidence. Sister Thérèse, therefore, ceased to speak of her "Way," but continued to venerate the humble Foundress. Having prayed fervently at her bedside during her last agony, the young nun felt an indescribable joy fill her soul at the moment that this holy Religious breathed her last. Should this be taken as a sign that the saintly Carmelite had gone straight to heaven or was it merely that she wished to give this mysterious token of her love to the little Saint whom she had not altogether understood when on earth? That evening, Sister Thérèse took a little piece of linen and wiped away a tear that still glistened beneath the closed eyelid of her venerated Mother; this she kept as a precious souvenir.

A dream, which she had shortly after Mother Genevieve's death, sealed the union between their two hearts. Thérèse dreamt that the holy foundress gave each nun something that had belonged to herself, but when she came to her youngest daughter her hands were empty. However, looking at her lovingly, Mother Genevieve said three times: "To you I leave my heart." In truth, the foundress gave her child not only her heart, so meek and humble, but also her strength of character, exceptionally firm and sincere.

A month later, the Saint had an unusual opportunity of proving her calm courage and her devotedness to the Community. A severe epidemic of influenza raged in the convent, where contagion was inevitable on account of the limited space. All the nuns, except two, fell ill; Thérèse had only a slight attack and so was able to go about. Like a young lieutenant when the superior officers have fallen, she saw to everything. The young nun, only nineteen years of age,[4] went fearlessly from one dying nun to another, laid out without shrinking the bodies of those who had succumbed, and arranged all by herself the burial services, of which there were three in the course of a few days. But as she said herself, she "felt the Hand of God and knew that His Heart was watching" over all.

Her courage and her capable arrangement of affairs in such difficult circumstances gained the general esteem. Even Father Delatroëtte, who came to console the afflicted nuns, was loud in his praise, and in later days always spoke of Sister Thérèse with admiration.

From divine providence, the valiant little Saint received a recompense of ineffable sweetness. The convent chaplain, Father Youf, who esteemed her greatly and knew the desires of her heart, allowed her to receive Holy Communion daily during the time of the epidemic and even for some time later. He might

---

[4] Thérèse's nineteenth birthday occurred at this time and was saddened by the death of the Sub-Prioress.

have accorded this privilege for an unlimited period, but Mother Mary Gonzaga intervened as superior of the community. She did not allow the daily reception of the Blessed Eucharist.[5]

"You will see, Mother, that I shall make you change your mind on that subject after my death," said Thérèse to her gently one day. The prophecy was fulfilled.

The young Carmelite of Lisieux was already a model of perfection. By her apostolic zeal, by her high ideals allied to sound common sense, and by the greatness of her desires, she was a true daughter of St. Teresa of Avila; by her interior mortification and her pure seeking after God, she was an intimate disciple of St. John of the Cross. Yet this innocent, sanctified life was only the preparation for the designs of providence. The day was approaching when this perfect flower would give forth its sweet perfume, when this true Carmelite would become the illustrious Foundress of a new spiritual way and the young Mother of a long lineage of souls, far greater in number than a religious order.

[5] Mother Mary Gonzaga's attitude was in accordance with the custom of the time.

CHAPTER XI

THÉRÈSE'S LITTLE WAY

WE HAVE seen to what an extent St. Thérèse of the Child Jesus found spiritual food for her soul in the works of St. John of the Cross. After mentioning this fact, the Saint adds: "Later on, all spiritual writers left me in my aridity. . . . Nowadays, I read without understanding or, if I understand, my mind is unable to meditate." After the joy of understanding the great Doctor of the mystic life at an unusually early age, the young Carmelite soon found it impossible to appreciate any spiritual authors. However, she was neither discouraged nor disappointed by this fact.

"In my helplessness," she wrote, "the Holy Scriptures and the *Imitation of Christ* are of the greatest assistance. . . . It is the Gospel more than any other book which helps me in time of prayer. . . . Jesus has no need of books or teachers to instruct our souls; He, the Teacher of all teachers, instructs us without the medium of words."

It was indeed Jesus Himself who taught her henceforth. Although she mentions this privilege quite simply, she realised that it was a very great grace. Studying the divine revelation contained in the Old and the New Testaments, she frequently discovered "new lights and hidden, mysterious meanings."

Realising that others have already spoken on this subject, I shall, nevertheless, humbly attempt to say something about these new lights and discoveries of the young Saint of Lisieux, guiding myself mainly by the explanation given by herself. That is possible, since divine providence has willed that this soul, which was so reserved and hidden for those around her, should now be laid bare to all. There is here no longer any hidden mystery; she invites us to draw unreservedly from her treasures. If we hesitate to partake of her riches and if our dazzled sight does not dare to gaze, her reassuring smile encourages us to accept the invitation given so lovingly to all.

1. *"If There Is a Little One . . ."*

In that part of her *Autobiography* which is addressed to Mother Mary Gonzaga, St. Thérèse traces the gradual development of her spiritual discoveries.

At the age of three, the desire to become a saint took possession of her soul. This desire, ardent and irresistible, increased with the years and caused her to leave all things to enter Carmel. There she strove to overcome herself in the constant practice of the most generous, unfailing virtue. Still, notwithstanding all her efforts, she considered there was just as great a difference between the saints and herself as between a mountain and a grain of sand. Her confidence, however, remained unshaken. She *wished* to become a great saint and she was convinced that her desire came from God, who does not inspire such desires without giving the corresponding graces.

By what means would she obtain her desire? She tells us herself:

"For me to become great is impossible. I must bear with myself and my numberless imperfections, but I intend to find a means of attaining heaven by a little way, very short and very straight, a little way which is wholly new."

This meant, therefore, that she was bent upon making a discovery.

"We live in an age of inventions," she continues; "now-a-days, rich people need not trouble to go up the stairs, for they have lifts instead. I should like to find a lift to raise me up to Jesus, for I am too small to climb the steep stairway of perfection."

The desire and the determination expressed in these ingenuous words were no doubt inspired by God Himself. With keen delight, then, in her study of Holy Scripture, the young Carmelite came upon the passage:

"Whoever is a little one, let him come unto Me."[1]

This was like a personal invitation to her. God calls to Himself "the little ones." Feeling that she was one of these little ones, Thérèse approached with confidence. But what next? What would God do for them? Then, searching further her eyes fell on the words in Isaias:

"As one whom the mother caresseth, so will I comfort you. You shall be carried at the breasts; and upon the knees they shall caress you."[2]

The God of infinite Power and Majesty, who made all things out of nothing, and before whom the angels veil their faces with their wings, in reverential awe and adoration, chose the comparison of a mother's tenderness for her little child, in order to show men His attitude toward them. No one was better fitted than Thérèse Martin to understand the full meaning of such a comparison. Her admirable parents had given her a perfect example of fatherly and motherly love.

"Never have I been consoled by words more tender and sweet," she exclaimed. "Thine arms, O Jesus, are the lift which will raise me up to heaven."

These words broke down all barriers and overthrew all obstacles. Joyously Thérèse cast herself into the arms of her God to remain there for all her life. Such was her unchanging attitude toward God. It was the truly new and characteristic manner of her sanctity.

2. *Her Message From God*

The light she had received was not for herself alone. *In God's name,* she invites all — sinners and innocent, ignorant and learned — to imitate her in this unlimited confidence, which had brought her to the heart of her heavenly Father.

"The *Way* that I wish to teach souls is that of confidence and complete abandonment. Confidence, and confidence alone, will bring us to Love. . . . If souls, as imperfect as I am, could feel

[1] Prov. 9:4.
[2] Isa. 66:12–13.

what I feel, not one of them would despair of reaching the summit of the Mount of Love, since Jesus asks only for abandonment and gratitude."

What light had the little Carmelite been given and what grace of understanding had she received that she could speak with such authority and utter such daring promises?

According to what she herself has told us, and what her judges have decreed concerning her — for she has been judged and proclaimed worthy of credence by the voice of infallible Pontiffs — the mystery revealed to St. Thérèse of the Child Jesus in a most special way was the truth of the unfathomable abyss of Divine Mercy, the fatherly tenderness of God toward His poor, little creatures. These two words, *"poor," "little,"* have been chosen purposely. It is the abyss of our misery that calls on the abyss of Divine Mercy.

By an exceptional grace the Saint most clearly perceived this truth, which was henceforth her guiding light. From then till the end of her life, the thought of the Mercy of Divine Goodness toward human weakness caused her such gratitude, confidence, and love that the words she used to give expression to these sentiments are among the most beautiful ever uttered by creature to the Creator.

"To me He hath given His mercy," she exclaimed triumphantly. This expression suffices to explain the extraordinarily fruitful influence of the Saint after her death. Saint Thérèse of Lisieux has become for humanity a channel of divine favours. There is every reason why we should listen attentively to her message; why we should strive to understand her appeal. Every word of this little Saint has been studied and examined by learned theologians. But above all, Rome has spoken urging all to learn and follow her Little Way of Spiritual Childhood.

It is St. Thérèse who saw and realised the truth contained in this. It is she whom God gave to us all as an example and a model, or, to use the expression of Pope Pius XI, as "a Mistress in spiritual things." For that reason we would keep our eyes fixed on the sweet, persuasive Saint and listen to her teaching. Her own holiness is the most eloquent commentary on the doctrine she holds out for our acceptance.

3. *Her Little Way for Little Souls*

"To remain in the arms of our Lord," she explains, "I do not need to grow up; on the contrary I must remain a little one and grow ever less."

She emphasizes the words "a little one." The expression is not pleasing to all; many even dislike it. But the Saint insists that she wishes to lay open her *"Little* Way" to *"little* souls." The word is repeated as a *leitmotiv,* the predominant idea in her explanation.

Could she not have made her lesson of love more attractive and more persuasive by insisting less on this? We can imagine the Saint's beautiful smile taking on an expression of gentle pity in reply to such a question. Our poor little minds would like so much to be considered *great!*

The Saint had read and reread the writings of St. John of the Cross until she knew them by heart. She was at home in the mode of expression used by him. But it was on purpose, and under the guidance of her interior Director, that she chose the most simple language. This well suits her "secret," which is much more subtle than one would think at first sight. To penetrate the meaning of this "secret," let us open the Book which rested on the Saint's heart day and night, the sacred Book of the Gospels, and then read with her the words that she meditated each day:

"Amen I say to you, unless you turn and become like little children, you will not enter into the Kingdom of Heaven."[3]

"Let the little children be, and do not hinder them from coming to me, for of such is the Kingdom of Heaven."[4]

And the great, solemn promise:

"Whoever, therefore, humbles himself as this little child, he is the greatest in the kingdom of heaven."[5]

[3] Matt. 18:3.   [4] Matt. 19:13.
[5] Matt. 18:4.

There can be no doubt whatever in the matter. It is the lowliest who will be the greatest. What hidden meaning is concealed in the word *"little"* that it has merited so much honour and is so loved by Jesus and His little disciple?

To be *little* means to be *humble*. The humility referred to here is not that of fear which shows itself in humble prostrations; nor is it that which proclaims its unworthiness by loud exclamations and gestures. It is the sweet, simple humility of children.

Jesus might have shown us, as the type of perfection, an old man of consummate virtue, such as Simeon who held Him with ecstatic love in his trembling arms, but He chose to give us as our model a child, a little child. This model is not left to our choice but is imposed on us, for it is a condition necessary for salvation. It is necessary and it is all-sufficing, for it will bring us to the highest sanctity, to that sanctity which obtains the foremost rank in heaven.

Every Christian knows the words of our divine Saviour, but how many understand and realise the depth of the truth contained in them? It is true that spiritual childhood has been practised by the saints — by many of them to an eminent degree — that many masters of the spiritual life have written on this subject, but, by a special permission of God's providence, no one has lived and proclaimed spiritual childhood with such candour and boldness, such penetrating logic and burning ardour, as St. Thérèse of the Child Jesus.

In a word: the teaching given by our Lord two thousand years ago has been placed in a brilliant light by the pure, clear-sighted genius of a young nun, only twenty years of age. *St. Thérèse's Message Is a Message From the Gospel*.

The authority of popes, like that of our Lord, has upheld Thérèse's Message.

Benedict XV declared: "We desire that the secret of the holiness of Sister Thérèse of the Child Jesus be understood by all our sons."

His successor, Pius XI, proclaimed: "It is Our desire that the faithful followers of Christ study her life attentively in order to imitate her and become themselves 'like little children,' since, according to our Lord's own words, that is the essential condition for reaching the Kingdom of heaven."

There is no question of making the Gospel insipid nor of belittling it, as some people fear. It is essential that we become "little ones," if we wish to fulfil our duties as true Christians. We must be "little" and "like children." These two expressions are linked together; it is the latter that gives the former all the tenderness, sweetness, and joy which make that state so desirable.

God asks of us a filial humility, because we are, in truth, His children. It is His desire that we realize our great destiny to be brethren of Christ, co-heirs with Him eternally.

In an admirable work, *Christ the Ideal of the Monk,* Dom Marmion has written: "The Masterpiece of the eternal thoughts which is Christ, the wonderful mysteries of the Incarnation, the Passion, the Resurrection, and the triumph of Jesus, the institution of the Church and the sacraments, grace, the virtues, the gifts of the Holy Spirit, all this marvellous supernatural order has come forth from this movement of the heart of God so as to make us His children."[6]

Speaking of the Love of God, St. John cries out: "Behold what manner of love the Father has bestowed upon us that we should be called children of God."[7]

And St. Paul proclaims: "You have received a spirit of adoption as sons, by virtue of which we cry, 'Abba: Father!' "[8] The teaching of St. Thérèse of Lisieux is in perfect harmony with this great doctrine of divine adoption, which is the very foundation of Christianity. This is proved in the short, but heroic, period of her life which remains to be recounted. Those who dislike "childishness" need not be disheartened; they will soon see that the way of spiritual childhood "is childlike only in name," as Pius XI so aptly remarked. It is linked inseparably with that true strength of soul, which relies on the divine strength for

[6] Christ, the Ideal of the monk (Chap. xi).
[7] First Epistle St. John 3:1.
[8] Rom. 8:15.

its power. Thérèse wished to be a child, but a child of grace, a royal child of the all-powerful Father!

4. *Some Multi-Coloured Months*

The encouragement given by Father Alexis to the young Carmelite with regard to her spiritual outlook was of the greatest importance, for it made her confidence boundless and brought her the assurance that her aspirations were indeed from God. Henceforth, she gave herself up, unreservedly, to the direct action of the Holy Spirit. Outwardly, her life was spent in accomplishing the seemingly monotonous, but sanctifying, Rule of the religious house she had chosen. In the summer of 1892, being no longer assistant sacristan, she was two months without any definite occupation and spent her time in painting.

As a child, she had longed to learn drawing. When her father was arranging for Céline to have drawing-lessons, he asked: "Would my little Queen like to learn also?" In her enthusiastic way, the child was about to exclaim a delighted "Yes," but Marie thought it right to make objections. Making a tremendous effort to overcome herself, Thérèse kept silence, offering the great sacrifice to Jesus. Eight years later, He made up to her for her childhood's sacrifice. As some pictures painted by the young nun showed real artistic talent, Mother Mary Gonzaga told her to paint a fresco in the oratory inside the convent. This work, undertaken by obedience, was carried out in a manner quite remarkable for a beginner. From this time till the end of her life, the saint had the consolation of painting and also of writing poems. But it was for a higher form of art that God destined her, none other than that of moulding souls to His own divine likeness.

However, before receiving the charge of the novices, she was given the duty of portress. In a convent, all communication with the outer world passes through the portress, who is constantly disturbed by every kind of visitor. For one so intensely drawn to silence and recollection, the constant attention needed for this duty must have required a continual practice of virtue and self-denial.

With Céline, the consoling angel of their poor paralysed father, her intercourse was as intimate and spiritual as in the early days of her religious life. After three years of martyrdom far from his family, Monsieur Martin had been brought back to Lisieux, though not to his own home, and was living near his brother-in-law. In August, 1892, he was with Léonie and Céline at a house called *Château de la Musse,* which belonged to Monsieur Guérin.

In a letter to Céline, dated August 15, 1892, the younger sister alluded to the beauty at dawn of the Norman skies, which she no longer saw except in memory, and quoted these words of St. John of the Cross:

> In my Beloved I have the mountains,
> The solitary, wooded valleys.

Another letter, about this time, quoted the following saying of St. John of the Cross, which filled her soul with a sense of exultation: "All is mine, all is for me. The heavens are mine; God Himself is mine; and the Mother of my God is mine." Then she explained to Céline one of her "simple ways" with regard to the Blessed Virgin. Sometimes in prayer she would say:

"Dearest Mother, I am more fortunate than you are. I have you for my Mother, and you have no Blessed Virgin to love as I have!"

Then thinking of the Immaculate Maiden, who dwelt beside the Temple of Jerusalem and who humbly wished to become the handmaid of the mother of the Messiah, the Saint cried out: "And I — poor little creature that I am — I have become your child, not your handmaid."

Thérèse never wearied of the title of *child.* For her, humility and trust were inseparable. Writing to her sister of the light given to her during the preceding retreat, she expressed some beautiful thoughts on the words of our Lord: "Make haste and come down, for I must stay in thy house today."

On January 2, 1893, Sister Thérèse of the Child Jesus and of the Holy Face celebrated her twentieth birthday. Her beauty had become more striking, and the black veil above the uncovered, smooth, white forehead enhanced her gracious charm.[9] Her soul, too, had progressed in holiness and beauty. She was in reality the greatest treasure of the convent, for she was a saint. But how many realised her sanctity? Probably no one but Sister Agnes of Jesus, who could read her little sister's soul as her very own!

When Mother Mary Gonzaga ended her term as Prioress in February of that year, a new superior had to be elected, in accordance with the Carmelite Rule. An election at Carmel is always an important event. In silence and prayer, each member of the Community implores the guidance of the Holy Spirit, and weighs the respective merits of her sisters in order to choose the Religious whom she considers the most worthy to govern and become the Mother of the Community. The nuns of Lisieux that year elected Sister Agnes of Jesus. The fact that she was only thirty-three shows how highly esteemed she was by those around her. What a joy it was for Thérèse to have her beloved "little Mother" as superior! It seemed as if an era of wonderful harmony was beginning after five years of silent suffering, and yet God decreed that she should see her Prioress less than any of the nuns. It was the Divine Master Himself who wished for this austere mortification.

5. *Spiritual Childhood Further Explained*

What position in the Community was to be given to Mother Mary Gonzaga, who had directed the convent for so long? Out of deference to the former superior, Mother Agnes gave her the title of Mistress of Novices. To Thérèse, who was still in the noviciate, she gave the charge of Assistant Novice Mistress, though she did not actually give her that title. It was a difficult position, but the new Prioress knew she could count on her

[9] The great St. Teresa of Avila did not like the foreheads to be covered, so Carmelites do not wear the usual religious headband.

little sister's virtue. To accomplish the task assigned to her without ever displeasing Mother Mary Gonzaga required untiring humility, patience, and charity. The Saint accomplished this difficult task and was in reality the Mistress of Novices, though she did not receive that name.

For the entire world, too, it was to prove of significance that she received this appointment, implying the charge of spiritual direction. For the essence of her "Little Way," which applies to all men, is admirably explained in her advice to the novices.

On receiving this charge, she realised that it was beyond her strength and exclaimed:

"Dear Lord, you see that I am too small to feed your little ones, but if, through me, you will give each one what is suitable for her, then fill my hands, and, without leaving your arms or even turning my head, I shall distribute your treasures to the souls who come to me for food."

In her *Autobiography*, the Saint further explains: "The knowledge that it was impossible to do anything of myself rendered the task easier. My sole interior occupation was to unite myself more and more closely to God, knowing that the rest would be given to me in abundant measure. . . . I have always found my hands filled when it was necessary to give nourishment to the souls of my sisters." Thus God responded to the trust of His child, who sought not to store up provisions, but counted on His guidance and inspiration at every minute.

Hers was a "Way" of abandonment and simplicity. Her soul was "passive" under God's action; but it must be remembered, as previously stated, the passive state of the interior life calls for very great spiritual energy.

"Ever since I placed myself in the Arms of Jesus, I have been like a watchman on the look out for the enemy from the highest turret of a fortified castle; nothing escapes my vigilance . . . I am often surprised at my own clear-sightedness."

Guided by the Holy Spirit, the young Novice Mistress led her novices by the light of Eternal Truth. She sought to train them to be perfect Carmelites according to the spirit of St. Teresa of Avila and of St. John of the Cross. Knowing that spiritual direction should be a discreet collaboration with the work of the Holy Spirit, she spoke to the novices of her own lights in so far only as they seemed likely to profit thereby.

The novices of Lisieux were the first disciples of the "Little Way," which is, in truth, a "simplifying." Simplicity, in spiritual matters, is an assured means of attaining union with God. Simplicity is like a straight clear path, which does not turn aside but goes straight ahead. It teaches the soul to go direct to God. God is simple. Things are complicated for us, because we are not simple.

As soon as a soul enters the way of spiritual childhood, servile fear disappears. By sanctifying grace, the child of God is established in confidence and love, and feels that she is in the House of her Father. Neither fear not discouragement can have any power over such a soul. One of the resolutions taken by Thérèse on the day of her first Holy Communion was: "I shall never let myself be discouraged." She was now able to share with others the secrets and the results of her heroic tenacity.

When a novice lamented that she always fell into the same faults, the young Novice Mistress took an incident from her own childhood to teach a lesson of perseverance. Remembering her home in the *Rue St. Blaise* and her childish efforts to go up the stairs alone to reach her mother, she recounted the repeatedly fruitless efforts she made to raise her little foot high enough to go up even the very first step, and then applied her lesson:

"By the practice of all the virtues, raise your little foot in an attempt to mount the stairway of sanctity, but do not imagine that you will be able to go up even the first step. God only asks for your good intentions. At the top of this stairway, He watches you lovingly. Soon, His love will be conquered by your vain efforts and He will come down Himself to carry you up in His arms."

Spiritual childhood "does not mean the presumption of hoping to attain a supernatural end by purely natural means,"[10] nor

[10] Benedict XV.

has it any connection with stoic pride. It means a continual and confident recourse to God's power. Our vain endeavours will act "as a prayer" on His fatherly Heart; our long-continued efforts will not fail to obtain His help.

The Saint confided to her novices the secrets of her own courageous little sacrifices, as she helped them to correct their imperfections. Cost what it might, she fought against sloth in the spiritual combat. Indifferent to flattery and altogether impartial in her conduct, she spared no pains in the accomplishment of her duty. Her personal experience and her exceptional gift of observation made her quick to detect the wiles of self-love: "A novice need not come to me for advice if she does not want to hear the truth," she exclaimed.

The novices did sometimes find her severe, for poor human nature is so likely to defend itself against those who strive to overcome its miserable self-seeking. The saintly Novice Mistress was perhaps surprised and saddened at not finding in others her own heroic generosity; it is the trial of saints that they do not often meet kindred souls.

What kindness the Saint united with her firmness! A novice, who had offended her, came to ask forgiveness. The pardon was instantly accorded with words that betrayed her emotion:

"If you only knew what my heart feels! I never understood so well with what love Jesus receives us when we ask His pardon after a fall! If a poor little creature like myself feels such tenderness for you when you come back to ask pardon, what must take place in God's Heart when a sinner returns to Him! Even quicker than I have done, He forgives all our infidelities and never thinks of them again . . . He even goes further, for He loves us more than ever . . ."

When human nature falls again and again, in spite of really good intentions, then we must "learn humility from humiliation."[11]

One of the most characteristic teachings of the Saint was that we should rejoice at everything that causes us humiliation

[11] Father Huvelin.

but does not offend God. The last precaution is typically Ignatian. Like St. Paul, she insisted that we should glory in our infirmities in order that the power of God may dwell in us: "When I am weak, then I am strong."[12]

"I rejoice greatly when people find me imperfect, and still more when I feel my own imperfection," admitted the Saint. She was convinced that our heavenly Father takes our weakness into account and that He will bless our sincere desires for perfection, even if it be only at the hour of death.

"If, throughout your whole life, you feel repugnance for suffering and humiliation, and if you feel regret that all the flowers of your desires and of your good intentions fall to the ground without producing any fruit, offer to God this sacrifice of never being able to gather the 'fruit' of your efforts. In an instant, at the hour of your death, He will cause the very best fruit to ripen on the tree of your soul."[13]

Through her humble but invincible trust, the zealous Novice Mistress had a reply ready for every difficulty and waged war on every expression of discouragement. Novices were never allowed to find fault with God's ways; they had to accept calmly their own spiritual "stature," without bitterness or envy of others. She had practised what she now taught: "I have always been pleased with whatever God has given me, even with the things that did not seem to me as desirable or as beautiful as those of others."

6. "To Be Little" Means —

Unceasingly she strove to teach humility, the virtue so dear to her heart. "When I think of all I still have to acquire!" exclaimed a novice: " — still to lose," interjected the Saint. "Jesus takes care to fill your soul according as you empty it of imperfections. . . . You have taken the wrong road. . . . You wish to climb a mountain, whereas God wishes you to descend . . ."

Thérèse did not mistake the way; she had learned "to descend." The third resolution taken on the day of her First Holy Com-

[12] II Cor. 12:10.
[13] Advice to a novice at Lisieux.

munion — "I will strive to humiliate my pride" — had been kept
as well as the first resolution; she had made herself "a little one."
How well she understood those words of Monsignor Gay: "The
spirit of childhood is even more efficacious than the spirit of
penance to overcome pride," and that other saying: "Nothing
makes a man so humble as being sincerely little."

Her profound teaching was not always understood at once,
even though she purposely couched her instructions in simple
form. A couple of months before her death, she was asked: "You
are always seeking to be like a little child, but tell us what must
be done to obtain Eternal Life."

We can visualise the picture of the novices, in their white
veils, gathered round the young Saint as they fixed their ques-
tioning looks on her, while she lowered her eyes in deep recollection as if to seek the reply in the depths of her soul. Her
words reveal the very foundation of her sanctity:

" 'Remaining little' means that we recognise our nothingness,
that we await everything from the goodness of God, *as a little
child expects everything from its father,* that we are not solicitous
about anything, and that we do not think about amassing spiritual riches. Even amongst the poor, a child receives what is
necessary while he is still small; once he is grown up, his father
will no longer keep him, but tells him to work and support himself. It was to avoid hearing this that I have never wished to
grow up, for I feel incapable of earning my livelihood, which
is Eternal Life. That is why I have remained little; my only
care has been to gather flowers of love and sacrifice and to offer
them to God for His good pleasure."

On another occasion, the Saint explained:

" 'To be little' means that we do not attribute to ourselves
the virtues we practise, as if we were capable of any good; we
recognise that God has placed this treasure in the hand of His
little child and that the treasure is always His. . . . 'To be little'
means that we are never discouraged at our faults, for, although
children often fall, they are too small to hurt themselves
seriously."

These quotations sum up the essential points of the Saint's teaching on spiritual childhood, which she practised unceasingly throughout her life, thus demonstrating its safe and enlightening precepts.

Her unerring sense of truth in matters of doctrine kept her safe from all error. There is neither quietism nor illuminism in her "Little Way," which, although it counts chiefly on God's grace and on the inspirations and impulses of the Holy Ghost, does not dispense us from personal effort and study, nor from submission to the authority of the Church. By this "Way," we live a truly angelic life. Pius XI called it "a way of golden simplicity," and Father Petitot says: "By the gift of Wisdom, this 'Way' unites the most spontaneous simplicity with the most consummate prudence."

The words of our Lord Himself are most instructive: "I praise Thee, Father, Lord of heaven and earth, that thou hast hid these things from the wise and prudent, and didst reveal them to little ones. Yes, Father, for such was thy good pleasure."[14]

[14] Matt. 11:25–26.

CHAPTER XII

THE GREAT OBLATION

1. *Thérèse As Convent Laureate*

THE year 1893 was marked for St. Thérèse of the Child Jesus by a development in her exterior activity which brought into action powers hitherto latent. Her talent as an artist had been realised earlier, but it was in this year that she manifested her remarkable gift for the training of souls. To this year also belongs her first poem, written by her for the Feast of the Purification of Our Lady.

The significance of its title, "The Divine Dew," is evident from the following verses (fourth stanza) addressed to Christ in Mary's arms. They connect the mystery of His death with the mystery of His coming to us in the flesh:

> Ah, little Brother, shielded safe from harms,
> In Thy deep eyes Thy future I foresee:
> Soon Thou wilt leave for us Thy Mother's arms;
> To suffer, Love already urges Thee.
> Around Thy very Cross, Thou fading Flower,
> Still clings the fragrance of Thy cradle-throne;
> I recognize the *pearls* of Thy first hour:
> This Blood drew life from Mary's milk, my Own![1]

The poem was written to be sung to the tune, *Noël d'Adam.*

To express in verse the aspirations of the soul and the intimate experiences of the interior life has become a custom in Carmelite convents, following the example of St. Teresa of Avila and St. John of the Cross. In loving imitation of these two great models of the ascetic life, Carmelites often solemnise the feasts of the Church, professions, anniversaries, and similar occasions, by the composition of verses, which help to give outward

[1] Translation by Susan L. Emery (adapted).

expression to their spirit of joy and mutual affection. These verses are then sung or recited in the large Community Room during recreation-hours, and especially on those feast days for which the rule of silence is somewhat relaxed. Naturally, only nuns with poetic talent are asked to compose such verses; in that way, St. Thérèse was called upon to write her poems.

The list of her metrical compositions is surprisingly long, considering that her poems were all written within the short space of four and a half years, and that no time was taken for them from the daily work of the Community. The Saint never asked for the least exemption on that point. While working, she reflected on the subject she wished to treat and composed the verses in her mind; in the evening, during the time allowed for personal occupations between eight and nine o'clock, she wrote out her poems on odd pieces of paper and on the backs of old envelopes. She once mentioned, though unintentionally, how trying this haphazard method had been to her.

In truth a very great facility in versification was necessary to succeed under such conditions. This facility St. Thérèse of the Child Jesus undoubtedly possessed. Speaking of her poetry, Father Jubaru says: "Her verses, flowing from an abundant source, are like a shower of fresh petals, dainty, gaily-coloured, and exquisitely fragrant." We might add: "with the fragrance of her own soul."[2] Great depth of thought and soundness of doctrine accompanied this graceful form of expression. For that reason, her poems have not been merely fleeting, though charming, pastimes; they have done good, permanent good, and form a fitting epilogue to the *Story of a Soul*,[3] being intimately connected with the Saint's miraculous, radiant influence.

The most severe critics admit that Thérèse Martin had an innate gift for poetry, in the style of Lamartine and Racine. "She does not reach the incomparable starkness of Racine's *Cantiques Spirituels*," Ghéon remarks, "but you are reminded

[2] One of St. Thérèse's poems, *La Rose Effenillée*, will be found in the Appendix, p. 250.
[3] *Histoire d'une Ame* is the title given to the original French edition of the Saint's *Autobiography*.

of them and are sorry that Thérèse had no competent and careful guidance when she wrote, for she might have excelled some of the acknowledged poets in France today."

One is almost tempted to regret that she did not receive a more complete literary education and did not devote herself to a more profound study of verse, by which means she would have reached that equality of style and precision of form which mark the perfection of such work.

"For His sake I have abandoned everything," the young Carmelite could say in all sincerity. All human things that pass away Thérèse of the Child Jesus had abandoned and despised in order to obtain the one thing necessary: that serene triumphant love, stronger than all things else, that weaves together the will of the soul and the will of her Divine Lord, uniting the soul so intimately to her Divine Spouse that she herself is completely effaced. A letter to Céline, dated April twenty-fifth of that year, shows this magnanimous disdain of worldly ambition:

"The Beloved has no need of our most wonderful works nor of our most beautiful thoughts. If He wishes for lofty conceptions, has He not got His angels, whose knowledge far surpasses that of the greatest genius in this world? It is neither wisdom nor talent that He looks for here below."

Being so richly endowed by nature, St. Thérèse of Lisieux might have become a great artist. She became something far greater. To God, who is Infinite Beauty, she gave the entire love of her heart; and *her holiness is her one, great, immortal masterpiece.*

2. *Concern for Léonie and Céline*

As in previous years, Monsieur Martin and Céline spent the summer months with Monsieur Guérin at the *Château de la Musse.* Léonie did not accompany them this year, as she had just entered the Convent of the Visitation at Caen. The petition made by Thérèse on her Profession Day for her elder sister had therefore been granted!

On August 13, the Carmelite wrote an affectionate letter, full of serious thoughts, to her sister at the Visitation Convent. Her happiness on account of Léonie's vocation was altogether spiritual since the two sisters would never see one another again on earth, being both in enclosed Orders. Their ways were different, but their goal was the same, and in heaven they would be reunited. In her letter, Thérèse dwells on the advantages of religious life, in which the soul, assisted on all sides by the exercise of her Rule and community life, has so many means of advancing rapidly on the way of perfection, and she concludes with this humble request: "Dearest sister, pray for your little Thérèse that she may draw profit from the abundant means given to her for meriting heaven."

Means were not lacking, indeed, to the fervent young Religious, constantly heroic in her exterior fidelity to Rule and in her interior fidelity to grace. In this connection, we must not overlook a very important point. Her boundless trust in God and her special graces of light concerning His Merciful Love in no way lightened the trial of spiritual aridity to which her soul was continually subjected; her life of the senses had no share in the strong food which nourished her faith. "Notwithstanding her extreme tenderness of heart and delicacy of feeling, a disposition which would seem apt to call down ineffable graces of Divine Tenderness, Thérèse lived a life of pure 'naked' faith."[4]

As to Léonie, so to Céline also she wished to be helpful, and for that purpose disclosed a little of her rugged path:

"Thérèse is not on the heights at present! But when I am in a state of spiritual dryness, unable to pray or to practise virtue, I look for little opportunities, for little trifles, to give pleasure to our Lord, for example, a smile or a kind word when I feel inclined to say nothing and to show annoyance. If I do not find these little opportunities, I tell Him over and over again that I love Him — that at least is easy and it sustains the fire of love in my heart. Even if this fire seemed completely dead, I would throw my little straws on the ashes and I am sure it would revive again. It is true I am not always faithful, but

[4] Process of Canonisation.

I never allow myself to be discouraged and I abandon myself entirely to my Saviour. He teaches me 'to draw profit from every thing, from the good and from the evil that He finds in me.' "[5]

Thus, with zealous ardour, the Saint shared with her sister the practical lessons of the spiritual life, showing her the daily, though often unnoticed, means of acquiring holiness, means that are real and efficacious and within the reach of all.

Thérèse had still one great desire — a wish long fostered in her mind. She longed for Céline to enter Carmel. But, quelling the dictates of her heart, she only prayed that her sister would be called to the religious life. She was determined to obtain a religious vocation for Céline as for Léonie. So, on one occasion, when her solicitude for the welfare of Céline's soul made her pour forth earnest prayers, these were answered in quite a strange and unexpected way. The incident is related at length in her *Autobiography*.

Céline, who danced well, had been obliged to accompany her aunt and cousins to a social gathering. She and her partner were just about to join in a dance when a strange, invisible force held them back. They both made serious endeavours to catch the rhythm, which had already carried off the other couples, but in vain; they were only able to walk demurely up and down before the astonished assembly. Embarrassed and mortified, the young man soon withdrew. What irresistible force had hindered them?

Thérèse, seized by a sudden impulse, had begged our Lord, with many tears, to grant that Céline would not be able to dance, lest she should be captivated by the spirit of the world! This incident, "unique of its kind," as the Saint wittily remarks, showed clearly that Céline was not intended for the world — a fact never doubted by her sister.

Much as Thérèse yearned that Céline might enter the Carmel of Lisieux, strong reasons existed which seemingly rendered such a consummation impossible. Nevertheless, she continued

[5] St. John of the Cross.

to cherish unremittently her unspoken desire, deep in her inmost heart, and, in the summer evenings, as she sat out on the monastery terrace awaiting the bell for Matins, she often gazed far into the star-lit sky, longing for this happy reunion.

"It was not for natural reasons that I desired this happiness," she explained one day to Mother Agnes of Jesus; "it was for the sake of her soul, that she might profit by my Little Way."

3. *Thérèse and Joan of Arc*

Once more, the penance of winter had to be endured. Then came spring, during which joyous season Thérèse wrote hymns and other poems in honour of the Venerable Joan of Arc, who had been the favourite heroine of her childhood's days. Under her habit of coarse texture, Thérèse Martin bore the heart of a warrior, notwithstanding the humility of her Way of Spiritual Childhood. The enthusiasm and ardour of her heart is seen in her spirited verses, in which the twin souls of Joan and Thérèse are clearly portrayed. Among these verses are some of poignant immolation:

> For love of Thee alone, my aged father's side
> I left, to offer Thee the springtime of my days,
> My chief desire the Cross, the path of sacrifice.
> Oh wounded, Suffering Love! disclose to me Thy ways.

Others glow with ardent patriotism, perfectly spiritualized in her:

> Beloved France! My Home! How I desire
> To keep thee ever rooted in Christ's Fold;
> I wish to serve thee ever, like brave Joan,
> That gallant fearless heart, in days of old.

No foreign invasion, nor prospect of future wars troubled the soul of Thérèse, such as had perturbed the mind of the Shepherdess of Domremy. "Far-famed generals then gave credence to my voice," the Saint of Lisieux makes her say. But what concerned Thérèse in the France of her day, and what alone concerned her, was the spread of irreligion, from which France's evils were to flow, and against which she so ardently

invoked the aid of the holy warrior maid: "Come," she calls
on her, "convert the land so dear to thee . . . a second time
save France!"

May 16, 1920, witnessed the Canonisation of this saint, for
which she had so longingly pleaded during her life as answering
the spiritual needs of the country. Her heaven-storming prayer
was not sent up in vain when she had prayed:

> Our tumults calm, her cause advance,
> The halo and the palm give unto Joan of France.

May 17, 1925, Thérèse's own Canonisation took place, only
five years later. Sisters, not in the blood but in the spirit, were
these two wonderful saints. Indeed, the day after Thérèse's
Canonisation Pope Pius XI, comparing them with each other,
gave St. Thérèse of the Child Jesus the very title that her
childish fancy had so often dreamed of, *"A second Joan of Arc,*
resplendent with glory."

But the only glory Thérèse ever coveted was the glory of
God alone. It was not renown of whatever kind, but death for
Him on the field or at the stake, that she ambitioned. "The
spirit of the Crusader burns within me," she wrote, "and I long
to die on the field of battle in defence of holy Church." That is
why the Voices calling Joan to combat awoke such echoes in
her own soul.

In the spiritual life, contrasting virtues unite to give perfect
balance to the soul, as, for instance, simplicity and prudence,
humility and greatness of mind. The sanctity of Thérèse of
Lisieux, uniting all virtues in a most gracious manner, gives us
a perfect example of this essential rule. A valiant warrior . . .
a little child. These contrasting terms are her own words and
they reveal her whole soul. As her interior heroism grew stronger,
the humility of her mind and heart deepened.

In a letter to Céline she wrote: "He gives abundantly as only
God can give, but He wishes to find humility of heart in us."
And in her recommendations to her novices, we find: "Let us
be little, so little that everyone can tread us underfoot without

our appearing to feel or even to notice it." Elsewhere, we find this little phrase laden with deep experience: "The only thing which is never envied is the lowest place." This lowest place Thérèse herself invariably sought, with quiet simplicity.

4. Thérèse Begins Her "Autobiography"

Thérèse was now fast reaching her full development, and the time was nearing when by God's providence she should be asked to commit to paper her own soul life. But before that a few events were still to transpire.

The summer of 1894 brought an intense sorrow to Thérèse and her sisters, for the soul of good Monsieur Martin was recalled to God on July 29 of that year. Since the beginning of his illness, he had only once been able to visit his daughters at Carmel. Helpless and overwhelmed with sorrow, in a voice choked by tears, he had uttered the farewell words:

"Good-bye, till we meet in heaven!"

In her *Autobiography*, the great-souled Thérèse has written that she would not have exchanged the years of her father's martyrdom for the most sublime ecstasies. Such supernatural heroism, however, did not lessen the intensity of her suffering. We might almost say that the Saint wrote those words with her heart's blood. That agony was now over. His suffering — and theirs — was ended; her holy and beloved father was in heaven. Thérèse was convinced of this, but she wished for a proof — and she also very much wished to have Céline at Carmel!

The fact that her sister had a religious vocation seemed clear, but there was opposition to Céline's entering at Lisieux, since it was against the established regulations to have four sisters in the same convent. The members of the Community Council made several reasonable objections, and one of the older nuns showed herself definitely hostile. In face of this opposition, with one of her impulses of apparent boldness which were in reality inspirations of the Holy Spirit, Thérèse said to our Lord one day after Holy Communion:

"My beloved Jesus, You know how I have hoped that my

father's trial would serve as his purgatory. I do not ask You to speak to me; I only ask for a sign. Sister N's opposition to Céline's entering here is well known to You. If she make no further objection, I shall take that change in her attitude as an assurance from You that my father's soul has gone straight to heaven."

The very first person she met just after her thanksgiving was Sister N who told her, with tears in her eyes, how pleased she would be if Céline should enter at Lisieux. God's answer!

The Saint seems to have had a presentiment already at that time that her own death was not far distant, for she wrote these prophetic words to her sister on August nineteenth:

"God has granted my greatest wish. Come, and we shall suffer together . . . and then Jesus will take one of us. Now pay great attention to what I have to say . . . if I should die before you, never think that we shall be separated . . . we shall be more united than ever."

On September 14, Céline Martin joined her sisters at the Carmel of Lisieux. It is easy to imagine with what joy Thérèse welcomed her. After the first embrace, however, true to her principles of complete detachment, the Saint was going to withdraw, when Mother Agnes of Jesus told her to take the new postulant to her cell. Thérèse would have been more self-denying than Jesus would have her to be. The tender Master granted her the pleasure of intercourse with her sister, who forthwith became her spiritual daughter in the noviciate.

The autumn slipped by, and winter brought the joys of Christmas-tide, with a slight relaxation of the strict rule of silence. At recreation one evening, Thérèse allowed herself the rare pleasure of chatting intimately with her two elder sisters, recalling their life at home and relating little incidents of her childhood. Indicating an unusually retentive memory, her words moved the hearts of her "Little Mother" and her godmother, causing them great pleasure. Suddenly the latter exclaimed:

"Oh Mother! you really ought to tell her to write her recollections of childhood!"

Taken by surprise, Mother Agnes of Jesus hesitated at first, but Sister Mary of the Sacred Heart, urged by the Holy Spirit, pleaded and prevailed. To her we owe a debt of gratitude. Mother Agnes of Jesus allowed herself to be persuaded, and some time later, using her authority as Prioress, told Sister Thérèse to write an account of her childhood's memories. The little manuscript was to be finished in a year, on January 20, 1896, the Eve of St. Agnes' feast. The humble Saint feared that such a task would distract her from her religious life, but obeyed quite simply when the order was actually given. She was left entirely at liberty to write whatever came into her mind. Her plans were soon made. She decided to write her thoughts upon the graces that God had given her rather than to delay on the actual events of her life. With an air of conviction surprising in a young nun of twenty-two, she remarked:

"I have reached a period of my life when I can cast a glance over the past . . . my soul has grown mature in the crucible of trial . . ."

At the first opportunity that occurred, she took a pen and a schoolgirl's penny exercise-book. Then, kneeling before the statue of our Lady that had smiled on her and cured her in her childhood, she prayed for guidance. On the first page of her *Autobiography,* we read:

"I implored the Queen of Heaven to guide my hand so that I should not pen a single line that would not be pleasing to her."

Next, opening at random the New Testament which she always kept beside her, the young Carmelite read these words: Jesus, "going up a mountain, called to him men of his own choosing."[6] How exactly those words described her own life! She recalled the day when she spoke to her father for the first time about her vocation, and he gave her a little flower, drawing her attention to the way divine providence had taken care of that frail blossom. Indeed, she still possessed that symbolic floweret.

With these thoughts uppermost in her mind and with intense

6 Mark 3:13.

gratitude filling her heart, Thérèse inscribed on the first page of her exercise-book the following title, which had such deep meaning for her: *The Story of the Springtime of a Little White Flower.*

Little did she dream at the moment that the manuscript, begun that day within the walls of her Carmelite cell, would be published in successive editions, translated into many languages, and touch more souls than a whole army of Missionaries could reach, winning finally for her youthful holiness the unparalleled admiration of the whole world.

The desire for literary glory was indeed far from her thoughts. Calmly and freely, in her own spontaneous style, she narrated the story of her soul for Mother Agnes of Jesus alone. Each day, according to her free time, she wrote a few pages, neat and regular, in her small straight handwriting, without alteration or addition. The extraordinary facility of style shown in her poems is even more striking in her prose, but the exceptional and inestimable value of this autobiography is due to the deep spirituality of the writer. Her own life-work on earth — her personal sanctification by God's grace — was almost completed. Divine providence decreed that it should be portrayed in writing.

By way of introduction, Thérèse resolutely broached the great question of predestination, undaunted by the difficulty of the problem. The question of the salvation of souls had been a subject of her serious reflection. Even during the years of her attendance at catechism, the problem occupied her thoughts. One day, at the Benedictine Convent, she exclaimed with childish simplicity: "If I were God, I think I would save them all!"

Why, indeed, does God appear to have His preferences? Why do not all souls receive the same graces? What is the reason for such sudden and extraordinary favours as those bestowed on sinners like St. Paul, St. Augustine, and St. Mary Magdalen? Then there are those privileged souls whom our Lord seems to cherish from the cradle to the grave, preserving their baptismal innocence from all stain of grievous sin! Thérèse knew that she was one of these cherished souls — for priests had assured her on this point — and the knowledge caused her unspeakable joy and gratitude. But those other souls! Why, for instance, do so many poor savages die without even having heard the name of God? To all these questions Jesus Himself deigned to give her a reply, for she tells us: "He showed me the book of nature, and I understood that every flower created by Him is beautiful." Yes, indeed, every one is beautiful in its own way, and their very diversity is essential for the harmony and splendour of the universe. With that, then, she draws the comparison:

"So it is in the world of souls, our Lord's living garden. The great saints are the lilies and the roses; the others, the lesser ones, must be content to be violets or daisies. . . . The more gladly they do His Will, the greater is their perfection . . . God's love is made manifest in a simple soul, which does not resist His grace, as surely as in one more highly gifted. Since condescension is a characteristic of love, God would not seem to stoop low enough in coming to souls, if they all resembled the holy Doctors who have enlightened the Church by their doctrine. He has created the little child, who knows nothing and can utter but feeble cries, and the poor savage who has only the natural law to guide him; it is to their hearts that He deigns to stoop. . . . As the sun shines on the cedar and on the floweret so does God enlighten every soul, whether great or small, and all things cooperate for the good of all, just as in nature the seasons are so disposed that on the appointed day the humblest daisy unfolds its petals."

In these simple but comprehensive words, the little Saint of Lisieux solved the problem that preoccupied her mind. Her love grouped together all the souls in the world as in one immense bouquet to be offered in homage to their Lord and God. In the new-born babe as in the most wretched savage — the latter holding a great place in her missionary heart — she discerned the work of Divine Goodness, and proclaimed the ineffable tenderness of the Creator. Her words are in accordance with those of our Lord Himself, when He gave His order to

St. Catherine of Siena: "Go and announce to all men that My decrees are guided by love alone."

After these general remarks, the author had to begin the story of her own soul, since she had been told to write her own life. What attitude was she to take? In the "garden of souls," she could not call herself an unattractive flower giving no perfume, for that would be at variance with truth. To deny or belittle the gifts of God would be ingratitude and false humility. How vividly she realised that God's grace had forestalled her every action and that she had been favoured with a love of predilection! She decided, therefore, to sing "the Mercies of the Lord," but only for the ears of Mother Agnes of Jesus. This same theme, the Mercies of the Lord, inspired our Blessed Lady to sing her immortal *Magnificat* in the privacy of Elizabeth's home.

5. *Holocaust to God's Merciful Love*

Thérèse's fears of distracting thoughts in the writing of her *Life* were quite unfounded, for, in that very year, she received special graces. God wished to complete the great work of her sanctification in two years and now bestowed on her an illuminating grace, which was at the same time a call to greater union with Himself. "In the year 1895, I received the grace to understand more than ever how much Jesus desires to be loved," she wrote toward the end of her *Autobiography*.

She longed to return love for love to her Divine Redeemer. What could she offer to her Divine Spouse that she had not already given Him? She knew that certain holy souls made the heroic act of offering themselves as victims to the Divine Justice in atonement for the sins of others, but she did not feel drawn to do this. Her desire was to atone for the numberless souls, who refuse to accept the love that God would lavish upon them, and to make reparation for the disdain of those that abandon Him.

"O my Divine Master," she exclaimed, with intense love, "shall Your Justice alone receive victims of holocaust? Has not Your Merciful Love also need of victims? On all sides It is despised and rejected . . . must It remain hidden in Your Heart? Ah, surely, if You found souls who would offer themselves as victims of holocaust to Your Love, you would consume them rapidly, being pleased to set free the flames of Infinite Tenderness that are imprisoned in Your Heart."

Thérèse already felt the ardour of these "flames of Infinite Tenderness." Her Little Way had brought her right up to the Furnace of Charity; she had only to cast herself into those glowing fires of Love.

"O Jesus, let me be that happy victim; consume Your holocaust with the fire of Divine Love."

This cry of oblation sprang spontaneously from her heart, one morning after Holy Communion, and was destined to enrich the Church with a new form of devotion.

Immediately on the completion of her thanksgiving, realising the value and importance of her complete oblation, she made a sign to Céline to accompany her and went to submit her action to the authority of her Prioress. The tender love of divine providence had decreed that the Prioress at that time should be Mother Agnes of Jesus. She and Céline both noticed that Thérèse's beautiful face was radiant with a special fervour. Like a youthful Moses, the Saint seemed to have come down from a Sinai of Love.

Mother Agnes of Jesus accorded the permission for this oblation and authorised a written formula, which, as Thérèse herself stipulated, was submitted to a theologian. This act on her part was characteristic of the calm wisdom the Saint always showed in even her most ardent desires. Accordingly Father Lemonnier, a missionary of *La Délivrande*,[1] examined and approved the long formula, dated June 9, 1895, the Feast of the Blessed Trinity.

For her great oblation, St. Thérèse of the Child Jesus and of the Holy Face chose the feast on which men adore God in the most sublime of all His Mysteries. She offered herself to God, Father, Son, and Holy Ghost. Nothing less could satisfy her fervour and her enlightened appreciation of dogma.

[1] La Délivrande is a town in Normandy, famous for its sanctuary in honour of our Lady.

What richness of contrast — lowliness and grandeur! Thérèse, the plaything of the Infant Jesus, was at the same time also the Victim of Love offered to the Most Holy Trinity. The purpose of this oblation was to establish her in a state of perfect charity: "In order that my life may be an act of perfect love, I offer myself as a Victim of Holocaust to Your merciful Love." Like the victims of holocaust which had to be entirely consumed by fire in the old Jewish law, Thérèse wished to abandon herself to the flames of Divine Love to be entirely consumed and to be transformed into fire.

God, who is Love Itself, is all-sufficient to Himself in His infinite perfections. No creature can add in the slightest degree to the infinite happiness of the Godhead, in the unity of the three distinct but equal Persons. Further, the act by which God inclines toward His creatures and communicates Himself to them is a gratuitous act of His Infinite Mercy. The words employed by St. Thérèse — "to Your merciful Love" — are therefore quite in accordance with theology. Commenting on the Latin word *misericors* (merciful), St. Augustine explains it thus: *miseris cor dare* (to give one's heart to those in misery). Thérèse, then, did not forsake her Little Way of Humility and Confidence, but rather advanced more surely on that path, since it was her worthlessness that she abandoned to infinite Mercy. Indeed, toward the end of her *Autobiography*, we read:

"It is my very weakness which emboldens me to offer myself, O Jesus, as a victim to Thy Love. In olden days, pure and spotless holocausts alone were acceptable to the Omnipotent God. . . . But the law of fear has given place to the law of love, and Love has chosen me, a weak and imperfect creature, as its victim. . . . In order that Love may be fully satisfied, it must stoop even unto nothingness to transform that nothingness into fire."

With this solid basis of true humility, the Saint's aspirations broke forth, eager, ardent, and irresistible:

"I desire to love You and to make You loved — to labour for the glory of Your holy Church. . . . I desire to accomplish

Your will perfectly. . . . I long to console You for ungrateful sinners. . . . I wish to labour for Your Love alone, with the sole aim of pleasing You, of consoling Your Sacred Heart, and of saving souls who will love You throughout eternity."

Since, in reality, there is only one Victim, Jesus Christ, Thérèse offered the merits of our Saviour, begging almighty God to look upon her only through the eyes of Jesus, her Spouse, and to see her in His Divine Heart. Intense longing surged up in her own heart, surpassing all she had hitherto experienced. Would she dare to name all her desires? As if to persuade herself that there need be no limit to her petitions, she cried out:

"Oh, my· God, I know that the more You wish to bestow, the more You make us desire."

Then, in an impulse of trustful expectation, fully appreciating the filial reverence and love due to our heavenly Father, she implored:

"I desire to be holy, but knowing how helpless I am, I beseech You, my God, to be Yourself my holiness. . . . I cannot receive You in Holy Communion as often as I wish, but, O Lord, are You not all powerful? Abide in me as You do in the Tabernacle — never abandon Your Little Victim. . . . I implore You to take from me all liberty of displeasing You; if I should fall through weakness, may a glance of Your eyes at once cleanse my soul and consume all my imperfections. . . . I hope to be like unto You in Paradise and to behold the sacred wounds of Your Passion shine on my glorified body. . . . I do not ask You, my God, to take account of my works. All our works of justice are sullied in Your eyes. I wish therefore to be clothed with Your own Justice, and to receive from Your Love the everlasting possession of Yourself."

Finally, as the last petition in this great act of self-surrender, Thérèse implored our Lord to consume her unceasingly and to allow the floods of divine tenderness imprisoned in His Heart to overflow into her soul.

"May I thus become a martyr of Your Love. May this martyrdom, after having prepared me to appear in Your presence, free me from this life at the last, and may my soul take its flight, without delay, into the eternal embrace of Your merciful Love!"[8]

A martyrdom of love! These words express a state of soul created by the disproportion between the infinite tenderness of God and the limits of the finite heart into which flow the streams of divine Love. The waves from this sea of love, growing ever greater, overwhelm the limited capacity of the soul with their inrush, sometimes even breaking asunder the mortal bonds of the body, thus allowing the soul to take its flight to God.

From the happy day of her great oblation, Thérèse was ready for the coming of Him to whom she had given herself so unreservedly. That perfect purity of conscience, which she had so anxiously sought in earlier years and so greatly desired at all times, was hers henceforth. She fully realised this, for she says:

"From that day, I have been penetrated and surrounded with Love. Every moment this merciful Love renews me and purifies me, leaving in my soul no trace of sin. . . . I cannot fear purgatory . . . the fire of Love is more sanctifying than that of purgatory. . . . I know that Jesus could not wish useless suffering for us, and He would not inspire me with the desires I feel, did He not wish to satisfy them."

6. *A Legion of Little Souls*

Such was the great oblation of Thérèse, "an unparalleled form of a binding pledge to perfect love."[9] Although the Act of Oblation made by the Saint of Lisieux may seem too heroic for us to imitate, it forms part of her special Message to the world. This complete oblation is within the power of all souls of good will, of all whom she calls "little souls." She herself declared:

"All that I do, little souls should be able to do."

Let us follow her without fear, since our wretchedness attracts God's Mercy. To encourage ourselves to follow in her footsteps, let us repeat the words she applied to herself:

"The poorer and the more wretched we are, the more fitting

[8] Act of Oblation. See Appendix, pp. 258–260.
[9] Father Desbuquois, S.J., *Documents concerning St. Thérèse of Lisieux,* January, 1933.

we are for the working of God's consuming and transforming Love. The desire to be a Victim suffices, but the most important point is to be willing to remain ever poor and helpless. There lies the difficulty. Let us love our littleness, let us be content to be without sensible joy; then shall we be truly poor in spirit, and Jesus will come to seek us, however far off we may be, and He will transform us into flames of love."[10]

As Father Desbuquois says: "These words are an admirable invitation to all imperfect souls and even to sinners — provided their intention is good and their humility sincere — to join the legion of 'little souls,' of which Thérèse of the Child Jesus is the leader and the model. These little souls offer themselves such as they are, humbly recognising their defects and weakness; they offer themselves to God to love Him, to make reparation to Him, and to give Him pleasure; they offer themselves as 'empty vessels' that He may fill them with the treasures of His Love. There is no question of offering ourselves for extraordinary suffering. We offer ourselves — through love — to the Merciful, Gentle, Compassionate Love, of Him who knows us through and through."

Ever attentive to our cry, He will incline unto us, and, with the cooperation of our own good will, He will take possession of our souls and sanctify the mind the way best adapted to our weakness. There is nothing in the Little Way which could frighten the most timid. True it is that all little souls will not reach that perfect degree of oblation attained by Thérèse. There are different degrees of love, for as she said herself:

"We are consumed by Love in the measure only in which we abandon ourselves to Love."

It is obvious, however, that even the beginning of such loving self-surrender glorifies God on account of this trustful abandonment of ourselves to the unfailing tenderness of God our Father, our Creator, our Saviour, and our Sanctifier. This is, indeed, the response of the soul to the appeal made by our Lord Himself: "I have come to cast fire upon the earth, and what will I, but

[10] Letter to Sister Mary of the Sacred Heart.

that it be kindled?"[11] We may, then, group ourselves fearlessly around the standard of Thérèse. That of Joan of Arc led her followers to victory over her country's enemies; the standard of Thérèse of Lisieux leads us to victory over the powers of darkness. We shall be wise, then, to join that Legion of little souls for which she prayed in one of her most fervent prayers:

"O Jesus, would that I could tell all little souls of Your ineffable condescension! I feel that if it were possible for You to find a soul weaker than mine You would take delight in lavishing still greater favours on her, *provided that she abandoned herself with entire confidence* to Your infinite Mercy. . . . I beseech You to let Your divine eyes rest upon a vast number of little souls; I entreat You to choose in this world a Legion of little victims worthy of Your Love."[12]

Of this petition His Holiness Pope Pius XI declared: "We adopt this prayer as our own."[13] The Church, by the voice of her sovereign pontiff, as well as by the indulgences with which she has enriched the Act of Oblation to God's Merciful Love, clearly shows her wish that this act of voluntary oblation should be propagated among the faithful throughout the world. We may rest assured that this act of self-surrender to God's loving Mercy is a source of abundant blessings for those who, even if it be only momentarily, unite themselves with a pure intention to this Legion of Love.

[11] Luke 12:49.
[12] Concluding passage in St. Thérèse's *Autobiography*.
[13] Sermon of the Mass of Canonisation.

CHAPTER XIII

A VICTIM OF DIVINE LOVE

1. *The Wound of Love*

THÉRÈSE had reached the summit of the mystical mountain, "the kingdom of the gifts of the Holy Ghost . . . transforming union."[1] She had long since entered the Unitive Way, the most perfect state that can be acquired here below; beyond it there is only the Beatific Vision.

Masters of the Spiritual life have been somewhat at a loss, however, in trying to distinguish the successive stages of spiritual progress in the life of the young Carmelite, by which she passed so swiftly to the top of that secret stairway mentioned by St. John of the Cross. "Do not look for me on the landings," the Saint could have said to them with her gay smile, "because I have taken the lift." The lift, as we know, was none other than her Divine Master's arms. Such words disclose the sweet secrets of the Little Way, which leads straight up to the lofty heights, provided that we follow it with unfailing perseverance, as Thérèse did.

The secret of her sanctity lay in her faithful correspondence to grace. Toward the end of her life, the question was put to her: "What would you do if you had to begin your life over again?" Already on the threshold of eternity, she was able to give this amazing reply:

"I think I should do as I have done."

"Conquered by the vain endeavours" of His little child and by her invincible confidence, God established her soul in the state of pure love, of which she was now to experience the wonderful effects. She realised that God acted freely in her

[1] Father Bernadot, O.P.

soul, that He was free to act as He would, and she exclaimed in delight and wonder: "My dwelling is entirely at peace."[2] St. John of the Cross explains that even the primary movements of a soul in this state, come from God: "God's fidelity ensures the fidelity of the soul." Without the medium of senses or faculties, God communicates Himself to the soul "by a contact of the Divine Substance with the substance of the soul," who thus truly participates in the nature of the Godhead.

Many writers have sought to describe these mysteries of perfect union with God; Thérèse, in her childlike simplicity, makes no attempt to do so, but her expressions of gratitude give us some idea of the favour bestowed upon her:

"O my God," she writes, "Your Love has gone before me, even from the days of my childhood. It has grown with me and is now an abyss whose depths I cannot fathom."[3]

Sanctity is a mystery; the saints themselves do not completely understand the workings of grace in their souls. How could they understand this mystery, since He who takes possession of them and acts within them is none other than the infinite and almighty God Himself? We know the saints only from what appears exteriorly, from their words and actions, or from what the Holy Spirit deigns to reveal concerning them. In His Goodness, God has vouchsafed to give us a precious testimony of the unfathomable abyss of love in Thérèse's soul. As she was beginning the stations of the Cross one day shortly after her oblation to God's Merciful Love, she felt herself wounded by a dart of fire so ardent that she thought she would die.

"I do not know how to explain this transport," she told Mother Agnes of Jesus; "it seemed as though an invisible force plunged me wholly into fire. . . . But oh! what fire! what sweetness! . . . One minute more — nay, one second more — and my soul would have been set free."

Father Bernadot says: "It seems allowable to consider that this mystic grace was the Wound of Love, mentioned by St.

[2] St. John of the Cross.
[3] *Autobiography*.

Teresa of Avila and St. John of the Cross. The latter considers that this grace is especially reserved for souls whose virtue and spirit of holiness are to be transmitted through the ages to their spiritual children. This was, indeed, the case with St. Teresa of Avila and with her namesake of Lisieux. A Seraph, in the form of a child, pierced the heart of the great Reformer of the Carmelite Order with a dart of gold; the young Apostle of the Way of Spiritual Childhood had no similar vision, but the Wound received was the same. The fire of love, enkindled in these two hearts, was destined to spread to the utmost confines of the earth. When Thérèse gave Mother Agnes of Jesus an account of what had taken place, the Prioress listened without appearing to attach any importance to the matter. As the Psalmist tells us: "All the glory of the King's Daughter is from within."[4] God Himself had decreed that the beauty of the soul of St. Thérèse should remain hidden as by a veil all during her life, but, through this veil of humility, there shone forth ever more and more intensely the reflection of Him who had become her very life, and at times there fell from her lips words of prophetic import, inspired by the Spirit of Truth.

2. *Flames of Zeal for Souls*

St. Thomas Aquinas has said: "As a flame shows the intensity of a fire, so zeal shows the glowing ardour of love." In the silence of her cloister, the flame of love in Thérèse's heart inspired her with an ever increasing zeal for souls. She yearned to save souls. Her zeal, however, was always in accordance with her Little Way. She knew that "the most ordinary sacrifices, if made for Love of God, delight His Divine Heart." Her aim was the salvation of souls; and for this end she offered her most ordinary actions — even the picking up of a pin — as acts of love to God's most Merciful Love. Her smallest actions were laden with eternal life.

At this period of her life, her patience seemed invincible; she showed herself so happy to oblige others that her amiability

[4] Ps. 44.

and gentleness made her an easy prey for inopportune requests. The sharp, youthful eyes of her novices sometimes observed her very narrowly to see if they could catch her unawares, but they never succeeded in finding her serenity ruffled.

"How is it," she was asked one day, "that you can be so patient?"

Her quiet answer reveals depths of self-abnegation: "Since I have abandoned all self-seeking, I live the happiest life possible."

Far from avoiding humiliations, she accepted them gladly. A novice once noticed her joyous attitude and was surprised to discover the reason — Thérèse had just been blamed unkindly by a Sister with whom she worked. At that very moment, the sister in question happened to pass, and, by the loving smile that was bestowed upon her, the novice was able to see for herself how saints forgive. Mother Mary of the Angels, who, as Novice-Mistress, had often noted the reaction of human nature to humiliating or reproachful words, declared that she had never found anyone, except Sister Thérèse of the Child Jesus, who could accept such remarks with real joy and delight.

St. Teresa of Avila remarks with her delightful candour: "In my opinion, it is a pure gift of God and a supernatural favour to be able to be indifferent to the evil that is said of us and even to rejoice that evil be said of us rather than good." In her daughter, Thérèse of Lisieux, she would have recognised this hall-mark of sanctity.

Two events, which brought great consolation to the young Carmelite in her mortified life, belong to this year of such abundant grace — the entrance of her cousin at Carmel and the adoption of a missionary "brother."

Thérèse had been of great assistance to her cousin, Marie Guérin, especially during a painful period of scruples, by encouraging her to receive Holy Communion frequently notwithstanding her troubled conscience, and explaining that her idle fears had surely been prompted by the devil. "What does offend Jesus," she wrote, "what wounds Him to the Heart is want of confidence."[5] The gentle soul of Marie Guérin, accepting humbly her saintly cousin's teaching, gradually grew strong in her love and confidence, and on August 15, 1895, she entered the convent at Lisieux.[6]

The month of October brought Thérèse an unexpected joy. One day, as she was occupied in the laundry, Mother Agnes of Jesus called her to explain that a young missionary seminarist had made the request that one of the nuns would be as a spiritual sister to him, by praying in a very special way for him and the mission that would be allotted to him. The request was granted, and Thérèse of the Child Jesus was chosen as that spiritual sister. The following year, she received another spiritual brother. Her letters to these brother missionaries are among the most beautiful of her correspondence. The Carmelite, who was destined to be proclaimed Patroness of the Foreign Missions by Pius XI, bestowed on these two young apostles the first-fruits of her intense activity in the world of souls. The exceptional ease and the tone of authority with which she wrote to them were due to her perfect freedom of spirit. The concluding pages of her *Autobiography,* finished at this time, also show the complete interior spiritual liberty to which she had attained.

3. *Highest Peak of Mountain of Love*

At the hour of the evening meditation on January 20, 1896, Sister Thérèse of the Child Jesus knelt down beside her Prioress in choir and silently handed her the manuscript, which a year previously had been requested for that date. Mother Agnes of Jesus placed it on the edge of her stall, without giving it a thought; on returning to her cell, she put it aside to be read at leisure moments. The term of her three years as Prioress was to expire in a few days; she was, therefore, exceedingly busy, and her mind was probably preoccupied in regulating matters for her successor.

The election of the Prioress that year presented some difficulty;

[5] Letter to Marie Guérin, 1888.
[6] Marie Guérin became Sister Mary of the Eucharist. She died on April 14, 1905, at the age of thirty-four.

the voting took place seven times before any name gained the necessary majority. Mother Agnes of Jesus had won the esteem of the community by her firmness and gentleness, but Mother Mary Gonzaga's personality was preferred by several of the nuns; finally, the latter was elected by a small majority.[7] Released from the duties of superior, Mother Agnes of Jesus could have found time to read her little sister's manuscript, but she did not give it a thought, owing to the important events which had just taken place. It was not till two months later that she remembered the matter; then her interest was aroused by the charming account which she gave to her two other sisters that they might share her pleasure.

On taking up the reins of government once more, the imperious Mother Mary Gonzaga decided to keep the monopoly of authority in her own hands; she retained the office of Mistress of Novices, keeping Sister Thérèse as her assistant. She appreciated the excellent religious spirit of the young Assistant Mistress, who had the gift of supporting authority without ever flattering. In talking to her novices, Thérèse once warned them of "the poisonous food of praise served daily to superiors."

Though she continued her duties as Assistant Mistress of Novices, Thérèse never received that title. In her humility, she had asked to be treated thus. She wished to remain among the novices "as one of themselves," taking the part of an elder sister. This modest view coincided with the ideas of Mother Mary Gonzaga. Thérèse remained in the Noviciate to the end of her life, and never took the place in the Chapter House that was hers by right. In addition to her work among the novices, she was also nominated again to help the Sister Sacristan.

"Although suffering is exceedingly meritorious for the human soul, when offered to God with love, still suffering is not pleasing to God for its own sake."[8] Thérèse of the Child Jesus would willingly have put her signature to these words which are an echo of her own inmost thoughts. Fearing that any one should

[7] Mother Agnes of Jesus was later re-elected Prioress. At the request of the Community, Pope Pius XI confirmed her in that office for life.
[8] Canon Paul Travert.

find God harsh and severe because He allows suffering, she took care to explain:

"Our suffering, in itself, does not give God pleasure. He sends us suffering as with eyes averted."

The extreme delicacy of her filial love wished to reconcile the distressing problem of human suffering with the belief in God's infinite tenderness for His creatures; her clear solution of the difficulty is in accordance with theological teaching. Suffering itself is not the work of God who is Infinite Goodness — the Loving Father from whom we receive all good things; suffering is the work of sin, the fruit of Adam's fall. This bitter fruit is utilised by the divine mercy as a healing remedy — an ennobling remedy sent by Love; it is an exceptional means of sanctification and prepares us for everlasting glory "Oh! what a consoling thought!" exclaimed the Saint. "I understand now why God allows us to suffer." She loved those words of St. Paul: "The sufferings of the present are not worthy to be compared with the glory to come that will be revealed in us."[9] Accepting this principle, Thérèse desired suffering, in order to profit to the full extent of this means of sanctification. With heroic love, she sought and welcomed this saving remedy. "O Holy Cross, sweet rest of my soul!" St. Teresa of Avila used to exclaim. "Suffering has become heaven on earth to me," declared St. Thérèse of Lisieux.

After her great oblation, however, her longing for suffering was lost in the one great desire of always accomplishing God's Adorable Will perfectly. Divine grace enlightened her soul ever more and more clearly with its penetrating rays. In her *Autobiography*, she tells us:

"I have no desire left, unless it be to love Jesus even unto folly! It is Love alone that draws me. I no longer wish for suffering or death, though I cherish both. For a long time, I called upon them as messengers of joy . . . now the spirit of abandonment alone is my guide; I can no longer desire anything ardently save the perfect accomplishment of God's designs upon my soul."

[9] Rom. 8:18.

In His instructions to His disciples, our Lord frequently taught them that this is perfect love.

In union with her Saviour, Thérèse wished to be obedient even unto death. Passive under the action of divine grace, "she wished to have no desires whatever of her own, not even the choice of her martyrdom."[10] Her will was entirely absorbed in the Divine Will; she had reached the state of perfect abandonment.

"The summit of the mountain of Love," explains Monsignor Gay, *"is complete Abandonment, and the highest peak of this summit is the Spirit of Childhood."*

In this height, Thérèse had established her dwelling; it might be more correct to say that our Lord Himself had taken her up and placed her there. What would God now decree for His little Victim of Holocaust, who, with her eyes closed, abandoned herself entirely to His unfailing Love, ready for the supreme sacrifice? As in our Lord's own life, the folly of the crib was to be followed by the folly of the cross!

4. *Approach of the Divine Spouse*

The Lenten season of 1896 was drawing to its close. Strengthened by her fervour and energy of will, Thérèse had taken part in all the penitential exercises of this holy season and was seemingly in perfect health. After remaining for hours in adoration before the Altar of Repose on Holy Thursday, she withdrew at midnight as she had not obtained permission to remain in prayer throughout the night. A quotation from her *Autobiography* tells us what then took place; no other words could equal the sublime simplicity of that account.

"I returned to our cell at midnight. Scarcely had I laid my head on the pillow than I felt a rush of blood surge to my lips. I thought I was going to die and my heart nearly broke with joy. However, as I had already put out the lamp, I mortified my curiosity until the morning, and quietly fell asleep."

"What stoic was ever capable of such self-restraint?" asks François Mauriac in his book *Maundy Thursday*.[11] "Was it really

[10] François Mauriac.   [11] *Le Jeudi Saint.*

blood she had coughed up? The answer to that question would be a messenger of life or death, and yet this prudent virgin did not relight her lamp but remained serenely calm in the darkness of that Holy Thursday night."

"Let us not underestimate the surpassing heroism of such self-control," remarks Father Petitot. "By the asceticism of her Little Way, Thérèse had acquired an exceptional command over her faculties." The gift of Fortitude had indeed been given her; docile to the interior inspiration which urged her to the most complete abandonment of self, she commended her future to God's hands and quietly fell asleep.

When the signal for rising sounded at five o'clock the next morning, she awoke and immediately remembered that she had "some good news to learn," as she tells us. Approaching the window, she perceived, by the pale light of dawn, that her handkerchief was stained with blood. It was indeed a hæmorrhage, one of the first signs of that dread malady, tuberculosis, the very name of which causes the most courageous to shudder. The words used by the Saint to relate this tragic discovery show that she lived on heights, far above this world; she calls it "a sweet distant murmur heralding the joyful approach of the Divine Spouse."

Quiet heroism indeed! And did not God mean her to be given as a sister, a protector, and an example to all those feverish sufferers whose mortal illness she shared? Thought of her, love of her, prayer for her intercession should be as rays of golden sunlight to those who languish in sanatoriums and live in constant anguish of approaching death!

On that Good Friday morning, after learning "the good news" of her fatal illness, the saintly little Carmelite, happy and serene, joined the Community in the Chapel for the recitation of the morning Office; it was only after Chapter that she went to tell her Prioress what had occurred. Narrating the incident, she writes: "I had been longing to cast myself on my knees to confide my happy secret to my Mother." Then she adds: "I easily obtained permission to finish Lent as I had begun."

The remark would seem to indicate that Mother Mary Gonzaga did not attach any importance to this alarming symptom. Of a strong constitution and without personal experience of illness herself, she was little inclined to trouble about the care and attention which prudence ought otherwise to have suggested. Her great aim was to uphold the austerity of the Rule. And then Thérèse herself was so serenely happy, assuring her that she felt neither fatigue nor pain. This alone may have banished in her any lurking suspicion. The sisterly eyes of Mother Agnes of Jesus, however, were not so easily deceived!

Without the least relaxation of their Rule, Thérèse followed all the austerities prescribed at Carmel for Good Friday. But, though transported with joy at the prospect of going to heaven so soon, she had nonetheless great difficulty in reaching the end of the day without mishap. Like the other nuns, she had taken nothing all day except a little bread and some cold water. In the evening, she was occupied in cleaning windows. A novice, who loved the Saint dearly, could not restrain her tears on seeing the poor sufferer so pale and exhausted. She begged Thérèse to allow her to inform the Prioress, but the young Novice Mistress would not hear of such a thing.

Later that evening, another hæmorrhage showed that the matter was serious. The young nun fully realised her state; in truth she had understood the danger from the outset, for her penetrating mind was not one to harbour an illusion. Moreover, she felt that her soul was ready to take its flight to heaven. Even in the early part of the year 1895, she had told one of the nuns that she did not expect to live more than two or three years at the most, on account of what was taking place in her soul.

She was soon to leave her dear Carmel of Lisieux in any case, for it had been decided that, if her health permitted, she would go to the Foreign Missions. The Carmelites of Hanoï in China had earnestly petitioned for her to be sent to them, and Mother Mary Gonzaga was ready to give her consent.

In her *Autobiography,* the Saint states her motives for wishing to go to a foreign land: she longed to be in a convent where she would be utterly unknown and where her heart would feel the loneliness of exile, far from her sisters and from the Carmel she loved. This desire was no mere suggestion of a lively imagination. She clearly states that her only aim was to accomplish the Divine Will, as this was made evident to her by the attraction she felt for a voluntary exile. She wished to offer her Beloved every kind of suffering of which her heart was capable. On the day of her profession, though little more than a child in years, she had asked for the martyrdom of her heart. This had long been hers, to such an extent, indeed, that God judged it sufficient. She had asked also for bodily martyrdom; that form of suffering was just beginning. There was yet a third martyrdom which she had not foreseen; that form of torture was now to add its all-but-crushing weight to her other sufferings — it was the martyrdom of her mind.

5. *Martyrdom of the Mind*

Thérèse's faith had always been a sure, unhesitating faith, and the thought of heaven was constantly with her. She could not believe that people really exist who are utterly devoid of faith. The suffering of her mind began suddenly in the happy Paschal Season that year, as she recounts in her *Autobiography.* "During the Paschal days, so full of light, our Lord made me understand that there really are souls bereft of faith and hope."

Scarcely had this reality been impressed on her mind than she was assailed by doubt. God had preserved her from all temptation of the flesh, and the witnesses of her life declare that she seemed "wrapt in innocence"; the terrible trial that awaited her was the temptation against faith.

Before beginning His public life, the Saviour was led by the Spirit into the desert to be tempted by the devil; before beginning the miraculous apostolate that was hers after death,

Thérèse of the Child Jesus was to be tormented by the father of lies. This trial caused an intensity of suffering she had never imagined. Her mind, so upright, straight forward, and sincere, was harassed by the most materialistic doubts, while diabolic voices sneered in derision: "Continue . . . continue as you are doing . . . rejoice in death, which will not give you the joy for which you hope, but the night of nothingness."

Who can imagine the anguish of such a trial? It was a heart-breaking, oppressive temptation to despair. She herself tried to describe its horror, but hesitated and laid down her pen, fearing to utter blasphemy. Was this not a proof that true faith was still hers? The heroic, strong-willed, intrepid Saint admits that such a temptation might have discouraged her earlier in life; at present, the heavy cross served to supernaturalise any feeling of natural satisfaction that she might have experienced in her longing for the heavenly Fatherland. The refining furnace of God's Love purifies till only the purest gold remains!

What burning zeal for souls is revealed in the humble, loving words of the prayer she addressed to her Lord and God:

"Lord, Your child asks pardon for her unbelieving brethren. For love of You she will sit at that table of bitterness where poor sinners take their food; she has no wish to rise from it until You give the sign. But may she not say in her own name and in the name of her guilty brethren: 'O God, be merciful to us sinners.' Send us away justified. . . . The only favour I ask of You is that I may never offend You."

For the salvation of souls, she was willing to endure the anguish of this suffering, by which her mind was to be tormented till her dying day. With the courage of a lion she fought relentlessly against her unseen enemy: "Though I had not the consolations of faith, I forced myself to perform works in accordance with faith." In one year, she made more Acts of Faith than in the whole of her previous life. To prove her determination to believe, she wrote with her own blood the formula of the Creed, which she bore on her heart as a testimony day and night. At each new onslaught of the tempter, she hastened to her Saviour for protection, assuring Him that she was ready to shed her blood to prove her belief in the existence of heaven. How many souls she must have saved by this agonizing torture!

Humbly, she proclaimed herself happy to endure such anguish if she could thus prevent or atone for one single sin against faith. Could joy be mingled with such bitterness? Her *Autobiography* asserts that this could be so:

"Notwithstanding this trial, which deprives me of all consolation, I can still say 'You have given me, O Lord, delight in all You do.' "

Joy and suffering can exist together in a soul only when love is stronger than both. St. Thérèse of the Child Jesus realised this fact; she considered that joy — one of the fruits of the Holy Ghost — is a supreme proof of love. Monsignor Gay has said: "The seeking after joy indicates a true understanding of the grace of baptism." Basis of true joy is the Divine Life infused into the soul at baptism. What is eternal happiness? It is God, Father, Son, and Holy Ghost, God who sees, knows, and loves Himself. Paradise is the sharing in this happiness. Even on earth, in those perfect souls, who "lose their life" to find it again in the Divine Life to which they have entirely surrendered themselves, "extreme suffering and extreme happiness co-exist in a harmony of peace which surpasseth all understanding."[12] Thus, from now till the end of her earthly life, suffering and joy were united inseparably in the soul of St. Thérèse of the Holy Child and of the Holy Face.

To the sufferings of the mind was added the alarming state of the young Carmelite's health. Of this she had said nothing to her sisters, but their affection for her could not fail to make them notice a dry, persistent cough which she could not conceal. Doctor de Cornière, who attended the Convent, and Doctor La Néele, her cousin's husband, were consulted. After a serious examination, in the hope of effecting a cure, they prescribed

[12] Father Bernadot.

the use of cupping-glasses, the applying of leeches and red-hot needles, and strengthening diet. The warm days of the summer months helped the treatment, and there was soon an improvement in her condition. On July 12, of that year, 1896, she wrote to Léonie:

"You ask for news of my health. You will be pleased to know that my cough has almost disappeared. However, that will not prevent our Lord from taking me to Himself whenever He wishes . . . my great desire is to remain as a tiny little child."

She abandoned herself to the divine Will, but felt sure that she would not get well, and almost regretted the improvement, for she exclaimed: "Sickness is, truly, too slow a liberator; I can only rely upon Love."

6. *The Chapter Wonderful*

It was in that same year that Sister Mary of the Sacred Heart felt herself drawn to confide in her god-child. Through the written reply of the latter, we know the godmother's humble confession. She was depressed at feeling a dislike for suffering and humiliation, and wished to experience the same longing desires as her little sister, especially the desire for martyrdom. With penetrating words of wisdom and conviction, Thérèse consoled her godmother, reminding her of the fact that "the martyrs suffered with joy, and the King of Martyrs in sorrow."

"My desire for martyrdom counts for nothing," she explained; "that is not the reason why God takes pleasure in my little soul. What pleases Him is the fact that I love my littleness and my poverty, and that I have a blind trust in His Mercy."[13]

She assured Sister Mary of the Sacred Heart that these humble dispositions could be hers if she wished. The latter, willing to follow her god-child's lucid doctrine, asked for a detailed explanation of the "Little Way." Having obtained permission for this work from Mother Mary Gonzaga, the Saint then wrote the admirable pages which form the eleventh chapter of her *Auto-*

[13] Letter written to Sister Mary of the Sacred Heart.

biography.[14] In this masterful exposition of her Little Way of confidence and love, her apostolic zeal is revealed in many beautiful passages.

In a simple but very affectionate manner, she expressed her delight at being able to have this little talk with her dearly loved godmother, who had pronounced the baptismal promises in her name, and who was her sister by the double bond of nature and of grace. Then she stressed her own state of constant aridity:

"My consolation is to feel that I have none on earth."

Passing then to her favourite theme of love and abandonment, she proclaimed that Love had ever been her sole ambition, since "Love alone can make us pleasing to God," and explained that our Lord had deigned to make her understand that the only means of acquiring this Divine Love is "the abandonment of a little child who sleeps trustfully in its father's arms." Further on in her explanation, she insists once more on the secret of her sanctity: "Jesus has no need of our works; He needs only our love." Having abandoned herself entirely to God's action in her soul, the Saint knew by experience what complete renunciation and hidden self-sacrifice are necessary before God takes entire possession of a soul; she knew that only souls stripped of all self-seeking can really please Him, but she had observed that such total abnegation is very rare.

"Alas!" she exclaimed, "even among His chosen ones, how few surrender themselves unreservedly to the tenderness of His infinite Love!"

On May 10, about a month after her painful way of the cross had started, a consoling dream assured her that Divine

[14] In the latest edition of the Autobiography, this forms the thirteenth chapter. It is now known that there were three separate manuscripts, though the earliest publication of this *Autobiography* joined the three manuscripts into one, with a somewhat different arrangement of the chapters. The first manuscript — Chapters I to VIII in the latest edition — was addressed in 1895 to her sister, Mother Agnes of Jesus; the second — Chapters IX to XII — was written, in 1897, for Mother Mary Gonzaga, then Prioress; the third — the beautiful Chapter XIII — was addressed to Sister Mary of the Sacred Heart, in 1897. An extract from this third manuscript has been inserted in the Appendix, pp. 252-258. — [Translator.]

Love was satisfied with the work accomplished in her soul. The Venerable Mother Anne of Jesus, foundress of the first Carmelite convent of the Reform in France and beloved daughter of St. Teresa of Avila, appeared to her in a dream, assuring her that her soul was very pleasing to God, who would soon call her to Himself. Then she caressed Thérèse and kissed her very tenderly. The remembrance of this sweet dream encouraged her to try to express in words, for her godmother's sake, the boundless desires that transported her soul.

"To be Your spouse, O my Jesus, and, through my union with You, to be the mother of souls, should not that be sufficient for me? And yet I feel in my heart other callings."

The most heroic works and every form of martyrdom appealed to her generous soul. She longed to be a champion of the faith, a priest, an apostle, a doctor of the Church, a martyr; she wished to preach the Gospel in every country in the world, and would have liked to be a missionary whose zealous work extended from the beginning of the world until the consummation of time!

"O my Jesus," she exclaimed, "open Your Book of Life, in which are written the deeds of Your saints; I should love to have accomplished all those actions for You."[15]

Was it not foolish to cherish these unbounded desires to do good in every age and in every land? Thérèse herself said to our Lord: "To such folly as mine, what will You reply?" And yet she felt sure that there was no exaggeration in her language, for peace reigned in her heart. Humble and docile to God's inspirations, she abandoned herself to the impulse of the Holy Ghost; it was truly His spirit that guided her soul in its lofty ascent.

Addressing her Divine Lord lovingly, she proclaimed:

"You did always accede to my childish desires, and to-day You will grant other desires more vast than the universe."

The ever increasing ardour of her aspirations became a real martyrdom, until she sought relief for her sufferings in the

[15] See Appendix, p. 252, for the whole of this very beautiful passage.

writings of St. Paul, who explains that the most perfect gifts are nothing without love and that charity is the most excellent way of going straight to God. Then, suddenly, she saw clearly that love includes all vocations, that love is everything, that love embraces all ages and reaches to the uttermost limits of the earth, because it is eternal.

"My vocation is Love," she exclaimed delightedly. "In the heart of the Church, my Mother, I shall be Love! Thus I shall be all things; thus will my dream be realised . . . I cannot preach the Gospel nor shed my blood. That does not matter. I shall remain close to the royal throne, like a little child, and I shall love You for all who are in the combat."

All her actions were enriched with this pure, perfect love. She wished to suffer with love — and with love she rejoiced. Joys that come to us from God's hand are indeed occasions of merit, if we receive them with thanksgiving. Thus, notwithstanding her "exceeding littleness," Thérèse dared to aspire to the plentitude of love. "I am not an eagle," she exclaimed, "I have but the eagle's eyes and heart."

That eaglelike gaze, which she fixed on the Divine Sun of Love, was her childlike confidence which never wavered. She knew that Jesus was the divine Eagle who would transport her on His wings; she knew that, satisfied with her weak endeavours, He would bestow on her His own merits and make her holy.

"O Word Eternal! O my Saviour! You are the Eagle whom I love and who draws me to Yourself. Descending to this land of exile, You wished to suffer and to die in order to bear away all souls and to plunge them into the very heart of the Blessed Trinity, the everlasting home of Love! . . . One day, I firmly hope, You will swoop down on me, and, carrying me off to the furnace of Love, You will plunge me at last into that burning abyss, so that I shall be forever Love's happy victim!"

In His work throughout the universe, God — whose every act is Love — associates with Himself souls who abandon themselves to His Love and follow His guidance in all things. With a prophet's vision, St. Thérèse foresaw the wonders that God wished to accomplish through her; in a penetrating gaze into the future, she caught a glimpse of the far-reaching influence that would be hers when she had left this world.

The Spirit of the Lord hovers over the closing pages of the *Autobiography* and causes us to prostrate before Him in wondering adoration, in deep emotion, almost in trembling awe.

Lord, we praise You, in Your saints, whose brightness comes from Your own Divine Light.

7. *Love Even Unto Folly*

But Thérèse was still on earth and had one more year to live here below, in suffering and in love! The month of October returned, and the chestnut trees of the cloister garden, whose autumn-tinted foliage stood out against the pale blue sky, began to shed their leaves. The autumn mists penetrated everywhere, making the mornings chilly and the evenings damp. Thérèse's cough returned, as she worked in her cold cell. By November, all the leaves had fallen and winter had set in, the bitter winter of 1896.

Thérèse's cell was somewhat apart from the other cells, so no one heard her coughing; she was glad that no one knew of the painful nights she endured. The cold penetrated her through and through. After Matins, shivering in her heavy, coarse habit, with its wide, open sleeves, she had to pass along icy-cold corridors to reach her cell. Her hands were numbed with the cold and she was so exhausted that she could scarcely undress. Then, on her hard bed covered by two blankets worn with use, she sometimes shivered all through the night. Nevertheless, at the first sound of the bell the next morning, she would rise promptly to begin another day of prayer and work. Looking at her crucifix, she would say:

"My Jesus, You worked and suffered . . . it is my turn now to suffer and to strive."

The folly of her love was satisfied in the daily martyrdom, in which she felt her physical strength growing weaker and her whole being breaking down and failing utterly. She did not ask

for any relief, for, in her childlike simplicity, she thought that
God would inspire her Superior to accord her the necessary care,
if that were His Divine Will. Mother Mary Gonzaga remained
blind to the seriousness of the matter. She was accustomed to
seeing Thérèse suffer and was deceived by the Saint's strength
of soul and incredible energy. In the depth of winter, the invalid
once did laundry work in the open air, having her hands in
icy-cold water for several hours. Under such circumstances, it is
no wonder that the remedies employed were powerless to cure
the malady. However, the work of Assistant Sacristan was considered too tiring for her, and she was relieved of that occupation; she was given needlework to do instead. Once, when she
was alone in her cell and occupied in sewing, a novice, who
happened to enter, was struck by her recollected attitude and
questioned her as to the subject of her thoughts. Raising her
beautiful eyes filled with happy tears, she replied:

"I am meditating on the Our Father. It is so consoling to be
able to call God 'Our Father.' "

In truth, she soared aloft beyond her sufferings and all created
things with supreme serenity, but, as her example was to remain
accessible to all, her sublime contemplation may be summed up
and expressed in this prayer, the simplest and yet the most
beautiful of Christianity. It was our Lord Himself who taught
it to His disciples, saying, "Thus therefore shall you pray: Our
Father, who art in heaven, hallowed be thy name . . ."[16]

To celebrate the Feast of the Nativity that year, Thérèse,
despite her serious physical condition, had the courageous energy
to compose verses in honor of the Divine Child. They are dated
December 25, 1896, the last Christmas that she was to celebrate
on earth.

The remaining winter months were spent in silent heroism;
only in heaven shall we know the details of that supreme period
of suffering and of love. Her soul was well-nigh crushed by the
weight of the trial she did not understand, and her body was
worn out by the course of the illness.

[16] Matt. 6:9.

Though scarcely able to stand, the heroic Saint continued her religious life. The evening before that on which she attended recreation for the last time, it took her more than half an hour to reach her cell; at almost every step of the stairs she was obliged to rest, for she was practically exhausted. A novice "who loved her dearly," Sister Mary of the Blessed Trinity, could no longer keep silence. Although forbidden by her mortified Novice Mistress to speak of the matter, she thought it time to inform the Prioress. Mother Mary Gonzaga at last realised the danger, and Thérèse was then given all the necessary care. But the disease had grown incurable. It was only in May that her three sisters were told of the hæmorrhage which had occurred in April of the previous year. Mother Agnes of Jesus reproached her little sister gently for having kept silence on such a matter. But the latter had concealed the fact in order not to grieve them; she was now unable to avoid wounding their hearts by the sorrowful news.

During the final months of intense suffering, the Saint upheld them with her tender affection. She felt that it was no longer necessary to deny herself the consolations derived from their mutual love. Her heart, wholly void of self and entirely penetrated by Divine Love, was free to bestow on those she loved a tenderness incomparably greater than if it had been "concentrated in a selfish and unfruitful love."

Thus the elder sisters had the consolation of resuming their familiar intercourse with their "little Thérèse," and had the joy of seeing that her extreme tenderness of affection had been purified and strengthened by her union with God, until it resembled something of His own divine Love. They surrounded their dearly loved, saintly, little sister with tender care, but were powerless to avert the approaching hour of her death. From her example and her teaching, they drew the strength to accept generously the heart-breaking separation which was inevitable.

CHAPTER XIV

LAST MEMORABLE SAYINGS

1. *Petals Scattered by the Rose*

MOTHER AGNES OF JESUS realised Thérèse's holiness; she understood something of the wonderful work wrought by God in the sublime simplicity of her sister's soul, and therefore decided to write down the precious sayings that fell from the latter's lips. Thérèse noticed this but made no objection, for praise could no longer cause her any self-satisfaction. She considered herself only "a poor little nothing" whom God might use for the good of souls if He so willed.

These sayings, *Novissima Verba,* recorded so carefully by Mother Agnes of Jesus, form a most precious spiritual testament. The first words, thus noted, were uttered on May 1, when the Saint felt a spiritual sweetness from the nearness of the Blessed Virgin and exclaimed: "My heart has been filled with celestial joy to-day."

What intense love she had ever felt for her heavenly Mother! Her last poem, full of tenderness and charm, was written in honour of the Mother of God in the spring of that year. Dwelling particularly on the humble life led by our Blessed Lady on earth, these verses tell us how the vast number of lowly souls here below "dare without fear or trembling" look up to her:

> For thou didst tread the common path,
> O peerless Mother mine,
> That little souls might follow thee
> Where Heaven's joys are thine.

Thérèse of the Child Jesus loved to meditate on the hidden life at Nazareth, where the presence of the Incarnate God and the wonderful holiness of His Mother were unnoticed in the lowliness of their surroundings. Her own eminent virtues and graces were likewise hidden under the simplicity of her actions. Imitating the Virgin Mary, she never thought of displaying her privileges to human eyes.

In a poem, written in May, to which she gave the title "The Rose Unpetaled," the gracious Saint compared herself to a rose which spends its sweetness in scattering its petals. In this charming way, she expressed her own longing to be despoiled of everything for God's glory, and her wish that, for the joy of the Holy Child, she might scatter, as it were, her petals before Him:

> So that Thy little foot, while gently treading,
> May press upon a flower.[1]

In showering its petals the rose yields up its life, "to be no more," and so these scattered petals seemed to Thérèse the image of a soul that has abandoned itself without reserve to God's good pleasure. "To be no more" had ever been her great desire. She wished that self would disappear entirely, so that God could reign supreme.

Thérèse had often meditated on the words spoken by God to Moses from the Burning Bush: "I am who am."[2] God alone has the right to say "I am"; everything else exists only through Him. God completed this definition in a revelation to St. Catherine of Siena when He said: "I am who am; thou art who art not." These concise words express the exact truth of the relation between the Creator and the creature — the All and the nothing. The bridge that spans the abyss is Love. "He, who is, is Love," says St. John. "He, who is, is Merciful Love," adds St. Thérèse of the Child Jesus, thus casting a ray of exceeding sweetness and hope upon everything. God Almighty is the Father of Mercy; He is our Father.

On May 15, Mother Agnes of Jesus noted the following words, which reveal — in striking terms — Thérèse's close union with God:

---

[1] The whole of this poem, *La Rose effeuillée*, is given in French together with an English translation, in the Appendix, pp. 250, 251.
[2] Exod. 3:14.

"I cannot think what more I shall have after my death; it is true I shall see God, but as to being with Him — that I am already here on earth."

Nevertheless, this consciousness of her intimate union with God did not prevent her from rejoicing exceedingly at the thought of going to heaven so soon. But some of the nuns, Mother Agnes of Jesus once mentioned to her, thought she would be afraid when the moment of death actually came.

"That may be," she replied; "I know how weak I am, but I wish to enjoy the present happiness that God gives me. When the time comes, it will be sufficient to bear that cross if it pleases God to send it."

"About the details of her funeral she spoke with the greatest calm and requested her friends not to buy wreaths for her grave, but to spend the money on the ransom of little Negro children. Frequently, she expressed her total abandonment to God:

"God has always helped me and has led me by the hand since my childhood; I depend entirely upon Him. I do not desire death more than life; I leave God to choose, and whatever His choice will be, that I shall love."

A few days later she exclaimed:

"I am as one risen; I am no longer where people think." In truth, no one realised the sublime heights to which she soared!

2. *Thérèse Completes Her "Autobiography"*

On May 27, Mother Agnes of Jesus noted a simple phrase that has meant much to the world, because it was the immediate cause of the continuation of her *Autobiography:*

"I am glad that I shall have a circular letter after my death."

It is namely the custom in Carmelite convents, on the death of a member of the community, to have a biographical notice printed and sent to all the convents of the Order, in the form of a circular letter. But as Mother Agnes of Jesus wrote the words, "a circular letter," she probably thought at once of the manuscript in her possession. She remembered that it was not complete and knew that Thérèse had so many other treasures to share. Accordingly, on June 2 toward midnight, urged by a supernatural inspiration and after fervent prayer, the elder sister went to her Prioress and mentioned that Thérèse had once written some "Recollections of Childhood" which might be of use in furnishing matter for the customary circular letter; she added that the manuscript contained little relating to the religious life and was therefore insufficient. She then humbly suggested that Mother Mary Gonzaga should tell Thérèse to write something more important, which would be of incomparably greater value.

The suggestion pleased the Prioress, who told Thérèse the very next day to continue writing her *Autobiography*. The young nun immediately obeyed without understanding at first why such a task had been given to her. "Mother," she said in her sweet simplicity, "I cannot help smiling at the idea of writing you an account of things that you know as well as I do. However, I shall obey."

In the course of her narrative, the humble child thanks Mother Mary Gonzaga for "not having spared her." Then she remarks that for the last few months — the last few months only! — the Divine Master "has completely changed His method for the cultivation of His little Flower," and again she thanks her Prioress for this changed attitude of confidence and affection.

Within a month, she wrote about fifty pages of her neat writing, in a style which was as fresh and spontaneous as when she had written, in good health, for her little Mother. The final pages, however, were completed only at the cost of very great effort. Much of this manuscript was written in the garden during the month of June, 1897, under the chestnut trees once more in bloom, as she sat in the invalid-chair used by Monsieur Martin during his illness. Toward the end she used a pencil, as even the effort of dipping her pen in the ink was too tiring for her ebbing vitality.

When, before beginning her writing, she had been told that

her manuscript would be used for the subject matter of her circular letter, she was not in the least disturbed. Nothing could now disturb her peace of soul.

"What shall I write about?" she had asked Mother Agnes of Jesus.

"On the novices or on charity," was the reply.

The accounts and the reflections then written by the saintly Carmelite form a wonderful little treatise on fraternal charity, showing sound practical spirituality and deep psychological insight into character. Arrived at the end of life's journey, she summed up all her teaching — as did St. John the Apostle — in the word Charity. She understood fully our Lord's words: "The Second Commandment is like unto the First," and that by a new precept — His own — Christ has commanded us to love our brethren, not only as ourselves, but as He Himself loves them. As He never commands us to do anything which is impossible, His little spouse turned to Him confidently for help, saying:

"You know that I shall never succeed in loving my sisters in the Community as You love them, unless You — dwelling in my heart — love them again within me." She was firmly convinced on that point: Jesus wished to love in her those whom He commanded her to love. Whenever she did an act of charity, it was Jesus who acted in her. "It is Jesus concealed in my poor, little heart," she would say.

However, it was not without effort and many a hard struggle that she had acquired this perfect charity toward her neighbour, as she herself relates. But now she realised that "true charity consists in bearing with the faults of others, in never being astonished at their weakness, and in being edified at their smallest virtues." It is not sufficient to love those who please us; we must love also those who displease or weary us, those whose ideals seem lower than our own, those who are still very imperfect, and even those for whom we feel a natural antipathy. Thérèse compared these characters to the lame and the paralytic who were invited to the feast as described by Jesus in the Gospel.[3]

[3] Luke 14:13, 14.

To them she offered the delightful banquet of sweet kindness and cheerful amiability, knowing that she would please her Divine Spouse by this most pure charity. It was of such virtues and sacrifices that the tissue of her life was woven. She calls them "little" sacrifices, but they will be appreciated at their value by those who know the difficulties and trials of community life.

All combat had long since ceased, for the generous-minded Saint had triumphed over her natural inclinations. Love reigned in her heart. In her *Autobiography*, we find this exclamation:

"My Jesus, I verily believe You could not bestow more love upon a soul than You have lavished upon mine."

She was astonished at her own words — written quite unintentionally — but she did not erase them, as they affirmed the boundless love with which God had favoured her soul" without any merit on her part." Her ardent desire was that this love should be bestowed equally on all whom she loved. "I beseech You, 'that the love with which Thou hast loved me may be in them,' "[4] she implored, making use of our Lord's own words to His heavenly Father.

The dying nun's remaining strength failed. Writing became impossible; she could not even hold her pencil. Her last effort had been for sinners, for whom she ever prayed so earnestly; the last passage of this manuscript is a touching appeal to them to have confidence in God's Mercy. She laid emphasis on the fact that it was not on account of her preservation from mortal sin — due to God's protecting grace — that she was able to lift up her heart to Him with confidence and love, and then exclaimed:

"I know that I should lose nothing of my confidence, even if I had on my conscience every crime that could be committed. Heart-broken with repentance, I would throw myself into the arms of my Saviour. I know that He loves the Prodigal Son; I have heard His words to St. Mary Magdalen, to the woman taken in adultery, and to the Samaritan woman. No one could

[4] John 17:26. Jesus addressed these words to the Eternal Father, but Thérèse used them in a prayer which she addressed to Jesus Himself.

make me fear, for I know what to believe concerning His love and His Mercy. I know that all that multitude of sins would disappear in an instant, as a drop of water cast into a flaming furnace."

3. *Triumph of Spiritual Childhood*

In the beginning of June, Thérèse had said words of parting to her three sisters. Notwithstanding her Little Way, which desired nothing exceptional in the events of life or at death, she asked the Blessed Virgin to obtain for her "a beautiful death," hoping thereby to console her sisters in their sorrow. Some time later, she remarked: "I shall not die at night; I have asked this favour from our Blessed Lady."

Thérèse knew that her death was approaching. She felt sure of this, although many of the nuns thought otherwise. Some did not even believe that she was really ill; others considered that she had suffered very little during her life. In reality, she had always known how to find joy in every form of bitterness.

One day, exhausted with pain, she was resting in her cell, when she overheard a remark made by the sister who worked in the kitchen:

"Sister Thérèse of the Child Jesus will not live long. I wonder what our Mother Prioress will find to say about her after her death. . . . This little sister is very amiable, but has certainly never done anything worth recounting."

The Saint smiled and said nothing, for the opinion of creatures did not trouble her. She left the judgement of her actions to Him who reads the secrets of hearts.

Seeing the danger of her state, those who loved her were distressed at the thought that she might die without receiving Extreme Unction. She herself had a great desire to receive the grace of this sacrament instituted for the sick, but waited humbly until others would decide that the time had come for administering that consoling sacrament.

"If you should find one morning that I had passed away during the night, do not be grieved at that," she once remarked with her heroic smile, presumably after a night of intense suffering. "Just think that God, my kind Father, my Papa, came to fetch me."

With feelings of inexpressibly sweet confidence, this perfect Child of God addressed her heavenly Father by the sweet name, Papa, which children of France give to their earthly father.

Her spirit of abandonment triumphed over every thought that might have caused anguish. She knew that everything that happens is a source of grace for a soul who loves God. She did not fear hell.

"Little children are not damned," she declared.

The thought of purgatory did not worry her; she was quite willing to go to its expiatory flames if God so decreed. "I shall sing the canticle of love there," she remarked. She had given all her merits[5] for the salvation of souls, reserving nothing for herself, and was able to state: "I have no works of my own." Her exceeding confidence is seen in the following remarks:

"If you only knew with what great indulgence I shall be judged. . . . Little ones will be judged with extreme tenderness."

In a photograph taken by Céline on June 7, we see the Saint on her knees in the garden, holding a twofold picture which represents the Child Jesus and the Holy Face. This picture, portraying the full name by which she had wished to be known, is an image of her soul. Suffering and love have moulded the perfect beauty of her countenance; her eyes reflect the holiness of her soul; her forehead, serene and pure, seems to express her interior peace of heart; there is something exceedingly dignified in her attitude, notwithstanding the fact that she was suffering and weakened by the consuming fever of her malady.

The same day, as she was walking in the garden, leaning for support on the arm of Mother Agnes of Jesus, she saw a white hen sheltering her tiny chickens under her wing. Remembering the comparison made by our Lord to illustrate His own tenderness for His creatures, she could not restrain her tears of gratitude.

[5] The word *merit* is not to be taken here in its strictly theological sense.

"That is exactly what He has done for me," she exclaimed. "He has covered me entirely with His wing."

Two days later, she made a remark to her godmother which has proved to be prophetic:

"You will see. After my death, I shall let fall a shower of roses."

Notwithstanding care and remedies and the fervent prayers offered for her recovery, Thérèse's state grew worse. She was exceedingly thin and had a high temperature constantly; the difficulty in breathing increased. The tuberculosis had become generalised.

To the question: "Are you suffering greatly?" she replied, "Yes, but I have so longed to suffer."

She had hoped to die in her cell, which was very dear to her, but on July 8 she was transferred to the Infirmary, where the miraculous statue of the Virgin, that had smiled on her in childhood, awaited her. Her Mother Mary was there to help her in the final combat.

In saying *Adieu* to the Community, the dying Saint addressed a few words of supernatural counsel to each of the nuns. About the middle of July, she wrote to one of her "missionary brothers," urging him to treat God with "the love and abandonment of a little child who knows that he is dearly loved by his Father." She was always faithful in praying for her spiritual brothers, and promised to make them understand from heaven the thoughts which she had not been able to express when on earth.

In her last letter to Léonie, dated July 17, she wrote these words of farewell advice to her sister:

"The only means of attaining true happiness on earth is to strive always to accept whatever God chooses for us as being the most delightful."

In this same month, Thérèse received a very touching letter from her kind uncle, Monsieur Guérin, who wrote to her for the last time:

" . . . You used to be the Little Queen of your aged father. . . . You are a privileged little soul. From your tenderest years you have gazed upon the Burning Bush; fascinated by its brightness, you have approached nearer and nearer, and soon you will become one with It. Farewell, my dearly loved child, from One who has the right, perhaps to call himself 'Your second Father.' "

4. *Words Large With Prophecy*

It was during the same month of July that Thérèse uttered words which are now known throughout the whole world:

"I feel that my mission is about to begin — my mission to make others love God as I love Him — to teach souls my *Little Way. I wish to spend my heaven in doing good upon earth.*"

Then she added the following remark, less often quoted but of the soundest doctrine:

"That will not be impossible, since the angels keep watch over us from the very heart of the Beatific Vision."

Her least utterances expressed such deep wisdom that the nuns urged her to speak on spiritual matters; her sisters, the novices, and even the older Religious came to her with questions, feeling that she was greatly enlightened by grace.

At last, the day dawned on which she was to receive the long-desired sacrament of extreme unction. On July 13, in the afternoon, Canon Maupas, Rector of St. James's Church at Lisieux and superior of the Carmelites of that town, administered the sacrament. For days, the dying nun had prepared for that grace with great fervour, and it was an unutterable joy for her to know that she was as pure "as a little child that has just been baptised."

The following day, she asked Mother Agnes of Jesus to paint a picture — after her death — for Doctor de Cornière, who attended her, and to inscribe the words: "What you have done unto the least of My little ones, you have done unto Me."

Then began the month of August. Patiently, Thérèse awaited death. Each morning, she hoped she would not reach the evening; each evening, she hoped not to see the dawn.

On August 3, she gave this beautiful definition of holiness:

"Sanctity does not consist in the practice of certain exercises of piety, but in a disposition of the heart which makes us humble and little in the arms of God, conscious of our weakness, but confiding — unhesitatingly — in His Fatherly Goodness."

On the eve of the Feast of the Transfiguration, with her usual thoughtfulness, Mother Agnes of Jesus placed beside Thérèse's bed a picture of the Holy Face. As the Saint gazed on this image to which she had such a great devotion — the likeness of her Beloved and her Model — she exclaimed: "Our Lord did well to close His Eyes in giving us the imprint of His Countenance, for the eyes are the mirror of the soul; if we had been able to gaze into His Soul, we should have died from joy." The tenderness of her love as Child of God was equalled by the ardour of her love as Spouse of Christ!

Sister Thérèse of the Child Jesus and of the Holy Face had hoped that God would call her to Himself on this wondrous feast of glory and joy. All night long, she contemplated the Face of her Beloved, but He seemed to abandon her altogether. "All night long, I waited for Jesus," she remarked the next morning. "I repelled many temptations . . . I made a great many acts of faith."

Jesus once asked two of His Apostles: "Can you drink of the cup of which I am about to drink?"[6] His Chalice, to drink this, means to be like unto Him even in being abandoned, to remain with Him in His agony, and to be identified with Him in desolation at the hour of death. It is the Holy Ghost who teaches us to follow Jesus until we become one with Him. Ever attentive to the inspirations of the Holy Spirit, Thérèse wished to have the most beautiful death that love can desire, the death of Jesus on the Cross. She did not wish to die in transports of love; she wished to be like her Divine Model in the anguish of that "Passion," which His Heart had desired to suffer, and which the divine Power allowed to be almost infinite in its agony.

The union of exceeding suffering and exceeding joy in her own soul made her understand something of the dereliction of Jesus on the Cross, as she herself states:

[6] Matt. 20:22.

"His soul was in possession of the supreme, infinite happiness of the Blessed Trinity; yet His agony was none the less terrible. That is a mystery, but I assure you I understand something of that mystery, from what I experience in my own soul."

Like St. Paul, she wished "to depart and to be with Christ."[7] Her own words were:

"What a joy it is to feel that I am wasting away!"

Striving to comfort her sisters, she exclaimed: "Do not grieve. See how happy God has made me. My dearest sisters, I should like you to rejoice!" As Father Petitot has written: "In her soul there seemed to be a glowing furnace of love for God and of holy joy which consumed all other things."

To encourage those who suffer, Thérèse wished them to know that she had *suffered greatly;* she explained that her joy and the transports of love existed only in the depths of her soul. In truth, she suffered to the very extreme limit. Covered with painful sores and parched with a burning thirst, she was so exhausted that she feared she would not retain the lucidity of her thoughts. For several days, her soul endured inexpressible anguish; mentally and physically, she felt as if she were in "a black hole."

All her life, to all God's wishes, she had responded with a sweet *Fiat* — "Be it done to me according to thy word" — as did the Virgin Mary at the Annunciation. But when the hour of death approached, she was to join her *Fiat* to that of her agonising Saviour in His Passion. "My God, my God, have pity on me. I can say no more," she murmured.

"Oh, how we should pray for those in their last agony. If people knew what they suffer!" she exclaimed one day. "I think Satan has asked God if he may tempt me with an excess of suffering to make me sin against patience and against faith."

The heroic Saint was never impatient, her faith never wavered; she seemed to be confirmed in confidence. The more God appeared to abandon her, the more she trusted in Him.

[7] Phil. 1:23.

"Oh! how good God is to help me to bear what I am enduring," she said. "Even if He should slay me, I would still trust in Him."

However, she never asked for greater suffering. "That would be self-willed suffering," she said. She considered that God owed her the grace necessary to bear the sufferings, which He Himself sent. The flood of suffering rose as the flood of love increased. She would smile graciously and murmur:

"What peace! what peace is mine!"

Her soul grew ever simpler.

"What do you say to Jesus?" asked one of the nuns.

"I say nothing; I just love Him," was the reply.

Notwithstanding the intensity of her suffering, she did not bear the sorrowful aspect of her crucified Lord. Her sweet face always retained its freshness and charm of expression. Was she not destined by God to charm all hearts?

"Oh! I know that everyone will love me," she remarked one day.

Several times she spoke to Mother Agnes of Jesus about the publication of her manuscript, which she considered "a very urgent and very important matter." On rereading it, she affirmed: *"These pages will do a great deal of good; God's Goodness will be better understood."* Then she added: "Every word I have written is true." On another day, she proclaimed:

"My Mission will be accomplished like that of Joan of Arc; God's Will shall be done, notwithstanding the jealousy of men. . . . *The saints encourage me, saying, 'As long as you are in the bonds of your mortal body, you cannot fulfil your mission; later on will come the time of your conquests.'"*

Unceasingly she prayed to the saints, whom she called her brothers and sisters. The dogma of the Communion of Saints delighted her.

"In heaven, we shall not be met with looks of cold indifference," she said, "for all the elect will recognise the fact that they owe to one another the graces which have enabled them to win their crown."

She loved to think that envy would be eternally banished from heaven. "How I long to be in that Kingdom of Love!" Her life was a perfect realisation of the words of her spiritual father, St. John of the Cross:

> Securely stay'd, yet without stay,
> Dark and unlighted all the day,
> Wholly am I consum'd away.[8]

5. *"To Die of Love"*

On August 19, St. Thérèse of the Child Jesus offered her Holy Communion for a well-known apostate of the time. This was the last time she received the Blessed Sacrament. During the year which had just passed, it had always cost her a very great effort to walk, even slowly, to the altar rails. Now the hæmorrhages were too frequent to allow her to communicate.

Thérèse had penetrated deeply into the meaning of our Lord's promise: "He who eats my flesh and drinks my blood, abides in me and I in him."[9] Now she was obliged to accept the very great privation of the absence of her Eucharistic Lord; she was to intensify her faith even to believing that God would henceforth communicate Himself to her and unite Himself to her soul without any intermediary means. She was fully conscious of this Divine Life within her, supporting and vivifying her.

At last came the month of September, the last that Thérèse was to spend on earth. "I long for heaven," she sighed. "Rend the veil which prevents me seeing You face to face, O my God."[10]

The doctor was amazed at the serenity of his patient. "She is an angel," he said; "if you knew what she is enduring!" He thought she had only one more day to live, but for thirty days more, without faltering, she was to mount her stern rugged path — stern and rugged for her soul, but fair and fruitful in God's eyes. "I make many little sacrifices," was her simple remark.

[8] The translation of these lines of St. John of the Cross is taken from the English version by Allison Peers.
[9] John 6:57.
[10] St. John of the Cross.

At times, however, she seemed again to have the consolation of foreseeing something of her future power. On the Feast of the Exaltation of the Holy Cross, September 14, she was given a rose. Tenderly, she detached the petals and shed them over her Crucifix. As some of the petals fell on the floor, she remarked:

"Be sure you pick up those petals; they will give pleasure later on."

Thirteen years later, a wonderful miracle was worked when an old man in the hospital at Lisieux was cured instantaneously of cancer of the tongue by touching one of these petals.

Another day, she made this extraordinary remark to her sisters who were at her bedside: "You know you are nursing a little saint." But this foreknowledge of her future greatness did not lessen the intensity of her sufferings. The feeling of suffocation was terrible and increased daily. No remedies could relieve her.

"You are suffering terribly," said one of the nuns.

"No," was the reply, "a little victim of love cannot think that any suffering is terrible since it comes to her from her Divine Spouse."

The dying Saint lived in the actual moment, accepting the suffering of each minute, without thought of the future. "We, who run in the way of love, should never allow ourselves to be troubled by anything," she wrote in her *Autobiography*. On another occasion, she affirmed the joy that existed in the depths of her soul:

"The angels cannot suffer; they are not as fortunate as I am!"

On the morning of September 29, she seemed in her agony; she could scarcely breathe.

"Mother, has my agony started?" she asked.

She felt her weakness, and sweetly acknowledged her littleness: "How shall I set about dying? I shall never know how to die."

She had always said she could do nothing alone. At the hour of death as in life, she counted on God alone, for she believed firmly in those words of our Lord to His disciples: "Without Me you can do nothing." After the doctor's visit, she asked her Prioress:

"Is it to-day, Mother?"

"Yes," replied Mother Mary Gonzaga.

"If it could be at once, what joy!" exclaimed the Saint.

When Sister Genevieve of the Holy Face asked her for a parting word, she replied:

"I have said all I have to say; all is accomplished; *it is Love alone that counts.*"

After Matins, she joined her hands and murmured:

"My God, my God, I wish all that You wish."

"You are in dreadful pain," said a Sister at her side.

"No," she answered, "not dreadful, just what I can bear."

Sister Mary of the Sacred Heart and Sister Genevieve of the Holy Face divided the hours of the night to watch at their dying sister's bedside. Then dawned the last day of Thérèse's earthly pilgrimage — a grey autumn morning. Mother Agnes of Jesus remained with her during Mass.

Fixing her eyes on the miraculous statue of the Virgin who had once smiled on her, the dying Carmelite murmured in intense anguish:

"I have prayed to her so earnestly, but I am in complete agony without the slightest consolation." Then she added: "But God will not abandon me; He has never abandoned me." And calling on His Mercy, she reminded Him of His divine goodness.

About three o'clock in the afternoon, she extended her arms in the form of a cross to resemble her Saviour, and then said to her Prioress:

"Oh, Mother, present me quickly to the Blessed Virgin; help me to die well."

Mother Mary Gonzaga told her she was ready to appear before her Judge because she had understood and practised the virtue of humility. After a moment's reflection, Thérèse replied humbly:

"Yes, I believe my soul has ever sought Truth; I have understood humility of heart. . . . All I have written about my longing for suffering is true."

Then, with conviction, she uttered these beautiful words:

"I do not regret having abandoned myself to Love."

"From that moment," says Mother Agnes of Jesus, *"it seemed as if it were no longer Thérèse who suffered."* She could, in very truth, repeat St. Paul's words: "It is now no longer I that live, but Christ lives in me."[11] It was indeed Jesus who lived and suffered in her. Then she repeated that memorable phrase:

"I do not regret having abandoned myself to Love . . . nay, on the contrary." And we know that her chalice was filled well-nigh to overflowing!

"I would never have believed that it was possible to suffer to such an extent," she murmured; "I can only understand it through my intense desire to save souls."

"I cannot breathe . . . I cannot die . . . I am quite willing to continue suffering. . . ."

"My slightest wishes have been realised; therefore my greatest wish — to die of Love — will surely be granted too."

At five o'clock, Mother Agnes of Jesus was alone with her dying sister when she noticed a sudden change. The agony had begun. The Community was called to the Infirmary, where Thérèse greeted each of the nuns with a sweet smile — for the last time. The sweat of death lay thick upon her brow; the sound of her death râle was heart-rending. When the Angelus rang at six o'clock, she turned her eyes toward the miraculous statue of our Lady. Shortly after seven o'clock, Mother Mary Gonzaga allowed the Community to retire, as death seemed to linger in coming. Thérèse sighed:

"Mother, is it not yet the hour of my agony? Am I not going to die? . . . Oh, I do not wish to suffer less!"

Then, fixing her eyes on the Crucifix, which she was clasping tightly in her hands, she uttered this final act of love:

"Oh, I love Him. . . . My God . . . I . . . love . . . You!"

The prayer of her First Holy Communion — the prayer that sums up all expressions of love — was her prayer at the hour of death.

These were her last words.

Her head fell gently back. Those who were present thought

[11] Gal. 2:20.

that her soul had passed to God. The Prioress had the bell rung to assemble the Community again, and ordered all the doors to be opened. The nuns gathered quickly and knelt to pray, with their eyes fixed on the pale face of their dying sister. Then every one of them saw her face light up with a joy that was not of this world; they saw her eyes radiant with life and rapture, in an ecstasy of Love.

Sister Thérèse of the Child Jesus and of the Holy Face remained in that state for the length of time it would take to say a *Credo* — and then closed her eyes.

It was twenty minutes past seven on Thursday evening, the last day of the month of September.

CHAPTER XV

LISIEUX, LAND OF HOPE

1. *The Shower of Roses Begins*

IMMEDIATELY after Thérèse's death, a beautiful smile spread over her face, like the seal of Triumphant Love. A freshness almost of childhood came back to her features, as Mother Agnes of Jesus and Sister Mary of the Sacred Heart prepared her for her tomb, with loving care. It was they who had rocked the baby's cradle in their home at Alençon, and they had watched over the delicate child with tender solicitude in their new home at Lisieux. Although their hearts were wrung with sorrow, the dawn of a mysterious joy was at hand, for signs of future glory were already apparent. In accordance with the Saint's prophecy that the weather would be fine at the hour of her death, the cloudy wet day suddenly changed toward evening and the stars shone forth in a cloudless sky.

A lay sister, who had once grieved Sister Thérèse by the sharpness of her words, suffered from cerebral anæmia; she was instantly cured, as she humbly bent down to rest her forehead upon the Saint's feet.

According to the custom in the Order, the coffin of the young nun was placed near the grating in the nuns' choir for two days. Devout crowds came to pray beside the body of the Saint and were greatly impressed by the majestic expression of her pure face. A poor woman, who tried to express what her feelings had been on looking at the Saint's bare, motionless feet, exclaimed enthusiastically: "Oh, how beautiful they were! They looked as if they had always walked upon light!"

At length the time came to cover her face. On October 4

a great many priests were present at the Office of the Dead and accompanied Sister Thérèse to the tomb, which they thought would be her last resting place. The Church's beautiful liturgical prayers were said as the body was lowered into the grave, on the hill which is called *La Colline des Rémouleux*.[1] Nature was adorned with autumn tints, when Sister Thérèse of the Child Jesus and of the Holy Face was laid to rest in her native Norman soil in the little cemetery which overlooks the town of Lisieux, apparently to await in that peaceful solitude the hour of the resurrection. On the simple wooden cross which marked her grave were inscribed these striking words, uttered by the Saint:

"I wish to spend my heaven in doing good upon earth."

With the permission of Mother Mary Gonzaga, Mother Agnes of Jesus carried out Thérèse's wishes by hastening the publication of the *Autobiography*, which she sent to all the convents of the Order, in the traditional form of a circular letter. Thérèse had once been impressed by the fact that the tiny flame of a small lamp was sufficient to light the candles of the whole Community. She alluded to this fact, almost in a prophetic manner, and referred to the idea in one of her poems:

O mystery of life, one tiny spark of light
Can kindle into flame a conflagration bright.

The little spark of the *Autobiography* was to enflame the world with its message of love and confidence. At first, the little manuscript was read in the monasteries. There it was so greatly appreciated that it was quickly passed on to friends. Souls were touched by its delicate charm, and soon the enthusiasm became general. Thérèse's intercession was invoked and miracles were wrought. These soon became so frequent that it was evident the young Carmelite nun was fulfilling her promise:

"After my death, I shall let fall a shower of roses."

An account was published of some of these miracles, but many — perhaps the greater number — will remain the secret of the

[1] Hill of the Knife-Grinders.

souls for whom they were wrought. Gradually, Lisieux became one of the chief places of pilgrimage in France. People came from all parts of the world to invoke the aid of "Little Sister Thérèse," who, by her promptitude in obtaining their petitions, was to them as a living friend.

During her lifetime, one of her sisters had said to her: "You will look down on us from heaven, will you not?"

"No, I shall come down," was her prompt reply.

She has indeed come down to us, not only to take her place in many a family circle, where her image sheds the radiance of her sweet smile, but in far more realistic ways. St. Thérèse has showered her favours on the lowly, the humble, and little children; she has helped missionaries and has converted sinners. Her charity has often been shown also to those in high places. She has assisted bishops by procuring for them unexpected funds; she has restored Princes of the Church to health; and she has wrought wonders in Seminaries and Colleges devoted to the study of religious truth. Numerous, too, are the appearances of her to souls in need or in distress.

Merely to enumerate the different kinds of miracles wrought by St. Thérèse of Lisieux would be well-nigh impossible. We are amazed at their number and variety, and captivated by the ingenious delicacy of the means she has employed. Not satisfied with bestowing isolated favours, she has chosen certain souls whom she seems to have adopted for life, strengthening, helping, and enlightening them under all circumstances, with untiring love and solicitude.

Once, toward the end of her life, Thérèse dreamt that she was setting out for a war, for which the troops were quite insufficient. During the Great War of 1914–1918 she was the incomparable protectress of soldiers on the battlefield, sometimes appearing to them during a battle to protect and encourage them. Many of the soldiers carried on them a picture of the Saint; when questioned, they would reply: "She is a relation of mine whom I love very dearly." Some of the men went so far as to write letters and postcards to her in their own simple style;

these were placed at her tomb in the cemetery of Lisieux. They even sent a petition to the Pope, begging for the beatification of their "little sister of the trenches."

England, Canada, Brazil — in fact all the nations of the world — sent testimonials of exceeding enthusiasm and gratitude, both to Rome and to Lisieux. Anticipating the Church's decree, Brazil presented a beautifully carved reliquary to bear her relics in procession.

Thérèse had promised that all who invoked her aid would receive an answer to their prayers. Her answers were so prompt and so numerous that, for her Canonisation, the Church shortened the delays customary in the Canonisation of Saints. Brought back to her monastery in triumph on March 26, 1923, Thérèse of the Child Jesus and of the Holy Face was declared Blessed on April 29 of the same year. On May 17, 1925, she was canonised in the Basilica of St. Peter in Rome, whose majestic walls were festooned with numberless roses for that occasion.

2. The Glorification of St. Thérèse

In the chapel of the Carmel of Lisieux, there is a statue of St. Thérèse of the Child Jesus in the brown and white habit of her Order. The casket containing her precious relics, which are venerated by thousands of pilgrims, has been placed beneath this statue representing the Saint in a reclining position. Of St. Thérèse's body, only the bones remain. When anyone spoke to her of miraculous conservation, she replied: "God will not perform such a miracle for me." Her reason was that this would render her too inimitable for little souls, and that consequently it would not be God's way of dealing with her.

In the hand of the statue of St. Thérèse is a golden rose, which Pope Pius XI sent by a special legate to the childlike Saint, so dear to his heart and so tenderly loved by the entire Christian world. This touching act of veneration symbolises the spiritual queenship which St. Thérèse of the Child Jesus has received as a faithful child of the Virgin Mary, Our Lady of Mount Carmel.

Above the reliquary is the statue of the Blessed Virgin that smiled on the ten-year-old child, leaving the reflection of that heavenly smile on her beautiful face. Thus the eyes of devout pilgrims pass from the little Queen of Lisieux to the great Queen of Heaven — the daughter cannot be separated from her Mother.

On approaching the relics of St. Thérèse of the Child Jesus, a feeling of veneration — amounting almost to awe — comes over the beholder when he realises that the child, who traversed the streets of Lisieux holding her father's hand and went to school like other children less than sixty years ago, is now venerated by thousands of Christians of all ranks and races. This same child has become a most powerful wonder-worker and is the Patroness of all the mission-fields throughout the world.

Numberless are the pilgrims who have knelt in this chapel where the flowers of unceasing veneration are strewn, as earnest supplications mount daily to heaven. St. Thérèse is there to welcome all and to obtain the petitions of all. She is there, not only by the presence of her glorious relics, but by that all-pervading though invisible Presence such as hovers over every great pilgrimage. Who has not felt this Presence at Lourdes, at Paray-le-Monial, and at Lisieux!

Though troubled at times by the wiles of the devil, France possesses to an unusual degree the secret of spiritual revival and holds proofs of revealed Truth.

At Lourdes, Faith stands forth triumphant — the faith of crowds who cry out and make supplication in the very same way as the people of Galilee, when they surged toward Him who passed along doing good. There, the attendants fill the water-pots, as it were, in preparation for the miracle that the Virgin Mother asks, confidently, of her Divine Son.

At Paray-le-Monial it is not quite the same. There, the pilgrim feels the revelation of glowing Charity, with all the mysterious confidence of Love. There, we feel that a Human Heart has loved us so much as to die for our salvation, and we know that it is none other than God made Man who has offered Himself in sacrifice to save mankind. From the moment of the Incarnation, the Divine Heart of Christ has never ceased to beat for love of us, and His Love will last forever.

Lisieux, in its turn, can be taken as the Land of Hope. Though the humblest of the theological virtues, Hope is the most audacious. Péguy speaks of Hope as a youthful maiden who runs before her two elder sisters, brooking neither obstacle nor delay.

Thérèse's sweet, serene countenance has been moulded by Hope. In her childhood's home in Lisieux — les Buissonnets — the souvenirs of her early life are charmingly displayed; and in the room where her toys and books are carefully preserved, her catechism lies open at the chapter on Hope. Her own thoughts on Confidence are most encouraging: "We obtain everything from God, according to the measure of our Confidence. . . . It is by Confidence — and by Confidence alone — that we reach Love." May the Saint's trustful words encourage us to remain with her in the abode of sweet and loving confidence!

Always and everywhere, human misery appeals to Divine Mercy. Mercy ever responds to that call. With what love, then, should we worship God's infinite Mercy! No matter how sinful a soul may be, as long as it retains the least ray of hope, it is separated from the Infinite Love of God merely by a sigh. Mauriac's saying that "one act of pure love can efface a whole life of sin" brings to mind Christ's pardon given to the Repentant Thief: "This day thou shalt be with me in paradise."[2] No wonder that this former sinner was among Thérèse's special favorites in heaven, "who to speak, stole it" she happily comments. To her also may we repeat that cry of Mauriac addressed to the Penitent Thief: "Make us hopeful even unto folly."[3]

Conversions at Lisieux are often as sudden as they are extraordinary. When faults and failings are cast into the furnace of Divine Love with the boundless confidence of a child toward its father, they are irrevocably consumed. The only condition necessary to obtain such pardon is filial confidence — the confi-

2 Luke 23:43.
3 Mauriac: Vie de Jésus.

dence of a child. It is always to children — to little ones — that
St. Thérèse makes her promises. It is a delicate stratagem on her
part, for by so doing she invites her suppliants to enlist in the
ranks of "Little Souls," and thus draws them to the path of
humility.

"God gives as He alone can give," says St. Thérèse, "but He
asks of us humility of heart." As we desire God's favor, let no
one be so haughty as to disdain the diminutive "little," that is
so dear to Christ Himself, who has said:

"Whoever does not accept the kingdom of God as a little
child will not enter into it."[4]

3. *Everything Through Love*

Over the high altar of a crypt, erected on a hill at Lisieux
and decorated in the soft tints of a Norman spring, stands a
statue of the Saint. Her eyes look heavenward and her arms
are raised, as if to teach us how to follow in her eagle flight to
the very throne of God. Above her head, the rounded curves
of the roof radiate in glittering mosaic the last words she uttered:
"Oh! I love Him. . . . My God, I love You!"

Suppliant pilgrims, their hearts burdened with many anxieties
yet beating high with great desires, come hither to plead for
aid in bodily or spiritual need. The prayer that most frequently
rises in song from the lips of the multitude, chanting in solemn
unison, is Thérèse's own favorite, "The Our Father." It is a
chant majestic in its simplicity. Soft and low at first, the voices
gradually increase in volume, as they unite in peaceful melody:
"Our Father, who art in heaven, hallowed be Thy name. . . ."
With deep understanding of the infinite tenderness of her
heavenly Father's love, Thérèse has shed her own pure light on
these words. And as the crowds fix their eyes on the statue of
the Saint their souls are stirred with hope and love.

Then follow the jubilant notes of thanksgiving: *Lauda Jerusalem Dominum! Hosanna! Magnificat.*

So the praying multitude pours out its heart in praise, and

[4] Luke 18:17

is enraptured by the atmosphere of joy — boundless, overflowing, spiritual joy. The joy of the Holy Ghost inundates each soul and fills it with new courage. A new fountain has sprung out of holy ground — a stream of living water of exceeding freshness — *Omen Novum!*

St. Thérèse of the Child Jesus promised this rich distribution of favours. "There will be abundant grace for everyone," she said. Her activity never wearies. She smiles upon sinners, touches men's hearts with sweetness, and offers them "the flowers" of graces, cures, and miracles. She ever finds new ways of forcing rebellious wills into submission, and of disarming the human malice that has risen in revolt against the goodness of God.

In reality she has but one aim: to teach men to love God. When she teaches Hope with such daring assurance, it is to lead us on to Love. On earth, she had only one object in view: to return Love for Love. From its very outset, her "Little Way" was the Way of Love: "Jesus, who is my Director, teaches me to do everything through Love." The secret of her sanctity ultimately lay in the ardor of her love.

Richly endowed by nature, the recipient of lavish graces, Thérèse was most intimately admitted into the secrecies of the Divine Love. She had besought her Divine Master to unite her to Himself "so closely that He alone might live and act" in her. To love Him worthily, she wished to borrow His own everlasting Love. In an unpublished letter to her sister Céline, she wrote: "Jesus alone exists — all the rest is nothing." Her one aim in life had been "to be no more" so that Jesus might be all, and her desire had been accomplished. The cross which she had clasped so lovingly — the cross made sacred by bearing the Body of Jesus, our Redeemer — had entered her heart and hallowed it completely. Grace had taken entire possession of the soul of this child, and Jesus had deigned to live again in her. When Death broke down the frail barrier that held Thérèse on earth, the miracle of grace shone forth; and, like unto Our risen Saviour, Thérèse of the Child Jesus has appeared to many!

EPILOGUE

ST. THÉRÈSE RETURNS TO EARTH
By the General Editor

1. *Prophecy and Fulfilment*

"ALL passes in this world, even little Thérèse — but she will come back."

On this point there was no hesitancy in the mind of the Little Flower.

"You will look down upon us from Heaven will you not?" someone asked her. And swiftly came back the answer:

"No, I will come down."

She had a mission to perform, a message to convey, and the time for that would not come until she had shaken off all the encumbrances of mortality.

"I feel that my mission is about to begin, my mission of making souls love God as I love Him, to teach my Little Way to souls."

If in heaven she could no longer work for God's glory — such was the sentiment with which God inspired her — then she preferred exile to home. And she counted without fail on the fulfilment of her desire simply because it so clearly came from God. That logic was irrefutable.

"I count on not being idle in heaven, for it is my wish to work for the Church and souls. I ask this grace of God, and *I am certain* that He will grant it."

And how long did she expect to continue her work here on earth? That question she had not overlooked. If her desires were fulfiled, she said, then would she spend her heaven on earth even until the end of the world. But that in itself was a weak statement, a conditional statement, and immediately she changed it into a most positive affirmation.

"Yes," she declared, sweeping aside every condition, and inspired evidently with a certainty the Spirit of God infused into her soul, *"I shall* spend my heaven in doing good on earth."

Then, pausing a moment to explain, she added: "This is not impossible, since from the midst of the Beatific Vision itself the angels watch over us." It was Christ's own testimony, as given in the Holy Scripture.

With her path thus cleared she proceeded straight toward her final pronouncement:

"No. I shall not be able to take any rest until the end of the world, so long as there are souls to save. But when the angel shall declare that 'Time shall be no more,' then I shall take my rest; then I shall be able to rejoice, because the number of the elect will be complete, and all shall have entered into their joy and their repose. My heart thrills at that thought."

And well it might!

"Later on, after death, then shall come the time of your conquest." That is what the saints were telling her; that is what the Spirit of God was whispering in her heart; that is what Christ, her Spouse, was making known to her in His silent communings with her soul.

Abraham heard God's voice and believed; and therefore God made him to be the father of a mighty progeny, the communion of the faithful through all the centuries, innumerable as the sands of the sea and stretching on to the end of time.

Mary believed, and all generations were to call her blessed.

And so, following in her own Little Way, conceiving herself the least and the weakest of all human creatures, rejoicing in her nothingness before God that she might rely on Him alone, the Little Flower, too, believed. And as she believed, so was it done to her.

"All the nations of the earth are pilgrims to her tomb," an observer wrote to the great secular Parisian daily *La Journal.* "Lisieux, with its 14,000 souls, has become as celebrated as Lourdes. [No fear that the child would derogate from its Mother's glory!] These pilgrims come to pray on the tomb of a Carmelite of twenty-four, whom the Pope has just canonised.

"Let one believe or not, can one deny that these ex-votos,

these gifts, these pilgrimages represent sufferings authentically cured or consoled? The holocaust of the little martyr was not then illusory . . . France has given the world the purest soul that has lived since Francis of Assisi."

Add to these words, penned by one who had gone to Lisieux as a sceptic, the summary testimony of a brilliant journalist, in an equally non-Catholic American review, who climaxed his report with the memorable words:

"In short she is the greatest woman of our times."

To challenge these statements, in a day of sceptic and scoffer, not one single voice was raised.

Rather, it was Thérèse herself, wrote the *Osservatore Romano,* who was God's own challenge to our times. And it was He who lifted up this child as His sign unto the nations plunged in material quests and bitter above all else against the cloistered life. And the extraordinary part of it is, continued the Vatican organ, "that the world has not ignored this Saint. Rather has it thrilled before her, and then has fallen on its knees in an enthusiasm that may be likened to a sweet delirium."

That indeed is the wonder of it all. And yet the Little Flower had predicted it plainly, when in the full simplicity of her child-like charm she observed, when glancing at her own completed *Autobiography:* "Ah, now I know it, all the world will love me!"

Too little to be vain, as she herself tells us, she saw in it all merely God's own doing, and gave to Him alone the praise.

Yet of all these wonderful tributes the most glorious were the words of Pope Pius XI, spoken in his Allocution of February 11, 1923:

"We thank God for the promise coming to us from that dear Star, Thérèse of the Child Jesus, *miracle of virtues and prodigy of miracles.* To her we recommend not only Our poor, unworthy person, not only the missions confided to the Carmel, and all missions, that were so dear to her and the inspiration of her most burning accents, but also the *Whole Church* — all the immense family which the Heart of God has confided to Our heart."

Declared patroness of the foreign missions, she was forthwith set by the side of that great glory of missionaries, St. Francis Xavier. Under her special protectorate were placed Russia and Mexico and the Alaskan icefields. In all the affairs of the Church she was the acknowledged counsellor of Pius XI who constantly wore her relic on his person, and kept before him on his desk a little marble statue of his *first* saint.

Tremendous, too, was the triumph of her canonization, when sixty thousand pilgrims enthusiastically thronged St. Peter's, with its myriad clusters of electric lights casting their radiance on the upturned faces of the assembled multitudes, on the scarlet robes of thirty-three princes of the Church there present, on the gleaming miters of twice a hundred bishops, and on the multi-colored uniforms of high representatives of the nations of the earth. And then, in the night, as the darkness slowly fell, there flamed up the soft light of the many tens of thousands of huge lighted torches, tracing out in living fire the exterior of the mighty Basilica, a scene not witnessed since 1870, while on the façade of the immense Cathedral was written an inscription ending with these mighty words of impetation, addressed to St. Thérèse:

> Guard Thou All God's Church,
> Aid Her Sacred Ministers,
> And Protect the Missions.

What a dazzling beginning of the realisation of her desires who in life had solemnly declared: *"My mission is to make others love God as I love Him. It is to return to earth to the end of time to make Love loved!"*

But there were still other days of special triumph for her, as the day when in the presence of fifty thousand pilgrims her relics were carried in procession through the streets of her city. Before they were taken up, a paralytic child, whom the mother fondly placed upon the Saint's coffin, leaped off, fully cured, and joined the singing throngs that followed after her remains. Three other cures were wrought that same day, but who could measure the invisible showers of roses that fell from heaven upon that multitude!

And still again, the nations of the earth were gathered together when the great Basilica of St. Thérèse was completed, at Lisieux, and from its commanding position overlooked far and wide, the countryside of Normandy.

2. *True Story of Gallipoli*[1]

In Southern Italy, on a little rocky Island in the gulf of Torento, is built the small town of Gallipoli, crowded into its restricted area. Within it, poor and insignificant, has stood for many years a Carmelite convent, long forgotten by the world. Its tiny rooms and narrow garden gave scant space for its inmates, whose commerce is with heaven. But though quite unknown before the death of St. Thérèse, Gallipoli was soon to become a word familiar in our day, and all because of her fidelity to the promise that she gave: "I will spend my heaven in doing good upon earth."

It was only a little more than two years since Thérèse had been laid in her grave. In the meantime the poverty of the Gallipoli Carmel had reached a stage at which it might better be called starvation. The distress of the nuns was extreme, and there was no help in sight. When dinnertime came and nothing was found on the tables, the Community silently filed into the chapel to pray.

By divine providence, however, someone had left with them a copy of the *Autobiography of Soeur Thérèse of the Child Jesus,* and the good nuns bethought themselves of invoking her assistance. So, too, did their Prioress, Mother M. Carmela of the Heart of Jesus. In making, therefore, a Triduum to the Most Holy Trinity, they took her for their mediatrix.

It was January 15, 1910. That same evening Mother Carmela had gone to rest quite ill and much worried by the urgent bills of creditors. Falling asleep, she dreamed toward the early

---

[1] This is an exact account, combining the statement of the Gallipoli Prioress with the descriptive factual data secured on his examination of the Carmel by the Vice-Postulator of the cause of the Little Flower.

morning hours that she felt a hand gently drawing the bed
clothes about her and tenderly covering her up. She took for
granted in her sleep, that it was one of the sisters and without
opening her eyes asked to be left alone, since she was in
perspiration and the movement created too much air.

"No, it is a good act I am doing," she heard a voice say in
reply. "Almighty God makes use of the inhabitants of heaven
as well as of those on earth to assist His servants. Here are 500
francs I give you, with which you will pay the debt of the
Community."

"The debt of the Community," answered the Prioress, still
in her sleep, "is about 300 francs."

"Well, the rest will be over and above. But since you may
not keep this money in your cell, come with me."

"How can I get up," thought the Prioress, "being all in a
perspiration?" But reading her thoughts the apparition smiled
and said: "Bilocation will help."

With that, Mother Carmela found herself outside her cell,
following a young Carmelite whose habit and veil shone with
a silvery brightness that served to light the way.

Descending a single flight of stairs, they came to the ground
floor, where they crossed over part of the monastery to "the
room of the turn." It was poor and small, and in it stood a low
writing table with drawers. The last of these the Vision opened,
disclosing on its bottom a little wooden chest. A cloth thrown
over it, had been removed by the hand of the angelic visitant,
who opened the small cash box without need of key. In it were
seven little copper sous, and by their side the bills of pressing
creditors. Here, finally, the apparition deposited her 500 francs.

"O our Holy Mother!" exclaimed the Prioress, casting herself on her knees.

"No," interrupted the Vision, "I am not our Holy Mother.
I am the Servant of God, Sister Thérèse of Lisieux. Today, in
heaven and upon earth, we celebrate the Holy Name of Jesus."

Gently touching the veil of the Prioress, as if to smoothen it
out, the visitor gave her a sisterly embrace and slowly withdrew.

"Wait," said Mother Carmela. "You might mistake the way."

"No, no," came the reply: *"My Way is sure — I am not mistaken in following it."*

The dream was over, but its reality was to be made manifest soon enough.

That morning two nuns, noticing the disturbed look of the Prioress, drew from her the story of her dream. The cash box was opened — and there the sum of 500 francs, made up in a roll of ten fifty-franco notes of the Bank of Naples,[2] was disclosed!

But the largess of Soeur Thérèse was not limited to this one gift. January, February, March, and April surpluses were discovered in the Community accounts. It was evident who must have been the cause of these, but finally Thérèse herself gave the definite assurance that the Community was indebted for the surpluses to almighty God through her.

With the need of this poorest of Carmels now sufficiently known, some alms were sent by the people and therewith, too, the surpluses ended. Yet once more, Thérèse appeared to the Mother Prioress. It was the eve of the exhumation of her remains, and she announced that "only her bones" would be found. So it proved to be. She further revealed what great and hidden sufferings she had endured on earth.

Spiritual benefits, also, were connected with these temporal benefactions, so that each member of the Community was able to acknowledge the remarkable graces personally received by her.

But there was further a notable denouement to this story, although it can be mentioned only very briefly here. The bishop,[3] namely, had sensed correctly that there was a mystic meaning

[2] "Where did Soeur Thérèse get her bank notes?" is the question that perplexed the Church of England *Guardian.* In heaven bank-notes do not circulate. On earth they are strictly limited in number, possessed by definite individuals and payable by definite banks. "A glance at the Note Circulation Account of every bank," wrote a former bank employee in *America* (Nov. 15, 1913), "shows that there are a good many notes issued that never come back. They are lost, and thus become *res nullius,* no man's property. Some are so effectively hidden away by misers that they are never found by their heirs; others are dropped and blown away by the wind; others are burned when houses catch fire; others go down with foundering ships. The lost notes give a supply exceeding all demands that miracles will ever make."

[3] Msgr. Nicolas Giannatasio, of Nardo, near Gallipoli.

in Thérèse's words to the Prioress on the first night: *"My Way is sure, I am not mistaken in following it."* He was not then aware, however, of the assurance Thérèse had given her novices that in case they were mistaken in following her Little Way, she herself would come back and tell them so. They were to know definitely "if my Way is sure."

In an envelope sealed in wax with the arms of the bishop and, for double precaution, locked up within the cash-box, the bishop had placed his visiting card, writing on it Thérèse's own words: "My Way Is Sure. I Am Not Mistaken."

Her confirmation of the correctness of the bishop's surmise was given in her own practical manner, by inserting within the sealed envelope, in the locked box, another 300 francs, leaving the wax seal unbroken and the box firmly locked. For exactly this sum the sisters had confidently asked Soeur Thérèse, wishing to use it for certain decorations in their destitute chapel.[4]

Since then Rome has spoken and has pronounced Thérèse's Little Way, her Way of Spiritual Childhood: *easy, swift,* and *sure* — both for attaining salvation, and for reaching the highest heights of perfection to which God has called us.

3. *An Incident of World War I*

When World War I broke out Thérèse had not yet been beatified, but from all sides Rome and heaven were importuned that this honor might be bestowed on her. Most earnestly the men in the field placed themselves under her protection. Aviation, artillery, infantry — all divisions found in her the Saint to whom a strong man could turn with utter confidence and purest love. From the front, letters regarding her were sent to the Holy Father, to the Carmel of Lisieux, and some were directly addressed to Soeur Thérèse herself and laid upon her grave.

[4] With the bishop's visiting card a sum of 500 francs was also placed in the envelope, before it was sealed by him with his armorial bearings. This sum he intended as an offering to the Carmel. The envelope was to be opened on the anniversary of the Apparition. When it was unsealed, his 500 francs were found in the envelope, together with Thérèse's 300 francs. Since the 500 francs are entirely irrelevant to the story, they are not mentioned above, to avoid confusion.

As sufficiently typical of the many marvellous accounts I shall offer one which, according to a statement in the *Irish Catholic,*[5] was well known in Belfast and neighbourhood, and well attested by ex-servicemen of the 7th Leinsters. It was in the trenches of Loos, at 1:30 o'clock on the morning of April 20, 1916, that the incident occurred, and the person concerned was Lance Corporal Francis Coyle. (Chaplain of the Regiment was Father Rafter, S.J.)

Corporal Coyle had shown great zeal in distributing pictures of the Little Flower among the men. When the fatal attack of that morning was launched, he felt that death was near and meant to say the prayer printed on the reverse side of the picture, but time was too short and he could only exclaim: "Soeur Thérèse, save us!"

"Instantly," to quote the Corporal's own words, "a shell burst over our trench, threw my comrade on his head, and smashed rifles and Lewis gun and everything around — sandbags and all.

"Not knowing that I was struck, I tried to lift my comrade and saw that he was wounded in the neck and wrist. The poor fellow died a few hours later from these wounds. Meanwhile I pulled out my clasp knife to loosen the field dressing. This knife was in my breast pocket directly over my heart, and what was my amazement to find that the two blades were knocked out and smashed. A purse in the same pocket, containing nine pennies, had two of the pennies completely twisted by shrapnel. I had not time to make a further search, but ran to my comrade and did all I could for him, and called for help to bring him to the stretcher-bearers.

"Then I made a further examination of my person and found that my tunic was fairly riddled with shrapnel. I counted eleven holes, but thanks and praise be to God and to the Little Flower, I was unhurt."

"He has had a miraculous escape," was the comment of Lieutenant Cullen, son of the Rev. Mr. Cullen, Methodist minister at Belfast. And when later Corporal Coyle made a

[5] May 30, 1925.

pilgrimage to Lisieux, with twenty-four wounded soldiers, Mother Agnes, sister of the Little Flower, greatly impressed by his account, wrote him the following note: "I ask my heavenly sister to give you a great share of the shower of roses which she has promised to send down to earth."

4. *The Canonisation Miracles*

Hardly had the body of Thérèse been laid upon its pallet when a fellow sister was instantly cured of a serious disease by touching her head to the feet of the Saint, whom she had grieved on one occasion by inconsiderate words. It was the beginning of what Pope Pius XI called the "innumerable wonders" worked by almighty God at her intercession, the "perpetual shower of roses, that is of graces." Before him, Pope Benedict XV had declared: "She has in her hands all the treasures of heaven."

Precisely because of these most exceptional manifestations Rome deemed it possible to modify or even entirely dispense with certain regulations of the Church, demanding more or less prolonged periods of years to intervene between the various processes that lead to canonisation. In fact, had she lived on earth to the date of her canonisation, May 17, 1925, she would have been only fifty-two years of age at that period. She was born in 1873, died in 1897, beatified in 1923, and canonized in 1925.

Day by day, to the present time, her showers of roses continue to fall in every part of the earth, and no true client of St. Thérèse need entertain the fear of being overlooked, whether the blessings bestowed be purely spiritual or temporal as well.

A glance at the two miracles selected for examination preparatory to the Canonisation may be of interest. The first is that worked in the instance of Mlle. Marie Pellemans, of Holland, then twenty-six years of age; the second is the cure of the Italian Sister Gabriella Trimusi, a religious of the Little Daughters of the Sacred Heart, at Parma.

At the age of thirteen Marie Pellemans had already displayed symptoms of consumption. By 1919 the doctors diagnosed it as pulmonary tuberculosis. In 1921 a tubercular enteritis set in, rendering vain all aid from the physicians. Speedy death became a certainty when in 1923 ulceration of the stomach was added, with vomiting and general debility. In fact, the end was then awaited hourly.

Yet despite this acute condition, or shall we say because of it, she swept aside the remonstrances of doctors, and resolved to join a pilgrimage to Lisieux — there to have herself taken to the grave of Thérèse that she might make her petition on that hallowed spot. Mindless of natural consequences as she had been, she cast herself upon her knees, and there, as she knelt, a voice made itself heard within her, bidding her to swallow a small fragment of the relic which she bore with her.

Marie obeyed, rose from her knees, and stood up — entirely cured of her mortal disease.

No less extreme was the case of Sister Gabriella. As early as 1913 a virulent disease attacked her left knee, necessitating its encasement in a plaster cast. But her suffering still increased. By 1919 her spine also had become involved. After many examinations and treatments, physicians pronounced her affection to be tubercular spondylitis (between the twelfth dorsal vertebra and the first lumbar). A plaster corset was prescribed to immobilize the spine, and this — after fruitless X-ray treatment — was changed into an armor of *iron*. The agonies of the poor nun can well be imagined. Thus she continued until June 24, 1923. That was the closing day of a novena held to obtain the cure of some sick religious. At the same time it was also meant to be the termination of a Solemn Triduum in honor of the Beatification of Blessed Thérèse. The devotions took place at the Carmel of Parma.

Sister Gabriella was present, and we can well understand the intensity of her prayers to the little wonder-worker of Lisieux. On leaving the chapel she felt a violent pain in the spine, increasing in its intensity as she returned home. At the same time, however, she experienced also a powerful impulse to remove the iron corset, even though she knew that without this she had never been able to remain erect a single instant. She obeyed the impulse within her, and to use her own words, "in four bounds was downstairs in the midst of the Community, perfectly cured."[6]

A radiographic examination of the spine and of the knee, thrice repeated, confirmed the complete cure of the disease, pronounced incurable by science.

Needless to say, the two cures described here proved permanent as they were perfect and instantaneous.

No one could possibly call in question their miraculous nature.

5. *Rose Showers Over the Missions*

At about the same time that examination of the preceding miracles was made by the Sacred Congregation at Rome, the Society for the Propagation of the Faith, at New York, published a number of authentic letters from missionaries in all parts of the earth, describing remarkable interventions of the Little Flower, the statements being all duly attested by bishops, superiors, physicians, or sworn witnesses.[7]

From India, from Oceanica, from China, from Africa, from Japan and Madagascar, from Brazil, Persia, Corea, Martinique, and whatever other mission countries, the marvellous accounts of spiritual and temporal favors had been sent in to the Little Flower's own Carmel of Lisieux, showing how in every language under the sun a hymn of praise and love goes up to "The Little Sister of the Missionaries."

How busy she must be! But it is by God's own power that all is done, and God is almighty. He can do all things, both sweetly and mightily, through instruments of His own choice. And such a one is the Little Flower. Let us follow her in spirit over the wide missionary fields and witness a few of the authentically recorded events described in the mission documents.

[6] *Carmel*, May, 1925: Carmelite Monastery, Wheeling, W. Va. Indebtedness is expressed here also to other issues of this small publication.
[7] *Shower of Roses Upon the Missions*. The letters were selected from the volumes of *Showers of Roses* in the Carmel at Lisieux.

So, then, from Gaboon, West Africa, comes in to her a request for *six* native girls whom the sisters wish to bring up in their boarding school. That is the precise number they are able to accept. A novena is begun, and before it has reached its end, the mail brings a letter from the Governor of the Ivory Coast. It inquires of the Sisters whether *six* girls, selected by the Administration, can be received in their establishment. But St. Thérèse does not do things by halves, as we have seen in the Gallipoli story, and so an allowance is promised by the government for the support of the children, who later can be relied upon to exercise an excellent Christian influence among the native women and children.

Next we find ourselves in Khandwa, Nagpur. It is a section of India to which some years previously a mission sister had come. But soon she began to suffer greatly, her pain steadily increased, and the doctors have just decided that her trouble is caused by an incurable cancer of the stomach. Human aid is past, and in the midst of her agony she turns to "the holy maiden of Lisieux." It is evening, yet she begins a novena, then places a relic of the Little Flower on the afflicted part, and so, filled with confidence, falls asleep. Suddenly it seems to her that she beholds Soeur Thérèse standing beside her, with outstretched hands and smiling countenance.

"What do you want me to do for you?"

"Oh, cure me, please, for I know that you can."

With that she wakes, completely cured, ready to resume all her work, as if the six years of cancer-suffering had all been merely an agonized dream.

In Ambatolampy, Madagascar, a novena to St. Ignatius has come to a close. It was made for a little girl named Adeline, stricken with a serious paralysis. In despair at not receiving an answer to her prayers, the mother of the girl, a native hospital nurse, turns to Thérèse for help and places her relic on the dear child. There is indeed no time to lose, for the doctor has just pronounced that the girl cannot live for ten more minutes.

A crucifix is placed on the gasping lips and instantly the child reaches out for the relic which she kisses three times. What now follows can best be likened to a resurrection from the dead.

But then comes the perplexing problem: Who cured the child? Was it St. Ignatius, whose novena had just been completed, or the Little Thérèse? The question is solved by St. Thérèse, herself, who appears both to the child and to the nurse's sister, assuring them that it was she who cured Adeline. "It is I who cured you." Up in heaven the chivalrous Ignatius is pleased that the honor should go to St. Thérèse.

And now we are at Seoul, Corea, in a small orphanage where a four-year-old girl, Agatha Yang, is suffering acutely from cataract. Total blindness is the doom the occulist forecasts. The sentence seems final. But on the right eye of the child, which is particularly painful, the Sister Infirmarian places a rose petal, gathered far away at the grave of the Carmelite nun of Lisieux. To her she and the orphans begin a novena. And when the ninth day arrives, the eye is well and the cataract has vanished. Indeed, the entire health of the once delicate child has become normal. The favourite saint of the orphanage is Soeur Thérèse.

In the Belgian Congo, at Lakandu, Africa, a missionary is lying on a mat unrolled upon the floor. He is worried — not because his case is pronounced hopeless by the doctors, so far as that concerns himself alone — but at the thought of what shall become of his black children who just now have need of him. There is no one who can do his work after he has departed. Fervently he begins a novena to the wonder-worker of Lisieux, to her who so deeply loves the missionaries.

The second day of the novena has arrived. Gathered before the tabernacle, the faithful are praying for him, where a picture of the Little Flower looks down on them. But there is still a second picture placed where the missionary himself can face it

in his room. As his eyes are raised to it, suddenly the picture
moves: it advances toward him: it becomes a living thing.
Distinctly he hears a voice saying:

"No, Father, you are not going to die yet. You must work
longer for the black people here."

When the last day of the novena arrives, it finds him completely out of danger.

Pella, South Africa. The little Christian convent children are
gathered around an altar of the Sacred Heart. They plan how
they can decorate it in the best way possible, and for that they
want roses. But in the convent garden stands one sole rosebush,
dried and withered. For six years now it has produced no single
blossom. So there is nothing that the sister can do to help them,
but why not ask the Little Flower? "She and roses are good
friends."

A fervent novena is begun, and on the seventh day four buds
are breaking out on the sterile stock. Rapidly they develop,
and their petals, as they unfold, seem to be of a tint and delicacy
such as the sister had never beheld. In fact, they are of a variety
different from any roses that had ever blossomed on that bush,
now flourishing anew, hale and vigorous.

What a beautiful symbol, surely, is that once dead and sterile
bush, abloom with roses of Paradise — a sign of what Thérèse
will do for souls that lovingly, trustingly, surrender themselves
to her guidance with childlike readiness! It is for that she gladly
comes to earth: to make God loved as she loves Him; to teach
men her Little Way.

1. *La Rose Effeuillée*

Jésus quand je te vois soutenu par ta Mère,
    Quitter ses bras,
Essayer en tremblant sur notre triste terre
    Tes premiers pas;
Devant toi je voudrais effeuiller une rose
    En sa fraîcheur,
Pour que ton petit pied bien doucement repose
    Sur une fleur.

Cette rose effeuillée est la fidèle image
    Divin Enfant!
Du coeur qui veut pour toi s'immoler sans partage
    A chaque instant.
Seigneur, sur tes autels plus d'une fraîche rose
    Aime à briller;
Elle se donne à toi mais je rêve autre chose:
    C'est m'effeuiller . . .

La rose en son éclat peut embellir ta fête,
    Aimable Enfant!
Mais la rose effeuillée, on l'oublie, on la jette
    Au gré du vent . . .
La rose, en s'effeuillant, sans recherche se donne
    Pour n'être plus.
Comme elle, avec bonheur, à toi je m'abandonne,
    Petit Jésus!

L'on marche sans regret sur des feuilles de rose,
    Et ces débris
Sont un simple ornement que sans art on dispose,
    Je l'ai compris . . .
Jésus, pour ton amour j'ai prodigué ma vie,
    Mon avenir;
Aux regards des mortels, rose à jamais flétrie,
    Je dois mourir!

Pour toi je dois mourir, Jésus, beauté suprême,
    Oh! quel bonheur!
Je veux en m'effeuillant te prouver que je t'aime
    De tout mon coeur.
Sous tes pas enfantins je veux avec mystère
    Vivre ici-bas;
Et je voudrais encor adoucir au Calvaire
    Tes derniers pas . . .

            Mai, 1897.

The Rose Unpetaled[1]

Jesus, when Thou didst leave Thy Mother's fond embrace,
    Let go her hand;
And first, on our hard earth, Thy little foot didst place,
    And trembling stand;
Within Thy pathway, then, fresh rose-leaves would I spread,
    Their Maker's dower,
That so Thy tiny feet might very softly tread
    Upon a flower.

These scattered rose-leaves form true image of a soul,
    O Child most dear!
That longs to immolate itself, complete and whole,
    Each moment here.
On Thy blest altars, Lord, fresh roses fain would shine,
    Radiant near Thee;
They gladly give themselves. Another dream is mine —
    To fade for Thee!

How gaily decks Thy feast, dear Child, a rose new-blown,
    Fragrant and fair!
But withered roses are forgot — the wild wind's own —
    Cast anywhere.
Their falling petals shed themselves unselfishly,
    To be no more.
Ah, little Jesus! so, I spend myself for Thee,
    And all my store.

These roses trampled lie beneath the passer's tread,
    Unmarked, unknown.
I comprehend their lot: — these leaves, though pale and dead,
    Are still Thine own.
For Thee they die; as I my time, my life, my all
    Have spent for Thee.
Men think a fading rose am I, whose leaves must fall
    At death's decree.

For Thee I die, for Thee, O Jesus, Fairest Fair,
    Joy beyond telling,
Thus fading would I prove my love beyond compare,
    All bliss excelling.
Beneath Thy feet, Thy way to smooth, through life's
    long night
    My heart would lie;
And softening Thy hard path up Calvary's awful height,
    I thus would die.

                    May, 1897.

[1] Translation by Susan L. Emery (slightly adapted).

2. *Concluding Words of Autobiography*

(This extract forms part of the manuscript[1] which the Saint
wrote for her eldest sister, Marie, known in Religion
as Sister Mary of the Sacred Heart.[2])

———

. . . O my Jesus, open Your Book of Life, in which the
actions of all Your saints are recorded; I should love to have
accomplished all those actions for You!

To such folly as mine, what will You reply? Is there on earth
a soul weaker than mine or more helpless? Yet, just because I am
so weak, You have been pleased to accord my childish desires,
and to-day You will grant other desires more vast than the
universe.

When these aspirations had become a real martyrdom, I opened
the Epistles of St. Paul one day in the hope of finding relief
to my longing, and my eyes fell on Chapter XII and Chapter XIII
of the First Epistle to the Corinthians, where I read that the
Church is composed of different members, that we cannot all
become Apostles, Prophets, and Doctors, and that the eye cannot
be the hand.

The answer was clear, but did not satisfy my desires nor bring
me the peace I sought. "Then, descending into the depths of
my nothingness, I was so lifted up that I was able to reach my
aim."[3] For I continued reading without being discouraged, and
this counsel brought me comfort: "Yet strive after the greater
gifts. And I point out to you a yet more excellent way."[4]

The Apostle then explains how all "the greater gifts" are
nothing without Love and that Charity is the most excellent
way of going surely to God. At last, I had found rest!

Reflecting on the mystical body of holy Church, I did not
recognise myself in any of its members as described by St. Paul,

[1] See note on p. 202, with regard to the three manuscripts.
[2] Sister Mary of the Sacred Heart died on Jan. 19, 1940. The Saint's other
sisters — Mother Agnes of Jesus, Sister Genevieve of the Holy Face, and
the Visitation nun, Sister Frances Teresa — were still alive at that date.
[3] St. John of the Cross.
[4] I Cor. 12:31.

or, rather, I wished to recognise myself in all. Charity gave me the key to *my vocation*. Since the Church is a body composed of different members, the most necessary and most noble of all the organs — the heart — cannot be wanting. I understood that the Church has a heart — and that this heart is on fire with love. I understood that Love alone gives life to its members, and that, if the fire of Love should ever be extinguished, apostles would no longer preach the Gospel and martyrs would refuse to shed their blood. I understood that Love includes all vocations, that Love is everything, and that it embraces all ages and all places, because it is eternal!

Then, in an ecstasy of joy, I cried out: "O Jesus, my Love, at last I have found my vocation! *My vocation is Love!* I have found my place in the bosom of the Church, and that place, O my God, You Yourself have given to me: in the heart of the Church, my Mother, *I shall be Love!* Thus, I shall be all things; thus, my dream will be realised!"

Why do I speak of "an ecstasy of joy"? Those words do not convey my exact meaning. I should rather say that peace has become my portion — the calm, quiet peace of the sailor when he sees the beacon which shows him the harbour. O luminous Beacon of Love! I know how to reach you; I have found the means of making your fire my own!

I am only a weak, helpless child; yet it is my very weakness which emboldens me to offer myself, O Jesus, as a victim to your Love! In olden days, only pure and spotless victims were acceptable to the Strong, All-powerful God; perfect sacrifices were necessary to satisfy the Divine Justice. But the law of fear has given place to the law of love, and Love has chosen me as a holocaust, weak and imperfect as I am! Is that choice not typical of God's Love? Yes, for in order that Love may be fully satisfied it must stoop even unto nothingness to transform that nothingness into fire.

O my God, I know that "Love is repaid by love alone."[5]

[5] St. John of the Cross. (St. Thérèse of Lisieux took these words as her motto.)

Therefore, I have sought and found the way to ease my heart, by returning You love for love.

After proclaiming that "the children of this world are in relation to their own generation more prudent than are the children of the light,"[6] You gave this advice to Your disciples, O Lord. "Use the riches, that cause men to be unjust, to make yourselves friends, who will receive you into everlasting dwellings."[7]

I am a child of light; I understood that my desires to be all things and to embrace all vocations were riches that might, indeed, make me unjust, so I employed them in the making of friends. Recalling the prayer of Eliseus when he asked the Prophet Elias for his double spirit, I presented myself before the angels and the assembly of saints and prayed thus: "I am the least of all creatures. I know my wretchedness, but I also know how noble and generous hearts love to do good. Therefore, I beseech you, O Blessed Inhabitants of the Heavenly City, adopt me as your child; all the glory you will help me to acquire will be yours. Deign to hear my prayer, and obtain for me, I implore you, a double share of your love for God.

O Lord, I cannot fathom the greatness of my request; I should fear to be crushed by the very weight of my audacious petitions. My only excuse is my title of *child:* children do not reflect on the exact meaning of their words. Yet if a father and a mother were to mount a throne and possess immense riches, they would not hesitate to grant the desires of their little ones, dearer to them than life itself. To please these little ones, they would commit acts of folly and of weakness.

I am a child of holy Church. The Church is a Queen, since she is Your Spouse, O Divine King of kings. It is not riches or glory for which my heart longs, not even the glory of heaven. Glory belongs by right to my brothers, the angels and saints. For me, glory will be the reflection of the radiance that comes from the countenance of my Mother, the Church. What I ask

[6] Luke 16:8.
[7] Luke 16:9. (The quotation is not quite literal.)

is Love. One desire alone remains for me — the desire to *love You*, O Jesus. Brilliant deeds are not for me; I cannot preach the Gospel nor shed my blood. That does not matter. My brothers work in my stead, while I — *a little child* — remain close to the royal throne and love You for all those who strive.

But how shall I testify to my love, since love is proved by acts? *The little child will strew flowers;* she will distill the sweet scent of her perfumes before the divine throne; she will sing the Canticle of Love in melodious tones!

Thus, O my Beloved, will my short life be spent in Your sight. The only way I have of proving my love is to scatter flowers before You; my flowers will be my little sacrifices, and I shall seize every opportunity for mortifying look or word. I wish to profit by the least of my actions and to do everything for Love. I wish to suffer through Love and even to rejoice through Love; in that way, I shall strew flowers. I shall scatter before You the petals of every flower I see. . . . And I shall sing. I shall sing always, even if my roses must be gathered amidst thorns; the longer and sharper the thorns, the sweeter will be my song.

But of what use will my flowers and songs be to You, O my Jesus? Ah, I know well that You will delight in this shower of fragrant flowers even though the frail petals be worthless, and that You will listen to my songs of love even though they come from such a poor little heart. Though trifles, they will be pleasing to You. The Church Triumphant will smile on her little child and gather up the petals of these roses; placing them in Your divine hands that they may acquire an infinite value, she will shower them on the Church Suffering to extinguish the flames, and on the Church Militant to obtain victory.

O my Jesus, I love You! I love the Church, my Mother. I know that "the least act of pure love is of more value to her than all other works together."[8]

But does my heart really possess this pure Love? Are not my boundless desires merely dreams and folly? If this be so, enlighten

[8] St. John of the Cross.

me; You know that I seek Truth. If my desires be rash, take them from my heart, for they are the most intense martyrdom. Yet I confess that if I do not one day reach these heights to which my soul aspires, I shall have tasted more sweetness in my martyrdom and in my folly than I shall ever taste in eternity, unless by a miracle You take from me all remembrance of my earthly hopes. Jesus, Jesus! If the mere desire to love You brings such delight, how great will be the happiness of possessing Love and enjoying it forever!

Yet how can a soul as imperfect as mine aspire to the plenitude of Love? Who can explain the mystery of Love? O my only Friend, why do You not reserve these intense yearnings for exalted souls, for the eagles that soar in the heights! Alas! I am but a tiny bird, a little fledgling. I am not an eagle; I have but the eagle's eyes and heart. Yet, notwithstanding my exceeding littleness, I dare to fix my eyes on the Divine Sun of Love; I long to soar to Him. I would imitate the eagles, by flying in the heights, but all I can do is to lift up my little wings; it is beyond my power to soar.

What is to become of me? Must I die on account of my helplessness? No, I shall not even lament. With daring abandonment, I shall remain there till death, gazing on the Divine Sun. Nothing will cause me to fear, neither wind nor rain. If heavy clouds come to conceal the rays of my Love and if the only reality seems to be the dark night of this life, that hour will be the hour of *perfect love;* it will be the time for urging my confidence to its uttermost bounds. I should not think of changing my position, knowing that — beyond the dark clouds — my sweet Sun still shines!

O my God, even up to that point, I understand Your Love for me. But You know how often I am led away from my sole desire. Leaving Your side, I wet my newly fledged wings in the muddy pools of this earth. Then I lament "like a young swallow"[9] and my lamentation tells You all; and You remember, O Infinite Mercy, that You came "to call sinners, not the just."[10]

[9] Isa. 38:14.   [10] Matt. 9:13.

Yet if You should remain deaf to the plaintive cries of Your weak creature, and if You should remain hidden, I am willing to remain bedraggled and numb with cold; I even rejoice at this well-deserved suffering, O Divine Sun, so dearly loved! I am happy to feel myself so small and weak in Your presence, and my heart is at peace. . . . I know that all the eagles of Your Heavenly Court feel compassion for me and that they protect and defend me, putting to flight the vultures — the demons — that would devour me. I do not fear these vultures; I am not destined to become their prey, but the prey of the Divine Eagle.

O Word Eternal! O my Saviour! You are the Eagle whom I love and who dost draw me to Yourself. Descending to this land of exile, You wished to suffer and to die in order to bear away all souls and to plunge them into the very heart of the Blessed Trinity, the everlasting home of Love! Returning to Your inaccessible light, You still remained in our valley of tears, hidden under the appearance of the white Host to nourish me with Your own Substance. O Jesus! Forgive me if I say that You love even unto folly. . . . In presence of such folly, what can my heart do but dart up to You? How could I put any limit to my confidence?

Ah! I know that the saints have loved You even unto folly; being "eagles," they have accomplished great deeds! I am too little for mighty deeds; my folly consists in hoping that Your Love will accept me as a victim. My folly counts on the angels and saints to help me to fly right up to You with Your own wings, O Eagle whom I adore! As long as You wish, I shall remain with my eyes fixed on You; I desire to be *fascinated* by Your divine eyes and to become the prey of Your Love. One day, I firmly hope, You will swoop down on me, and, carrying me off to the furnace of Love, You will plunge me at last into that burning abyss, so that I shall be forever Love's happy victim.

O Jesus, would that I could tell all little souls of Your ineffable condescension! I feel that if it were possible for You to find a soul weaker than mine, You would take delight in lavishing still greater favours on her, provided that she abandoned herself with entire confidence to Your Infinite Mercy.

But why do I desire to manifest Your secrets of Love, O my Beloved? Since it is You alone who didst teach them to me, can You not reveal them also to others? I know You can and I implore You to do so. *I beseech You to let Your divine eyes rest upon a vast number of little souls; I entreat You to choose in this world a legion of little victims worthy of Your love.*

3. *Act of Oblation to God's Merciful Love*

The Church has enriched with indulgences the concluding passage of the following Prayer, which was composed by St. Thérèse of Lisieux and kept in her book of the Holy Gospels, which she constantly carried on her breast, night and day.

For an account of this oblation of herself as Victim of Holocaust to God's Merciful Love, see Chapter XII.

O my God, Most Blessed Trinity, I desire to love Thee and to make Thee loved, to labour for the glory of Thy holy Church by saving souls here on earth and by delivering souls suffering in Purgatory. I desire to accomplish Thy Will perfectly and to attain the degree of glory Thou hast prepared for me in Thy Kingdom. In a word, I desire to be holy, but, knowing how helpless I am, I beseech Thee, my God, to be Thyself my holiness.

Since Thou hast so loved me as to give me Thine Only-Begotten Son to be my Saviour and my Spouse, the Infinite Treasures of His merits are mine. These I offer to Thee with joy, beseeching Thee to look upon me only through the eyes of Jesus, and in His Heart of burning Love.

I offer Thee also all the merits of the saints in heaven and on earth, together with their acts of love, and those of the holy angels. Finally, I offer Thee, O Most Blessed Trinity, the love and the merits of the Blessed Virgin, my dearest Mother. In her hands I place my oblation, entreating her to present it to Thee.

Her Divine Son, my well-beloved Spouse, during His life on earth spoke these words: "If you ask the Father anything in my name, he will give it you."[1] Therefore I am certain Thou wilt grant my prayer. O my God, I know that the more Thou wishest to bestow, the more Thou dost make us desire.

Boundless are the desires of my heart, and I confidently entreat Thee to take possession of my soul. I cannot receive Thee in Holy Communion as often as I wish, but O Lord, art Thou not all-powerful? Abide in me as Thou dost in the Tabernacle; never abandon Thy little Victim.

I long to console Thee for ungrateful sinners, and I implore Thee to take from me all liberty of displeasing Thee. If I should fall through weakness, may a glance of Thine eyes at once cleanse my soul and consume all my imperfections, as fire transforms all things into itself!

I thank Thee, O my God, for all the graces Thou hast bestowed on me, especially for having purified me in the crucible, of suffering. On the Last Day, I shall behold Thee with joy bearing Thy sceptre, the Cross; and since Thou hast deigned to allow me to share Thy Precious Cross, I hope to be like unto Thee in Paradise and to behold the Sacred Wounds of Thy Passion shine on my glorified body.

After this earthly exile, I hope to enjoy Thy Presence in our eternal Fatherland, but I do not wish to amass merits for heaven; I wish to labour for Thy Love alone, with the sole aim of pleasing Thee, of consoling Thy Sacred Heart, and of saving souls who will love Thee throughout eternity.

When the evening of life comes, I shall appear before Thee devoid of merit, for I do not ask Thee, my God, to take account of my works. All our works of justice are sullied in Thine eyes. I wish therefore to be clothed with Thine own justice, and to receive from Thy Love the everlasting possession of Thyself. I desire no other throne or crown but Thee alone, my Beloved!

In Thy sight, time is nothing: "A day is as a thousand years"; in a single instant, therefore, Thou canst prepare me to appear before Thee.

[1] John 16:23.

† In order that my life may be one act of perfect love, I offer myself as a victim of holocaust to Thy Merciful Love imploring Thee to consume me unceasingly and to allow the floods of Infinite Tenderness gathered up in Thee to overflow into my soul, that so I may become a very martyr of Thy Love, O my God!

May this martyrdom, after having prepared me to appear in Thy Presence, free me from this life at the last, and may my soul take its flight, without delay, into the eternal embrace of Thy Merciful Love!

O my Beloved, I desire at every beat of my heart to renew this oblation an infinite number of times, "till the shadows retire" and everlastingly I can tell Thee my love face to face.

[Signed]   *Marie-François-Thérèse de l'Enfant Jesus et de la Sainte Face.*

(Mary Frances Thérèse of the Child Jesus and of the Holy Face.)

Feast of the Most Blessed Trinity,
The ninth day of June, in the year of grace 1895.

† The Church has attached the following Indulgences to the concluding passage of this Oblation (from the words "In order that my life may be an act of perfect love" to the end).
Three years indulgence.
A plenary indulgence, once a month, on the ordinary conditions, if recited each day for a month. Given at Rome (S. Paen.) July 31, 1923 and Dec. 23, 1935.

MEMORABLE DATA

Day of Birth . . . .   January 2, 1873

Day of Baptism . . . .   January 4, 1873

Miraculous Cure by Our Lady . . . .   May 10, 1883

First Communion . . . .   May 8, 1884

Confirmation . . . .   June 14, 1884

Reception Into Children of Mary Sodality   May 31, 1886

Audience With Pope Leo XIII . . . .   November 20, 1887

Entrance Into Carmel . . . .   April 9,* 1888

Clothing . . . .   January 10, 1889

Profession . . . .   September 8, 1890

Reception of Black Veil . . . .   September 24, 1890

Departure for Heaven . . . .   September 30, 1897

Congregation of Sacred Rites Approves
   Thérèse's Writings . . . .   December 10, 1913

Cause Introduced by Pope Pius X . . . .   June 10, 1914

Decree by Pope Benedict XV Concerning
   the Heroicity of Her Virtues . . . .   August 14, 1921

Decree Approving Miracles Authorized
   by Pope Pius XI . . . .   February 11, 1923

Beatification by Pope Pius XI . . . .   April 29, 1923

Canonisation by Pope Pius XI . . . .   May 17, 1925

Beginning of Present Date of Liturgical
   Cult in Catholic Churches . . . .   October 3, 1927

* Feast of the Annunciation. It was transferred that year because March 25 fell on Palm Sunday.